P9-DTA-763

FEB 2 7 2021

NO LONGER PROPERTY OF
SEATTLE PUBLIC LIBRARY

BUNDINI

TODD D. SNYDER

BUN

~~DON'T~~ BELIEVE THE HYPE

DINI

HAMILCAR
PUBLICATIONS
BOSTON

Copyright © 2020 Todd D. Snyder

All rights reserved. No part of this book may be reproduced in any form or by any means, electronic or mechanical, including photocopying, recording, or by any information storage and retrieval system without permission in writing from the publisher.

ISBN: 978-1-949590-20-3

Publisher's Cataloging-in-Publication Data
Names: Snyder, Todd, 1981–, author.
Title: Bundini : don't believe the hype / Todd D. Snyder.
Description: Includes bibliographical references. | Boston, MA: Hamilcar Publications
Identifiers: LCCN: 2020936073 | ISBN: 978-1949590203
Subjects: LCSH Brown, Drew Bundini. | Boxing—United States—Biography. | Boxing—United States—History. | Ali, Muhammad, 1942–2016. | Robinson, Sugar Ray, 1920–1989. | African Americans—Biography. | BISAC SPORTS & RECREATION / Boxing | BIOGRAPHY & AUTOBIOGRAPHY / Sports | BIOGRAPHY & AUTOBIOGRAPHY / Cultural, Ethnic & Regional / African American & Black
Classification: LCC GV1131.B76 2020 | DDC 796.8/3/0922—dc23

Hamilcar Publications
An imprint of Hannibal Boxing Media
Ten Post Office Square, 8th Floor South
Boston, MA 02109
www.hamilcarpubs.com

Printed in the United States of America

On the cover: Muhammad Ali yells with Drew Bundini Brown during a press conference before his first fight with Sonny Liston at the Convention Center in Miami Beach on February 25, 1964. *Stanley Weston/Getty Images*

To Stephanie Nicole and Huntington Jay,
for always being in my corner

CONTENTS

Introduction   *Requiem for a Hype Man*..................................*1*

1   *Do the Best You Can for Him*.....................................*10*

2   *A Rosebud in Harlem*...*30*

3   *Honey and Sugar*..*50*

4   *Metamorphosis*..*72*

5   *Blue Eyes and Brown Eyes,*
       See Grass Green..*98*

6   *Bundini's World*..*120*

7   *Make Sure You Be There, Waitin'*...............................*146*

8   *The Road to Heaven*...*172*

9   *God's Act*...*194*

10   *Everyone Sees but Only a Few Know*...........................*218*

11   *The Fighting Cowboy*...*246*

12   *From the Root to the Fruit*....................................*270*

Acknowledgments..*295*

Works Referenced..*297*

Notes...*303*

INTRODUCTION

Requiem for a Hype Man

ntroducing myself to you, the reader, is no easy task, provided that
I occupy many contradictory selves in embarking on this journey.
First and foremost, I am a professor of rhetoric and composition at
Siena College in Albany, New York, where I teach a course titled "Rhetoric(s)
of Hip-Hop Culture." As part of my college's cross-cultural-solidarity
initiative, I have worked with a variety of hip-hop legends, Grandmaster
Flash (Grandmaster Flash and the Furious Five), Sha Rock (of the Funky
4 + 1), Masta Killa (of the Wu-Tang Clan), and Biz Markie (The Juice
Crew), just to name a few. Students in my course come to understand
hip-hop as a full-blown culture, with its own set of pre-formation pioneers
and practitioners. On the first day of class, I begin with a discussion of
the social, political, and artistic movements that serve as the foundational
backdrop to the rise of hip-hop culture. For members of the Millennial
generation, who have never known a world bereft of rap music, exploring
this history can be an enlightening experience.

"Where does hip-hop come from?" my incoming students often ask.

My goal, as a professor, is to tell that story.

On a diasporic flowchart, one could trace hip-hop's origins from Africa
to the Caribbean and on to the United States. Aside from its larger global
influences, hip-hop, as a musical genre, has its roots in gospel, blues,
ragtime, jazz, rock 'n' roll, funk, reggae, R&B, and disco. More important

to our classroom discussion, however, is close attention to the sociopolitical influences that impacted hip-hop's stylistic formation. One cannot outline this history without first discussing the Harlem Renaissance, urban folk poetry of the late 1960s, or the key orators of the Black Power and American civil rights movements. Hip-hop, I tell my students, was not born in a vacuum.

Each semester, I end my initial classroom lecture with a clip from ESPN's 2006 documentary *Ali Rap*. Hosted by hip-hop icon Chuck D (of Public Enemy), the film aims to position Muhammad Ali as the first rapper. Throughout the documentary, hip-hop artists, such as Jermaine Dupri, MC Lyte, Ludacris, Doug E. Fresh, and Rakim, recite some of Ali's most famous poetic lines, demonstrating how the Ali formula served as a template for early MCs. Hip-hop is something you live, rap is something you do, the great KRS-One famously states. And you can't talk rap without first talking Ali. There isn't a reputable hip-hop history book that doesn't, in some form or fashion, pay homage to Muhammad Ali's influence.

In the spring of 2014, Chuck D, the man behind *Ali Rap*, served as the keynote speaker for Siena College's annual "Hip-Hop Week" ceremonies. As part of his on-campus duties, Chuck D had dinner with me and my students in Lonnstrom Dining Hall. Because my students were familiar with his documentary, the dinner conversation eventually turned to the topic of Muhammad Ali.

"In our textbook, D.M.C [of the iconic duo Run-D.M.C] argues that 'Float like a butterfly, sting like a bee' is the most famous rap lyric ever," one of my more outgoing seniors recalled, attempting to glean some measure of insight into whether our dinner guest agreed with his former Def Jam labelmate.[1]

Chuck D smiled, nodded his head, and took a moment to ponder the statement.

"That's a great line. Hard to beat that one," Chuck D replied.[2]

"But it actually comes from Bundini Brown," I injected, speaking without thinking.

To this, Chuck D flashed a smirk of approval, one that roughly translates to "you know your boxing, professor." Today, most boxing aficionados are aware that it was, in fact, Drew Bundini Brown, Ali's outspoken corner-man, who coined the famous rhyme.

"Wait, Ali didn't come up with that?" another student interrupted, feeling lost in the conversation.

None of my students were familiar with the name Bundini—it is not mentioned in the ESPN documentary.

"If Ali is the first rapper, that makes Bundini the first *hype man*," I continued, referencing Chuck D's notorious Public Enemy sidekick, Flavor Flav.

My comparison garnered a hardy laugh from the 2013 Rock & Roll Hall of Fame inductee. He was genuinely amused by the analogy.

"Somebody should do a book on Bundini," Chuck D replied, wiping tears of laughter from his eyes.

■ ■ ■

The true meaning of the term *hype man* is difficult to pin down. Renowned music scholar Mickey Hess describes the hype man as a "figure who plays a central but supporting role within a group [or for a headlining solo artist], making his own interventions, generally aimed at hyping up the crowd while also drawing attention to the words of the MC."[3] During the early days of live performances, the job of the hype man was to warm up the audience before the headlining rapper hit the stage. Over the years, the term gradually came to have competing definitions. In *How to Rap: The Art and Science of the Hip-Hop MC*, Royce da 5'9" positions the role of the hype man as that of a "motivator," an onstage presence who ensures that the momentum of the show continues.[4] In fulfilling this duty, the hype man both energizes the crowd and the artist. The hype man's job is thus metaphysical; his work exists in the realm of spirit and emotion.

While Kidd Creole of the pioneering rap group Grandmaster Flash and the Furious Five likely serves as the genre's original hype man, hip-hop history is full of such figures. The Notorious B.I.G. had Lil' Cease. Jay-Z had Memphis Bleek. Eminem had Proof. And, of course, my friend Chuck D had the zany, oversized-clock-medallion-wearing Flavor Flav. As the rhetorical tradition expanded over the years, the term *hype man* eventually became synonymous with the concept of a loyal sidekick or trusted companion. During the 2012 presidential election, for example, Vice President Joe Biden was often referred to as Barack Obama's hype man;

some internet memes specifically compared the Obama–Biden dynamic to that of Ali and Bundini.

As is often the case with language, the pop-culture signifier, like all slang terms, came to embody counter meanings, many of which took on their own negative connotations. For some, the term *hype man* is synonymous with the role of a yes-man—a person who serves no function other than affirming the greatness of a headlining celebrity. These notions were present in the early days of hip-hop as well. When Public Enemy began negotiating their record deal with Def Jam Records in the early-1980s, the label was, at first, unwilling to take on Flavor Flav. "What does he do?" record company executives asked. "I don't know but it works," Chuck D famously replied.[5]

In many ways, Chuck D is describing how most boxing experts feel about Muhammad Ali's enigmatic cornerman. Drew Bundini Brown wasn't a boxing trainer, not in the traditional sense. He never boxed as an amateur or as a professional. Not once. With that being said, Bundini was more than a fringe member of the entourage. He was a constant, if not dominating, voice in Ali's corner, working forty-four of Ali's sixty-one professional bouts. Aside from Ali's first bout with Floyd Patterson, Bundini was present for all of Ali's most significant fights. With respect to training, Bundini worked side by side with Ali, waking him up for morning roadwork and shadowing him in the gym for every workout routine. Rhetoric, a concept Aristotle defines as "the persuasive element of discourse," was Bundini's chief talent. In his lifetime, Bundini would play the role of master motivator to two of the greatest boxers in the history of the sport.

Before ever meeting Muhammad Ali, Drew Bundini Brown worked as a member of Sugar Ray Robinson's entourage, a partnership that lasted seven consecutive years. Sugar Ray Robinson and Muhammad Ali are, of course, two of the most celebrated boxing icons in the history of the sport. The common denominator among these legendary champions is Bundini. Unbeknownst to many casual boxing fans, Bundini also worked with former welterweight champion Johnny "Honey Boy" Bratton, as well as heavyweight contenders Jeff Merritt, George Chuvalo, and James "Quick" Tillis.

To pretend that Bundini was nothing more than a hype man, in the negative sense of the term, is to undermine his place in boxing history.

He was more than a lackey. Bundini's contributions to Ali's legacy were both motivational and stylistic. The poetic side of Ali's prefight routine was taken to new heights when Bundini joined the fray. In giving us the simile that would forever encapsulate the way we think of Ali's graceful fighting style, Bundini helped shape the *idea* of Muhammad Ali.

"*Float like a butterfly, sting like a bee* is generally attributed to Bundini. If he never did anything else, that contribution alone would certainly be an extraordinary one. I can't think of a phrase more associated with Ali," boxing historian and Muhammad Ali biographer Thomas Hauser once said to me.

During their time together, Muhammad Ali and Drew Bundini Brown played a pivotal role in shaping the Black poetic tradition. The 1963 release of *I Am the Greatest,* Ali's spoken word album for Columbia Records, created a marketplace for acts such as The Last Poets (1968) and Gil Scott-Heron (1970), both of which paved the way for the emergence of hip-hop. From his proud Afrocentricity, to the hypermasculine boasting, to the comical trash talk, Ali's rhymes, flow, and braggadocio provided a model for rappers such as Kurtis Blow and LL Cool J. The list of contemporary hip-hop artists who reference Ali in their music, or directly borrow from his lyrical formula in their craft, is far too large to mention in this introduction. Bundini unquestionably played the role of chief second to Muhammad Ali, the street poet.

"It was like a marriage. It was maybe Muhammad Ali's best marriage. Ali, like all great jazz musicians, was a great borrower. That's one of the reasons he kept Bundini all of those years. Ali didn't write those poems, Bundini came up with many of them. Ali borrowed what he needed from Bundini," Jonathan Eig, author of *Ali: A Life,* suggested to me.

Aside from his work with Ali, one could argue that Bundini was a cultural icon in his own right. As an actor, appearing in six feature films, Bundini made a unique imprint on popular culture. His biggest contribution would come through his reoccurring role as the Harlem gangster Willy, in Gordon Parks's iconic *Shaft* franchise, a groundbreaking series of films that would give rise to the so-called blaxploitation genre. The commercial success of *Shaft* would demonstrate the rapidly growing market for movies with Black heroes, plots centered on Black communities. Blaxploitation films were also famous for their soundtracks, the first to feature funk and soul music. In this regard, Bundini is also connected to the formation of hip-hop culture. Blaxploitation film was a precursor to the mainstream visibility afforded to rap artists in the culture industries.

Later in life, Bundini would deliver a cameo performance, alongside Oprah Winfrey, in Stephen Spielberg's adaptation of Alice Walker's novel *The Color Purple*. Bundini was also a featured character in *Superman vs. Muhammad Ali*, published by DC Comics in 1978. Name another cornerman who can say he has worked with the likes of Sugar Ray Robinson, Muhammad Ali, John Shaft, Oprah Winfrey, Stephen Spielberg, and Superman!

Drew Bundini Brown lived an amazing American life, one that not even the best Hollywood writers could have invented for the silver screen.

■ ■ ■

As is often the case with hype men, history has not been kind to Bundini's legacy. In the 1996 HBO original film *Only in America*, Bundini, played by actor and comedian Bernie Mac, is depicted as a fickle turncoat. In director Michael Mann's widely celebrated Muhammad Ali biopic, released in December of 2000, Bundini, played by Academy Award–winner Jamie Foxx, is portrayed as a heroin addict. When Bundini's life is written about in boxing books or magazines, the story is often brief, centering on his propensity for drinking, alleged drug use, his affinity for white women, or his knack for pawning Ali memorabilia as a side gig. For example, Alex Wallau, president of the ABC network, in an interview with Thomas Hauser, once stated the following: "Bundini, to me, was the most obvious exploiter. I'm not saying he didn't have genuine feeling for Ali, and he was an entertaining guy, but Bundini knew no limits when it came to exploitation."[6]

Over the years, a number of boxing historians have been quick to label Bundini a leech, cheerleader, or even court jester. *Sports Illustrated*, for example, once compared Bundini to Svengali, the fictional character in George du Maurier's 1895 novel *Trilby*—the term "Svengali," as literary critics well know, has, over the years, become synonymous with the term *con artist*.

For the young men and women in my hip-hop class, those who research Bundini and find these overly simplistic characterizations, I feel sympathy. Drew Bundini Brown was no con artist; he was a hustler—a term my fellow hip-hop historians will likely recognize and understand. A *hustler* is someone given very few advantages but always finds a way to maximize their opportunities. For all that he achieved in his improbable life, Bundini, in my scholarly opinion, deserves better than the legacy of a Svengali.

Long before viewing ESPN's *Ali Rap*, or meeting and conversing with the legendary Public Enemy front man Chuck D, I understood Bundini's vicarious influence on hip-hop culture. I come to this exploration as more than a hip-hop professor. I am also the son of a small-town West Virginia boxing trainer, Mike "Lo" Snyder, a man who mined coal by day and trained amateur fighters by night. My father loved Muhammad Ali. As a young boy, he would parry and feint and glide his way around the perimeter of a cattle rack, pretending to be the heavyweight champion of the world. He would toss a dingy pair of Everlast gloves over his shoulder and walk down to the local basketball courts, searching for a Joe Frazier. In Mrs. Thompson's English class, my father signed all of his term papers *The Greatest*. Mike "Lo" Snyder was a fifth-generation West Virginia coal miner, from a long line of extractive-industry fighters. He'd come up in one of the poorest towns in one of the poorest states in Appalachia; fighting was a life philosophy that made perfect sense to him, and Muhammad Ali was his pugilistic idol. The first book I ever read cover to cover was my father's tattered copy of Ali's 1975 autobiography. I had no choice but to become an Ali scholar.

Growing up in Cowen, West Virginia, it was not easy for my father to be a fan of Muhammad Ali. The Cowen of my father's youth was an all-white community that prided itself on a working-class brand of humility. "Getting too big for your britches" was a cardinal sin. Thus, for many Cowen residents, Ali's boasting was unforgivable. And there was, of course, Ali's stance on the Vietnam War. My uncle, Denny, was wounded while serving in Vietnam. For many folks in town, Ali's refusal to accept induction into the U.S. military was the primary reason they cheered against the so-called Louisville Lip. Ali's religion didn't do him any favors in Cowen, either. In a community with deep Christian roots, overwhelmingly Protestant, cheering for a Black Muslim was hardly a popular move. Yet my father persisted. Ali's bravery and bravado spoke to him in a deeply spiritual way. Ali was the champion of underdogs, the little guys—those victimized by the powers that be. My father's admiration for Muhammad Ali got him into more than a few playground scuffles.

Hip-hop was never a taboo subject in my family. This is probably because my father was so enamored with Muhammad Ali. Most of my friends had parents who forbid rap music in their homes. I know this because my friends would often sneak hip-hop cassettes into their bedrooms as if they were contraband. My father, on the other hand, felt some measure of familiarity with both the style and rhetorical aim of hip-hop music. He enjoyed Ali and Bundini's prefight poetics just as much as he did the fights themselves. Hip-hop, like boxing, was an aesthetic space where underdogs had the opportunity to demonstrate their greatness to the world.

"Those rappers are just doing a version of the Ali–Bundini routine, set to a beat," my father would often say.

When my father's boxing career ended, he opened up a series of makeshift gyms and began mentoring local youth. Lo's Gym Boxing Club was his contribution to our poor mountain community. Back in those days, hip-hop music served as the soundtrack to our nightly training sessions. Hip-hop was my first love. Boxing was his. Amid the ricochet of speed bags and jump ropes skimming a hardwood floor, two passions that transformed our lives combined into one. Drew Bundini Brown served as the connective link between my father's inspiration and my own. It is with deep appreciation for Bundini's contributions to hip-hop and boxing that I accepted the task of writing his life story.

The book you are about to read is the product of fourteen months spent visiting, interviewing, and conversing with Drew Timothy Brown III, the son of Drew Bundini Brown. It does not aim to hide behind the illusion of neutrality. I want you, the reader, to see Bundini through the eyes of his son. Drew's memories of his father are, in my opinion, as historically significant as any account of Bundini one might stumble upon while conducting archival research. They are most certainly as worthy of publication as Alex Wallau's assessment of Bundini's character.

By exploring Bundini's relationship with his son, we move closer to understanding Bundini beyond his cultural mythos. I do not think of this text as a biography, not in the traditional sense. I don't consider myself an investigative journalist. I am a storyteller and these are the stories Drew Brown III and his family are ready to share with the world. For an unconventional character like Bundini, the traditional approach simply wouldn't do.

I invite you, the reader, to discover Bundini with me, making your own judgments based on my conversations with his family. I don't confuse oral history with irrefutable evidence. I present this collection of family stories, corroborated by a variety of Bundini insiders, as evidence of an oral tradition that keeps Bundini alive in the hearts and minds of those who loved him most.

My goal is not to redeem Bundini's reputation. Nor am I interested in vilifying him for the benefit of Muhammad Ali's legacy, as so many others have done. My goal is to de-mythologize Bundini. It is time to have a funeral for the term *hype man*. It is past time we remove the *hype* and explore the life of the actual *man*.

Bundini's improbable story, as Chuck D suggested to my students, is one worth telling.

1

Do the Best You Can for Him

The white Rolls-Royce weaved out of the slow-moving airport traffic and came to a rolling stop. The suicide doors opened, providing a sneak peek of the interior. He was tall, thin, handsome, and gangly like his father. Drew Timothy Brown III, Drew Bundini Brown's son, smiled and brushed his right hand through his hair, briefly fingering the bald patch.

"We used to think my daddy's hair fell out because of those chemicals he put in it, back when the conk was a thing," Drew said to me, lifting the carry-on bag from my shoulder as if he were a chauffeur.[1]

"Now we know it's genetic. Looks just like his, doesn't it?" he added.

I climbed into the luxury vehicle, awkwardly. The car doors shut themselves.

Drew's resemblance to his father was uncanny. I instantly noticed he was wearing his father's jewelry, the famous Star of David necklace, a gold watch, and a diamond-encrusted bracelet bearing the family name. Drew had grown his hair out for me, I suspected. This was his way of introducing me to his father.

"I didn't anticipate getting scooped up in a Double R," I said, half-jokingly, attempting to stave off the kind of silence that often lingers between strangers thrust into close proximity.

"After the first Ali–Frazier fight, my father bought a brand-spanking-new Fleetwood Brougham Cadillac. He named the car "Black Beauty." Daddy named all of his cars. But this one was the bomb. Black with gray interior. It had psychedelic lighting in the rear passenger section. It had the disco package, they called it. The lights would go with the music. Daddy loved that car," Drew responded, suggesting my statement had triggered a memory.

The white Rolls-Royce exited Hartsfield-Jackson Atlanta International Airport and made its way onto I-85 South.

"Let me tell you a story about that car," Drew continued.

Moments into our time together we became old friends. Drew's enthusiasm for his own story was infectious.

"When I received my driver's license, I was looking for one of those *Brady Bunch* moments, so I asked my daddy, when he came to visit, if I could drive Black Beauty," Drew continued.

"No, boy. You don't get to drive *this* car. You didn't work for this. You gotta work hard, you gotta do something great, to drive a car like this. I'm not going to let you drive around in this car, acting like you did something," Bundini scolded his son.

Listening to Drew relive the memory, seated in the passenger side of his Rolls-Royce, I was suddenly reminded of the fact that I was in the presence of Drew Timothy Brown III, not Drew Bundini Brown.

"I had never been more upset in my life. I just wanted that *Brady Bunch, Father Knows Best* type of moment. 'Dad, can I borrow the car?' That kind of thing. I would have just taken the car around the dang block," Drew said.

"Is this a painful memory for you?" I asked, sensing my research was now officially underway. To this, Drew flashed a Cheshire grin.

"Fast-forward a few years, after I graduated college, when I was working in Las Vegas, I bought this beautiful red Cadillac. I remember picking daddy up from the airport. He said, 'Dang, son, this is *nice*. Let me drive it," Drew continued.

I guessed the crescendo of the parable long before the words left his lips. In telling the Black Beauty story, Drew had given me my first lesson on Bundini.

"I told daddy, 'Hell, no. This is my ride. You gotta do something great to drive a car like this.' And, you wouldn't believe it, the biggest smile you'd ever seen crossed Daddy's face," Drew said, chuckling as he delivered the punchline.

"I didn't understand what he was trying to tell me before. But at that moment, it felt wonderful. Daddy was proud. And in the end, I was proud of myself. Daddy was absolutely right," Drew added.

Drew Brown III has, without question, achieved greatness in his own life. He was a college basketball star, earning a full athletic scholarship to Southern University of New Orleans. After becoming the first member of his family to graduate from college, earning a degree in business with a minor in economics, Drew later joined the U.S. Navy, earning his Wings of Gold in 1983. Early into his career, Drew was assigned to Attack Squadron 35, known as the "Black Panthers," the oldest attack squadron in naval aviation history. Because the young pilot was known around the squadron for being tall, dark, and handsome—Drew stands at six feet five—he was given the call sign "Dark Gable." At the time, Drew was the only Black Navy jet pilot flying the A-6 Intruder attack aircraft on the East Coast.

His would be an illustrious naval career. He was awarded the Meritorious Service Medal by the president of the United States, the Freedom Foundation Medal by the U.S. Supreme Court, and the Congressional Black Caucus Foundation Male Achievement Award, as well as the U.S. Chamber of Commerce Special Salute for outstanding leadership. After his naval career came to an end, Drew was hired as a airline pilot for FedEx, a career that would span three decades. While Drew spent much of his adult life above the clouds, it would be on the ground, in front of junior high, high school, and college students, that the former Navy pilot would make his biggest impact.

In 1991, Drew Brown III published a best-selling book titled *You Gotta Believe!*, which launched his career as a motivational speaker. After the book was released, Drew appeared on NBC's *Today Show*, *NBC Nightly News*, *CBS This Morning*, and hundreds of local radio and television programs. His work was also featured in the *New York Times*, *Washington Post*, and *Fortune* magazine. At the height of his popularity, Drew was interviewed by media luminaries such as Jane Pauley, Phil Donahue, and Connie Chung. When it came to rhetoric, the apple did not fall far from the family tree. Drew is much like his father: he is a fast and eloquent talker, his vocal presence commanding.

"Bundini's son is the person you should be writing the book about. He was an extraordinary young man. He made a path for himself in life," Gene Kilroy, Muhammad Ali's longtime business manager, said to me over the phone, just days prior to my visit to Atlanta. Drew Brown III's home was breathtaking. It was the most beautiful home I had ever visited. We entered the property via cast-iron gates, griffins perched on each side of the entrance, a double "B" insignia prominently featured on each of the dual swing driveway doors. Drew's multistory home featured a gym, a small movie theater, and a man-made lake in the backyard. Each room was handsomely furnished, adorned with antiques and artifacts from around the world. Regarding the decor, there were plenty of visual cues calling back to Drew's days in the Navy, but little to no evidence of his life around boxing.

"I'd be embarrassed to show this place off to you if my father had left me this, if I hadn't earned it myself," Drew insisted, petting Beaux, one of his six Great Danes, animals who were in every way as impressive as his home.

In suggesting he had *earned* his fortune, Drew Brown III was not being disingenuous. When Bundini died in September of 1987, he left his son absolutely nothing in terms of money. Drew's father died penniless, in a modest motel room located in a crime-ridden section of Los Angeles. His mother, Rhoda Palestine, was no better with finances than her mercurial husband. Drew and his mother spent much of his childhood living in the Carver Housing Authority projects in Spanish Harlem. My host, despite all of his impressive material possessions, was hardly of blue-blood lineage; his wealth had nothing to do with trust funds or celebrity privilege.

"My father's life ended in misery, like my mother's, because in the end they didn't plan for the future. They lived in the *now*. If you gave my father money, he either gave it away or spent it. One of the reasons I am successful is because I watched my parents struggle," Drew said to me as we made our way around the property.

It was on the final leg of the tour that I found the opening to my story. As we made our way into Drew's private library, the photographs lining his bookshelves all but jumped into my hands. There were images of Drew and his father palling around with the likes of Sugar Ray Robinson, Muhammad Ali, Colin Powell, and even Liberace. Drew showed little energy when rehashing celebrity encounters. He showed even less interest in talking boxing. When describing the personalities of family members, however, Drew came alive, his verbal and physical enthusiasm noticeably changed.

"I'm not biracial, Todd," Drew corrected me. "There is one race, the human race. I'm bicultural," he insisted.

The diversity found within the frozen images lining his library book-shelves was nothing short of spectacular. Each photograph contained visual representations of seemingly disparate worlds in harmony.

"Growing up, I never once thought of myself as less than," Drew assured me, providing a hard pause after making his declaration.

"My parents, if anything, taught me that I was *better*. I had the Black side and the Jewish side. I had the best of both worlds," Drew added, handing over, one by one, my cast of characters.

"To tell my father's story—to really understand his life—you've got to go back to the beginning," Drew III insisted, removing one last framed photograph from the top shelf.

"To really get the story right, you've got to take it back to Sanford," he added.

■   ■   ■

He pours a dipper of water into the top of the cast-iron pump. His sandpaper hands grip the thin red handle and begin to do their work. The first two attempts produce no results. In short, erratic bursts, water pours into the galvanized washtub carefully positioned below the spigot. Bathed in the hazy Florida sunlight, the metal flickers and flashes, maintaining a bucket-gray hue. The waters of the makeshift bathtub are warmed by the same elements that nurture the nearby citrus groves, acres of rolling farmland where box fillers earn as little as twelve cents an hour. Beads of sweat sag their way down his bald head like reluctant travelers. He is a short, wiry Black man, compact and muscular, a stiff jaw and intimidating scowl, a constant expression of disapproval marked by thick slanting eyebrows. From the shadows of the screened-in front porch, a small boy studies his father, each movement the personified spirit of strength.

Hunkered down on one knee, applying the smooth oils to his son's naked back, casting a silhouette that dances its way along the ripples of soapy water, the man approaches his task with the careful precision of a blacksmith. His life has been reduced to a routine, a series of steps and procedures to be followed and repeated. Routine is all that keeps the anger locked away, his only productive means of coping. Work the railroads. Collect oranges. Wash grapefruits. Harvest stalks of celery. End up on a chain gang, or tarred and feathered, or with a noose around your neck, strung up a sycamore tree. The small boy splashes and fidgets and squints his eyes. No words are spoken. The man pays no mind to the patrol car making its way down the dirt road, giving birth to a cloud of dust along the way.

A car pulls up. Sheriff Baker's long ropey arms fold themselves behind his thin torso. He stands a good fifteen yards back from the washtub, waiting to be acknowledged. The gold star pinned to his left breast pocket glistens in the sunlight. His face is hairless and thin, his eyes misty blue. The sheriff removes his hat before speaking. "Drew," he calls, his thick southern accent breaking the stony silence. The man does not flinch. The small boy playfully splashes. "Drew," the sheriff repeats. The man continues bathing his son. He slowly moves the washrag from armpit to fingertip. The small boy complies with the familiar maneuvers. "You know why I'm here," the sheriff calls. There is no response. "Come on, Drew," he adds, his voice wavering. "It's time for you to go down to jail. You know what you did last night," he urges.

For a few tense moments, the sheriff is having a conversation with no one but himself.

"You get the hell off my land," the man finally answers, a bellowing voice marked by a notable lisp. A few seconds pass.

"I'll come down when I've finished washing my boy," the man says, his speech slow and stern, the oration heightened by the intentional pause.

The sheriff's arms unfold.

"Now, you go on . . . get the hell off my land," the man repeats, adding a little extra bass to his voice, glancing over his shoulder for the first time.

To this, the sheriff places his hat back on top of his head. The ignition starts and the patrol car makes its way back down the dirt road.

The thin cotton blanket rests just below the small boy's bottom lip, his mouth slightly ajar. Even the most fantastic of dreams will not be able to compete with the journey that awaits. In the next room over, the man stands facing a crooked mirror, sizing himself up. He removes the starched, freshly ironed white shirt from the hanger. He puts it on. He holds the Prince Albert cigar to his lips. He strikes the match. He places his knife in its holster. Out on the cinderblock steps, he pauses, taking in the galvanized washup in the front yard, stagnant waters reflecting the pink and blue of a Florida sunset. The man takes another drag off his cigar, makes his way down the cinderblock steps, and onto the long dirt road that leads to the jailhouse.

■ ■ ■

Known as "Celery City," for it was once the nation's leading producer of the crop, the town of Sanford, Florida, rests on the southern shore of

Lake Monroe and at the head of the St. John's River. Located twenty miles northeast of Orlando, the city maintains a long and complicated history of racial tension. Baseball aficionados likely remember the historic Sanford Field as the site where Jackie Robinson began his minor league career. Because of the constant harassment by locals, in the form of death threats and outright violence, Robinson was forced to leave Sanford on two different occasions. Contemporary generations likely know Sanford as the site of the 2012 shooting of seventeen-year-old Trayvon Martin, a highly publicized incident that, in many ways, served as the beginning of the Black Lives Matter movement.

This history of violence and racism is not unique to the city. Rather, it is a microcosm of a larger regional discord with roots dating back to the second half of the nineteenth century and early twentieth century. Florida was the site of more lynchings, per capita, than any of the southern states during this time period.[2] Many of these graphic murders took place in Sanford and in the surrounding counties, where the presence of the Ku Klux Klan loomed large. Recognizing this history is a necessary precursor to any discussion of Drew Bundini Brown, for his father's rage, and the impact that rage would have on the trajectory of his young life, was the by-product of these harsh sociocultural realities.

Drew Brown Sr., Bundini's father, was born on December 25, 1894, in Thomasville, Georgia. He was the first of Ellen Brown's six children: Drew, Willy, Johnnie, Alonzo, Coley, and Sadie. The only child born out of wedlock, Drew Sr. grew up feeling an underlying sense of detachment from his siblings. His biological father, a West Indian man whom he would never meet, held no place in his life whatsoever.

Stern, short-tempered, and at times emotionally distant, Drew Sr. came to be seen as an intimidating figure in both his family and community. As a young man, he hunted alligators in the nearby swamps, alone and at night. He sold their hides to help support the family. Drew Sr.'s reputation as a hunter was surpassed only by his reputation as a fighter. He was a "man's man," for lack of a better cliché. Drew Sr. drank whiskey and smoked cigars. He carried a sheathed knife on his side at all times. If someone wanted trouble, he was quick to remove the knife from its holster. Nobody in Seminole County messed with Drew Brown.

Looking back on his own childhood in Sanford, Willy Brown III, Drew Sr.'s nephew, recalls his uncle's domineering reputation: "Blacks would go into the little downtown area and there was a certain way you had to conduct yourself. We had to be very careful and very skilled at negotiating that situation. We knew that we had to be careful about what you did and said around white people. Sanford was two separate worlds back then. The white world and the Black world. But Uncle Drew was *known*. He was different than his brothers, or anybody else for that matter. He'd get into these beefs with people and somebody would end up cut. The police would come up to Uncle Drew's house and ask him to turn himself in. That's the kind of respect Uncle Drew commanded in Sanford."

If there was one thing Drew Brown Sr. hated more than his absentee father, it was *crackers*. According to family legend, his great-grandfather, on Ellen Brown's side of the genetic fence, was a runaway slave from a plantation in Georgia. He and two other slaves escaped to Florida after killing a white man. Prior to the Second Seminole War of the 1830s, runaway slaves often sought refuge among the Native American communities in central Florida.[3] It is possible that Drew's family lineage follows this trend. Ellen Brown, with her long, silky black hair, was often mistaken for a Native American woman.

Like his ancestors, Drew Sr. carried with him deep-seated feelings of hatred and mistrust toward the white man. He'd never met a white person who treated him with any measure of respect. The story of his childhood was that of "Colored Only" water fountains and bathrooms; segregated buses, schools, and restaurants; and poll taxes and literacy tests that kept uneducated Blacks from participating in local politics. "Hey there, boy," whites would call. "What you doing, boy?" they'd goad. If a white man was making his way down the sidewalk, his Black counterpart was expected to passively step aside and out of his way. Be it conscious or subconscious, Drew Brown Sr.'s bravado, his sullen and violent temper, was a mask cultivated and worn daily to hide the pain.

Racial tension aside, life in Sanford was an arduous existence. Hard work was *the* reality, agriculture *the* way of life. When opportunities were not available in the local farms or citrus groves, contracting groups recruited young Black men as migrant laborers, partaking in three-month excursions to northern locations, such as the outskirts of Rochester, New York. Harvesting beans and celery in the unforgiving sun, Drew Sr. considered himself no different than a slave. The system had found a way to return him to the plantation. As Drew Sr. entered his mid-twenties, he was in constant search of some semblance of agency and freedom in his life. For a period of time, he worked as a porter on the Atlantic Coast Railway. When World War I broke out, he briefly served in the military. To escape the pain and anger that marked his daily existence, Drew inevitably found refuge in the bottle. His drinking steadily progressed after leaving Sanford to find his way in the world.

The first major turning point in Drew Sr.'s adult life, a tragic story in its own right, came in the form of his ill-fated marriage to Elizabeth Brown. A beautiful young teacher who taught at a "colored school" in West Palm Beach, Florida, Elizabeth, unlike her husband, was soft-spoken, educated, and nonconfrontational. She was raised in the church and came from a family with deep religious faith. Elizabeth believed Blacks could find happiness by working within the system. Her mantra was to "do the right thing," follow the rules, and treat others as you would like to be treated. This philosophy best describes Elizabeth's turn-the-other-cheek Christian worldview. She did not approve of her husband's violent temper nor did she think his lashing out could lead to anything more than trouble. Elizabeth was raised to believe Black folks should carry themselves in a humble and respectable manner, education being the only true path to liberation. Drew Sr.'s anger was a puzzle that Elizabeth would not solve.

Drew and Elizabeth's first child, Drew Brown Jr., the boy who would later come to be known as Bundini, was born on March 21, 1928, in West Palm Beach, Florida. The couple's second child, Elbert, would arrive two years later.[4] Rearing children did little to mend their ideological differences. The brief amount of time the Brown family coexisted under one roof, eight years in total, was plagued by verbal and physical abuse. America's Great Depression was well underway and opportunities, even for educated whites living in large metropolitan cities, were scarce. As Drew Sr. struggled to find work, often taking to the Florida forests to hunt for food, he became increasingly angered by the social limitations that surrounded his life. The barroom fights became more frequent, and he often returned home angry and drunk.

Recalling the turmoil, Drew Brown III discussed with me the family dynamics into which his father was born: "[Elizabeth] feared the violence that erupted from within Granddaddy Drew when he came home drunk and frustrated from fighting so hard. I'm sure that he loved his wife and children, but alcohol-propelled anger caused him to abuse and beat them. Society's injustices had cut too deep. Something within Granddaddy Drew would not allow him to quit striking out, even after he was back home with the people who loved him."

As Drew Brown Sr.'s drinking progressed, the abuse, for both his wife and children, became more frequent. The culminating incident of domestic violence occurred in the spring of 1935. It is a horrific family story that, in many respects, marks the beginning of Bundini's journey around the world.

■　■　■

"I'm not taking this anymore, Drew. I'm leaving and taking the kids with me," Elizabeth screamed from underneath a bed, curled into a fetal position, her two sons sobbing in the doorway.[5]

Blocking Elizabeth's escape, his knife drawn as if he were hunting alligators, Drew Brown Sr. gave his wife a final ultimatum: "*You* can leave but you ain't taking my first born."

It was a decision that would forever change the course of each of their lives. Elizabeth crawled out from underneath the bed, took her youngest son, Elbert, by the hand, and on unsteady legs, walked out of their home, never to return.

Day after day, young Drew Brown Jr. waited out by the mailbox at the end of the dirt road leading to his house. He imagined his mother and younger brother would return home. He imagined a letter arriving in the mailbox, signaling their whereabouts. No such letter arrived.

The psychological trauma Drew Jr. experienced by the sudden loss of his mother and younger brother is immeasurable. After the divorce, Drew Jr. stopped attending school altogether. He was just seven years old. The young boy suddenly found himself alone with a father who was unable to reconcile his anger. Regardless of whether he was conditioned to believe so or came up with the hypothesis on his own accord, Drew Jr. grew up feeling abandoned. His mother had made a calculated choice, to save herself and Elbert, and to leave him behind.

Placing the photograph of his grandfather back on the bookshelf, Drew Brown III turned to me, his thin face tight with emotion. "This is part of very deep issues with my father and women. It was a major problem in his life. We really didn't talk about it because he'd have nothing to say, but I know that feeling of abandonment was a key source of Daddy's pain," Drew III suggested.

Ironically, it would be Elbert Brown, who fled with his mother and was given the privilege of continuing his formal schooling, who would end up spending much of his life in prison. Meanwhile, his older brother, Drew Brown Jr., who was left to fend for himself in West Palm Beach, would go on to become famous the world over, rubbing shoulders with leaders of nations as well as some of the most talented and celebrated figures of his generation.

It is likely that Drew Brown Sr. came to regret his ultimatum to his wife. He was, in every sense of the word, ill-prepared for the challenges of being a single parent. One night, for example, while slushing through the murky Florida swamps in search of alligators, Drew Sr. spotted a barefoot child hiding in the tall grass. His son, only seven years old at the time, had snuck out of his bed and followed him into the woods, disobeying his father's orders to stay inside. Rather than give his son a lecture on the potential dangers of his actions, Drew Sr. devised an unorthodox parental solution: Each night before an alligator hunt, he would take his son to the roof of their home and tie him to a vent. This, in Drew Sr.'s estimation, was the only way to assure his son would not end up becoming alligator food.

In late summer of 1935, a few months after Elizabeth fled West Palm Beach, Drew Brown Sr. once again turned himself in to local authorities on charges of assault and battery. The arrest, his first after the divorce, served as the proverbial straw that broke the camel's back. Unwilling to send his eldest son back to his mother, whom he no longer had contact with, Drew Sr. arranged for his son to be sent to Sanford to live with his grandmother, Ellen Brown. In a solemn and perhaps sentimental gesture, Drew Sr. dressed his boy in his best outfit and attached a note to the chest pocket of his flannel button-up shirt with a paper clip. The note read, "Do the best you can for him." Drew Sr. then walked his son into town, bought one greyhound bus ticket, and watched the small boy climb aboard. When the 162-mile trip was complete, Ellen Brown was waiting at the Sanford bus station for her grandson.

In a 1971 *Sports Illustrated* profile piece, Drew Jr.—Bundini—hinted at the story of how he came to Sanford. The quote is paraphrased at the beginning of Director Michael Mann's 2001 Muhammad Ali biopic.

"I was what I call a pillar-to-post baby. You know, born on a doorstep with a note on your chest that says, Do the best you can for him," Bundini stated.[6] By his own estimation, the note marked the beginning of what would become a nomadic life journey.

"Self-experience is one of the great things in the world, but I wouldn't say all people should live like me. Of ten born like me two will make it and only one [will] really make it. It's an exciting life. You meet all kinds and learn to know the truth, not just from words in a book. There's man's truth, and there's God's truth. I live by God's truth," Bundini added.

Moving to Sanford gave Drew Brown Jr. some measure of stability. His grandmother, Ellen Brown, had already taken in another grandson, Willy Brown Jr., whose mother had died of appendicitis when he was a small boy. At the time, there were no Black doctors in Sanford and, unless circumstances were dire, Black families were left with little to no medical resources. The two boys, close in age, came to think of each other as brothers.

In Sanford, Drew Jr. was no longer alone. Surrounded by his uncles Willy, Collie, Johnny, Alonzo, and Aunt Sade, along with their children, he developed an outgoing and boisterous personality. Even as a child, his voice was *the* commanding voice in the room. "You could hear Drew Jr. coming before he arrived," a family member suggested. Fiercely independent and prone to mischief, the young boy was known for his booming laugh and motormouth to match. Perhaps making up for lost time, Drew Brown Jr. quickly came to be known as the *talker* of the family.

With that being said, life in Sanford was hardly easy. By the age of eleven, during the end of the Depression years, Drew Jr. shined shoes and carried water for Civilian Conservation Corps crews building bridges in the Florida swamps. Their nickname for the boy was "Baby Gator." With a shoeshine rag over his bony shoulder, and a tin can full of change, the young boy sharpened his skills as a hustler, survival instincts bred by necessity.

■ ■ ■

Bundini's life in Sanford, Florida, was defined by two cornerstone moments, the first occurring on the night of June 22, 1938. Down at the Sanford Crossroads Store, one of the few venues where Black customers were welcome, a ten-year-old Drew Brown Jr. joined his father and his uncles Alonzo, Willie, Johnnie, and Coley as they huddled around the showroom radio. Thick cigar smoke and a palpable tension filled the air. The men shadowboxed and drank rounds of scotch and beer; the children played marbles and did their best to imitate the men.

Arguably the most sociopolitically significant sporting event of the early twentieth century, much was at stake in the rematch between Joe Louis and Max Schmeling. More so than in any moment in the history of professional boxing, the combatants personified the hopes and ambitions of their homelands. An aspect of the Louis–Schmeling fight that has been widely debated over the years, however, is the extent to which the fight encouraged the United States of America to put aside its racial differences to support the "Brown Bomber" as he sought redemption from the fighting pride of Nazi Germany. Patrick Myler, for example, argues that white Americans' admiration for Louis "did not galvanize them into demanding an immediate end to the widespread discrimination against their fellow black citizens."[7] While much of White America wanted to see the Nazi challenger defeated, Louis clearly meant something different to Blacks. Drew Brown Jr. was lost in the pageantry and spectacle of the occasion.

The first chapter of Joe Louis's life was heavily impacted by the prejudice and racism endemic of the time period. He was born in rural Alabama, where the Ku Klux Klan terrorized his family. When Louis was just a boy, his family fled to Detroit to escape the overt racism of the American south. In Detroit, Louis cultivated his boxing skills, compiling a professional record of thirty-one victories with only one defeat before capturing the heavyweight championship of the world from "The Cinderella Man," Jim Braddock, becoming only the second Black man to hold the storied crown. The lone blemish on Louis's resume was, of course, a twelfth-round knockout loss to the German Max Schmeling, occurring two years before the highly anticipated rematch. In their first fight, Schmeling used his jab to outbox the rising star, finally landing a powerful hook to the body, followed by a jarring right hand to Louis's jaw. Down for the first time in his young career, Louis was unable to beat the referee's count.

Schmeling, thirty-one years old at the time of his upset victory, instantly became a national hero in his native Germany. Following his upset victory over Louis, Schmeling was invited to a private dinner with Joseph Goebbels and Adolph Hitler and later, "with Schmeling at his side, Hitler watched a film of the fight, slapping his thigh with glee every time Schmeling connected."[8]

When Hitler ordered that a film titled *Schmeling's Victory: A German Victory* be shown in theaters throughout the country, Schmeling, largely apolitical, found himself in the unfortunate situation of being trapped within the Nazi propaganda machine, his victory touted as proof of Aryan superiority. Louis rebounded from the loss, winning his next eleven bouts and capturing the heavyweight title. Schmeling's life would never again be the same. American anti-Nazi groups threatened to boycott any Braddock–Schmeling title fight. Thus, Schmeling was, in the two years following his victory over Louis, forced to play the waiting game. When Louis dethroned Braddock, however, the rematch became inevitable. "Don't call me champion until I beat Schmeling," Louis told reporters.[9]

The buildup to Louis–Schmeling II was unprecedented. Weeks before the fight, Louis visited the White House, where President Franklin Roosevelt told the young champion, "Joe, we need muscles like yours to beat Germany." Schmeling arrived at Yankee Stadium for the rematch, accompanied by a Nazi Party publicist who issued statements that suggested Schmeling's purse would be used to build Nazi tanks. When the two rivals finally entered the ring, amid a sold-out crowd of over 70,000 spectators, the world seemingly stopped turning. The bout was broadcast by radio to millions of listeners throughout the world, with announcers reporting in multiple languages.

Down at the Sanford Crossroads Store, the men fell silent. Their hopes and dreams hung on the ring announcer's every word. Drew Brown Sr., not one for parental lectures, wrapped his sturdy sandpaper hand across his son's mouth to ensure the young chatterbox complied with the shared understanding of the room.

"Keep quiet, boy," Drew Sr. instructed his son before the bell rang.

Drew Jr., despite the momentary gag order, would never forget the excitement he felt. The boxing match lasted two minutes and four seconds. "The Brown Bomber" obliterated the the German, sending shock waves of racial and national pride throughout the country. When the call came across the radio, the men screamed and hollered and hugged each other, drinking and celebrating well into the night. After the fight, Louis received a police escort to the Hotel Teresa on 125th Street in Harlem, where Budd Schulberg conducted the postfight interview. In Sanford, the radio stayed on.

"I don't know what was said in that interview. My father didn't remember details, but whatever my father heard on the radio that night, he never forgot how the sounds from Harlem made him feel," Drew Brown III reflected.

Drew Brown Jr.—Bundini—had never seen his own father so joyful. For one fleeting second, his father had nothing to fight against. He'd won. Everyone at the Sanford Crossroads Store had won. The great Joe Louis would forever hold a special place in Drew Brown Jr.'s heart. Boxing was magic, the young boy figured.

And maybe there was magic in the air that night. The young Sanford boy couldn't have possibly dreamed that he would one day walk the streets of Harlem, or meet and befriend the great Joe Louis, let alone serve a key role in the lives of the two greatest boxers, of any race, to ever to walk the face of planet Earth.

■ ■ ■

The second, and perhaps most directly impactful, moment of Bundini's Sanford years occurred on November 3, 1942. When Naval Air Station Sanford was officially commissioned as an active naval base, the economic makeup of the town shifted instantly. During peak wartime, Naval Air Station Sanford enlisted 360 officers, and 14,000 enlisted men, both Navy and Marine Corps. Sanford, once a sleepy lakeside farm town, quickly transformed into a hub of naval activity.[10]

It was the white cotton hat, the jumper, and freshly pressed trousers. It was the dangling medals and aura of superiority these artifacts aroused in strangers. The uniform captured the young boy's imagination. An ultimate opportunist, Drew Brown Jr. took to the streets, shining the shoes of the enlisted men who made their way through town. This was a different brand of masculinity, a lifestyle in every way different from the inevitable fate Black men faced in the citrus groves of small-town Sanford.

"The naval base, when it started, Black folks didn't really pay it no mind. Black folks in Sanford worked in citrus groves and on the farms. That naval base wasn't for us. But Uncle Drew looked around and saw the kind of life that was waiting for him. Uncle Drew was not that kind of guy," Willy Brown III told me.

At thirteen years old, three months after the United States entered World War II, Drew Jr. arrived at Naval Air Station Sanford, eager to sign up for duty. Over six feet tall and with a stocky physique, Drew Jr. lied to Navy officials, telling them he was eighteen years old.

"He was tall for his age, probably looked nineteen or twenty years old, so they took him in as a steward," Willy Brown III added.

Dressed in white slacks, a matching button-up dress shirt and suit jacket, complete with a black bow tie, Drew Brown Jr. must have felt like he had accomplished something magnificent. The truth, however, was that he was brought aboard the ship to essentially fulfill the role of a servant. The Navy being the last of the U.S. military branches to fully integrate, Blacks in the 1940s were relegated to second-class citizenship there. Despite the showy uniform, Drew Brown Jr.'s job was anything but glamorous. As a naval steward, he prepared and served food, was responsible for cleaning the living quarters of officers, and shining their shoes just as he had done back in the streets of Sanford.

In an interview with *Sports Illustrated*, Bundini once outlined his brief career in the Navy, two years in total, consisting of service on three ships in three of the Pacific Islands invasions. Much of Drew Jr.'s service occurred in battles fought in the southwest Pacific and in Southeast Asia. In wartime, Bundini worked as "an ammunition loader locked between decks during battles." When things were calm, his role was that of a "mess boy dishing out soup and biscuits to officers."

Despite the menial work, imminent danger, and disparaging treatment, Drew Jr. was enraptured by his adventures at sea. His heart was truly beating for the first time. He was alive. "I loved the sea. Fell in love with it. The world becomes so small," he reflected.

Until joining the Navy, the teenager had never left the state of Florida, which is astounding considering the fact that Drew Jr. is given his famous moniker of Bundini thousands of miles away from the citrus groves and Crossroads stores of Sanford.

The Asia–Pacific War transformed Drew Brown Jr. in every way imaginable. It turned a wide-eyed country boy from central Florida into a man named *Bundini*.

Because of a broken screw in a torpedo, the ship was idle for just under a week. The temporary delay gave the handsome fifteen-year-old boy, dressed to impress in his all-white steward getup, a chance to explore the small port in India. For Drew Jr., this meant an opportunity to mingle with the beautiful Indian girls hanging around the docks. The attraction, it appears, was mutual.

"Bundini! Bundini! Bundini" a few Indian girls cried as the Navy ship pulled away.

On deck, a few of the officers observed the flirtatious farewell. *Bundini* was the name the young girls had bestowed upon Drew Brown Jr.

Word of mouth soon spread around the ship and a few of the officers took to teasing the young steward. The nickname Bundini (famously pronounced Bow-deenee by Muhammad Ali) would stick. Drew Brown Jr. was known as "Bundini Brown" for the rest of his tour of duty, and for the rest of his life for that matter.

"Daddy was very proud of the name," Drew Brown III recalled. "He always told me the word meant lover. It was like a Beatles moment for him, the girls were shouting—lover, lover, lover."

Playful teasing aside, the outright discrimination Bundini faced in the Navy would eventually prove too much for the young man. When he wasn't being called Bundini, he was being called "nigger." One officer, in particular, went out of his way to ensure that Bundini knew his place. The tension between the two would, over time, build and eventually bubble over.

"He was the ignorantest man I ever met," Bundini once told reporters, rehashing the buildup to his discharge.

The harassment, which began in the form of name-calling, steadily progressed. For some time, Bundini held his anger in check.

"If I was as ignorant as he was I'd've spit in his coffee and put glass in his food. I was just a nigger to him. I didn't understand *the word* then or I'd've laughed and kept going. A nigger is an ignorant man, not of color, and he was the nigger," Bundini told reporters.

"In the Navy, his duties were actually that of a ship's porter. One day, while he was shining a lieutenant's shoes, a white officer slapped him and called him a nigger. My father responded by throwing the man overboard. After that incident, the only thing that saved my father from being jailed and court-martialed was that he had lied about his age in order to join. His records confirmed that he wasn't eighteen," Drew Brown III said to me.

When the officer finally made it back onto the ship, Bundini was restrained. Some stories suggest that Bundini fetched a cleaver from the kitchen as a measure of self-defense. Regardless of the details, the incident would mark the end of Bundini's time in the Navy. The worst punishment, Bundini would later suggest, was losing the fancy uniform, his white getup and black bow tie.

"That was the worst part. Girls like uniforms, and I was only fifteen," Bundini would joke years later.

Despite the murky details surrounding Bundini's expulsion from the Navy, the undisputable truth is that he was only a boy.

"Daddy once told me that he took a black pen like a magic marker, and tried to make dots around his crotch that looked like pubic hair so that when he showered the rest of the porters would think he was a grown man," Drew III said to me. "Daddy turned that experience into one of his favorite expressions. 'Pen up,' he'd say. That meant, 'be a man,'" Drew added.

While Bundini's naval career was over, his life on the water continued. Neglecting to mention the incident, Bundini quickly signed up with the Merchant Marines. As a member of "the Merch," as Bundini would call it, he assisted in moving cargo and passengers between nations and also within the United States. The next twelve years of his life were spent at sea, sailing from one port to the next. According to Bundini, he traveled the world twenty-seven times as a member of the Merchant Marines. Between voyages, Bundini spent much of his free time in Philadelphia and New York City.

"I was on top of the world," Bundini reflected.

"New York was a play toy to me, like Paris and London. Japan was just another seaport. I was a pirate. When a man is a traveler, the world is his house and the sky is his roof, and where he hangs his hat is home and all people are his family," Bundini argued.

Sanford, Florida, would never get Drew Brown Jr. back, not completely. He'd escaped the citrus groves. He'd escaped the Ku Klux Klan. He'd escaped cyclical poverty. He'd found a way out of the swamps. He'd escaped his abusive father, the small-town sheriffs, and the racist naval officers. Bundini now fancied himself a cosmopolitan, a world traveler.

Perhaps the only way to survive in a society that says you do not belong is to live as if you belong nowhere.

2

A Rosebud in Harlem

In the rubble of the war-torn city of Kiev, nationalist soldiers viciously beat and torture an old Jewish man with the butts of their rifles. A thick stratus of smoke hangs above the city like a gloomy specter. The soldiers laugh and drink vodka. They bellow obscenities while spitting on their hostage. Blood fills the mouth of the Jew. He is gagging, unable to beg for mercy. Behind the broken glass of a twisted, rusted window frame and inside the ruins of a bombed-out warehouse hides a small child and his parents, some twenty-five yards away. Their home has been burned to the ground. All that remains is a smoldering pile of ash. The carnage will last for three days. Forty-five Jews will be massacred. Thirty-five women and young girls will be raped.[1]

Deep in the woods of Seminole County, Florida, members of the Ku Klux Klan place a noose around the neck of a twenty-year-old Black man named John West. Earlier in the day, the jury returned a verdict of "not guilty" on a charge of rape and the judge declared West free to return home. At 9 p.m., John West boards the Sanford Short Railroad Line. Sheriff Karel buys the ticket, tells him to get on out of here. When the locomotive arrives at the Sanford depot, an angry mob awaits. West's hands are tied behind his back. His clothes are ripped and frayed. He is shoeless. His pants are pulled down to his ankles and he is castrated. Illuminated by the dancing shadows of cruel flames, the body of a gangly, unimposing figure makes its way up the large sycamore tree.

The old Jew is shot and the Black man swings and shakes until he is dead.

"Brighton Beach, not Europe or Palestine, is the real promised land for Jews . . . where we may practice the religion of our forefathers without interference from narrow-minded bigots or maniacs," Dr. Maxwell Ross reflects during the dedication of the newest of Brighton's synagogues in 1937.[2] For the massive influx of Jewish refugees fleeing Europe as a result of the tyrannical reign of Adolf Hitler, Brighton Beach, New York, located in the southernmost portion of Brooklyn, is a safe haven from European repression. Conveniently positioned along the Coney Island peninsula, facing the Atlantic Ocean, the neighborhood was once a summer hotspot for New York City tourists. With the market crash of 1929, however, property values significantly plummet and migrant Jewish workers, often by way of the Lower East Side, settle in the area. Jobless families, composed of first- and second-generation Russian immigrants, consolidate households. During the years just before and after the Great Depression, new apartment buildings are erected, shifting the social dynamics of the neighborhood, transforming Brighton Beach into "Little Odessa."

For a downtrodden race of people, delivered from slavery but not yet fully American, Harlem, New York, is the promised land. What was once a predominantly white neighborhood composed of Lutheran churches and Dutch settlers is quickly transformed into a burgeoning community of Black cultural and intellectual life, a strange mix of poverty and promise. Harlem's massive demographic shift is, in large part, connected to a post–World War I exodus of rural Black families fleeing the institutionalized racism of the South. In Uptown Manhattan, Blacks form a new society, "not just as transients, or even residents, but as proprietors."[3] By the late 1920s, seventy percent of Harlem's real estate is under Black control. The poetry, fiction, art, music, and history born amid these conditions, "reflecting a forward-thinking optimism and deeply felt community pride," can only be properly described as a renaissance. Eleven housing projects. Twelve thousand low- and moderate-rent apartments. Thirty thousand Black and brown faces packed into a twenty-four-block radius. Harlem is coming of age.

Be they redemptive, reformative, or revolutionary, social movements are more than surface waves of the human condition, caused by winds of change. Social movements are the result of a larger gravitational pull. Freedom is the most basic of human needs. In this regard, we are all pushed and pulled by the violent undertows of war. This is a story of freedom. It is a story of worlds colliding; star-crossed lovers, the descendants of slaves, in search of nothing more than freedom. On the gentle shores of Brighton Beach and in the wild jazz joints of fair Harlem, we lay our scene. This is the story of Drew Bundini Brown and his Rosebud.

■ ■ ■

Jack Palestine was born in the tiny village of Rohachiv, located thirty miles from the city of Kiev, on March 24, 1905. These were cruel and unforgiving times to be born the son of Orthodox Jews. From 1791 to 1917, Jewish residency was restricted beyond the western region of the country, a firmly mandated set of boundaries known as "the Pale of Settlement." Jews were denied the opportunity to reside within a number of cities in the Pale as well. The constricts of Jewish life in Imperialist Russia transformed cities, such as Kiev, into easy targets for the growing plague of anti-Semitic violence rapidly spreading throughout early-twentieth-century Europe. Just seven months after Jack Palestine's birth, for example, a two-day massacre ravaged the nearby city of Kiev. Approximately one hundred Jews were slaughtered in a two-day riot directed against the factories, shops, and homes of Jewish residents. In the coming years, a three-party civil war would erupt, making way for a revolution that would forever transform Russia. Looking to escape the bigotry and brutality surrounding their daily lives in Rohachiv, the Palestine family, like many Jewish families in the area, fled their mother country in hopes of finding refuge in the United States. Freedom was the wave that brought Jack Palestine to the docks of Ellis Island on March 12, 1913, just eleven days shy of his eighth birthday.

Mildred Stromberg was a beautiful Jewish girl with a bewitching smile and an outgoing personality to match. Her parents were also Jewish immigrants from the war-ravaged village of Rohachiv, but she and her older brothers, Maxie and Sidney, were born in Brooklyn. Mildred's Brighton Beach childhood could not have been more different than that of her parents. A rich cultural and religious presence and a profound sense of freedom and hope permeated the streets of her neighborhood. Yiddish-speaking bookstores, restaurants, banks, schools, synagogues, and social clubs were the norm. In 1918, for instance, the Brighton Beach Music Hall was converted into a Yiddish theater, the first of its kind in the United States. Brighton Beach was theirs, sandy beaches and peaceful shores. Immigrant Jews had little reason to leave the comfort and safety of their carefully constructed safe haven. In this regard, the lives of second-generation immigrant Jews could, at times, feel quite determined. One day Mildred Stromberg would marry a hard-working Jewish boy from the neighborhood and they would have children, continuing the cycle. Traditions would be passed on from generation to generation and Brighton Beach would never have to end. Much of Mildred's young life followed this blueprint.

On March 10, 1929, Mildred Stromberg married the love of her life, a twenty-four-year-old Brighton boy named Jack Palestine, the son of immigrants from her parents' native village. Jack was a kind man, with a thin face and thick-rimmed glasses. He carried himself with a quiet confidence.

"Did you know that I used to box?" Jack Palestine joked with children in the neighborhood.

"I boxed oranges" was his punchline.

In some ways, Palestine was a traditionally masculine figure; he maintained the strong physique of a manual laborer. Yet his words were soft. There was no ego or hypermasculine rhetoric in his speech. Aside from "garshdarnit"—Jack's favorite utterance of frustration—he never came close to cursing or raising his voice. Of the two, Mildred was the extrovert. Short in stature and big on personality, Mildred's beautiful auburn hair bounced about her shoulders as she espoused her opinions. You didn't have to guess what Mildred Palestine was thinking. She was, as the cliché goes, a straight shooter. After the marriage ceremony, the Palestine family settled into their new home at Waldorf Apartments, located in an all-white Jewish neighborhood at the southern end of the boardwalk, a seemingly perfect location to carry on the hopes and dreams of their lineage. Their first child, Rhoda May Palestine, was born on February 4, 1930. Rhoda's brother, Herbert, arrived three years later.

The Palestines were, in many respects, a typical Brighton Beach family. Mildred and Jack spoke Yiddish and perfect English. As was the custom in Brighton households, however, Yiddish was mostly spoken as a code language that would allow for parents to discuss matters in front of their children. English was paramount. The true success of Brighton parents came in the form of the success of their Americanized offspring. Children were raised to have courage and to believe they had the intelligence and talent necessary to break through and do things they never dreamed possible. With this freedom came appropriate boundaries, areas never to be transgressed, lines never to be crossed, as dictated by the traditions of the Jewish faith. Herbie Palestine, as he was called by friends and family, was a good Jewish boy. He was loving, kind, and dependable. Herbie did as he was told and worked hard to make his parents proud. His big sister, Rhoda, on the other hand, was a free spirit from the start. As a young girl, she was as brilliant as she was beautiful, an extroverted wild child with a rebellious spirit. She and Mildred mixed like oil and water, perhaps because underneath the surface they were so much alike.

The personality dynamics of the household can best be exemplified by the story of Jack Palestine's near-death accident at the fruit company where he worked for many years. When Mildred and her brothers arrived at the hospital, Jack was unconscious. His body had been smashed between two trucks at the loading docks. The family gathered around the bed. A rabbi was called into the room to say *mitzvahs* (prayers). The doctor, his face a canvas of concern, spoke frankly with Mildred.

"Your husband is in critical condition. These are very serious injuries, Mrs. Palestine. You need to go find a suit to bury him in. Jack might not recover," he added.

To this prognosis, Mildred gave no reply. She simply walked around the hospital bed and slapped her husband square in the face.

Smack!

"Get up, *goddamit*, get up! What the hell do you think you're doing, Jack Palestine? You can't leave me with these two kids. Oh, no. I won't stand for it. So just get yourself up, right this minute. And don't you think about dying. You hear me, Jack?"

And, like a poorly written scene from a Hollywood movie, Jack Palestine opened his eyes and lived for another thirty years. He and his son were pacifists; the women of the Palestine family were firecrackers.

Irwin Levowitz, Rhoda Palestine's second cousin, lived in an apartment located one floor above Jack and Mildred's unit in Brighton Beach. In our conversations, Irwin outlined the family dynamic.

"Bubba [Mildred] was loving, but she could be tough. She would bang on the ceiling of her apartment with a broom, shouting for us to quiet down! Poppa Jack was the complete opposite. If there ever was such a thing as a Jewish saint, it was him. Poor Jack had to have the patience of a saint to deal with his wife and daughter, who were both very volatile characters. Herbie took after his father, but Rhoda definitely took after her mother," Levowitz recalled.

During her early teenage years, Rhoda incited more pride than paranoia. In 1943, she enrolled in Abraham Lincoln High School, where she became the editor of the school paper, *The Lincoln Log*. Her dream was to become a journalist. Rhoda was going to make a difference—she was going to save the world. As a birthday present, Mildred and Jack bought her an Underwood typewriter, and thus began Rhoda's career as a writer. As a young woman, she wrote the following essay:

An Ongoing Philosophical Search for the Best That This Life Has to Offer[4]

What is our purpose having once left our mother's womb and been granted life on Earth? Is it not to have in some way made a difference by our existence, using our minds and bodies within reason? Hopefully and rationally we found a decent set of values which we then put into action and left this world in a little better condition than we found it. These values indicated that we not only were responsible for our own actions but were responsible for the actions of others, if it denied some people the entitlement of all human rights to live with dignity, integrity, virtue, and respect and the right to pursue their own chosen work without harassment. It is our social responsibility to call these brothers and sisters to task and communicate the need for responsible individual and community action.

Beauty and harmony—the truth to music to our ears, peaceful co-existence and understanding the richness of the difference of all cultures. Socrates said, "Music First," to stimulate the rhythms of the soul and then gymnastics for a healthy balanced state to aid us in the struggle of daily living.

In Plato's "The Republic," he states that it was impossible for one man to do many arts well. Whatever the craft it requires knowledge of its science and practice to keep reaching for a more profound goal. The guardian's role is to be qualified by nature with gifts of flexible perception and insight and having the ability to use it. Plato again suggests that the soul thirsts for reason, desire, and a high spirit. We are also the guardians of our own souls, with intellect and strong heart and that bubbling ocean and sometimes death sea calm.

Aside from her promise as a writer and thinker, Rhoda was, at times, a handful for her teachers. She was often punished for dancing in the hallways and scolded by teachers for her theatrical behavior in the classroom.

"I'm the reincarnation of Genghis Khan or Sitting Bull," Rhoda often joked, demonstrating a rebellious attitude that often didn't sit well with teachers—or in her Orthodox household.[5]

In her late teens, Rhoda frequently attended USO centers and Coast Guard dances at the Maritime in Manhattan Beach. During World War II, Rhoda worked the monitor board at the USO center near her home. With her long red hair, big doe eyes and curly lashes, and teasing smile and infectious laugh, Rhoda's presence did not go unnoticed by the naval officers. Men flocked to Rhoda and she quickly came to understand and enjoy the power of her seduction. Unlike her younger brother, Herbie, who did his best to avoid the scorn of his parents, Rhoda was in a hurry to become her own woman, driven to discover the world outside of Brighton Beach. In 1946, Rhoda graduated from Abraham Lincoln High School, a year early.

After graduation, Rhoda worked at several New York City nightclubs, often as a camera girl. Her job was to flirt with customers, get them to pose for a picture, and then present them with the finished product later in the night. It was the perfect line of work for a young, beautiful woman with an outgoing personality. Getting paid to listen to, and sometimes socialize with, famous jazz musicians touring New York City was certainly an added bonus. Despite her somewhat sheltered upbringing, Rhoda was no stranger to the jazz scene. Unbeknownst to her parents, Rhoda had, for some time, been taking secret excursions to Harlem. At eighteen years old, she knew all of the hottest jazz joints and had met Miles Davis, Duke Ellington, and Count Basie. Rhoda's musical hero, however, was the legendary jazz songstress Billie Holiday.

"I knew conventional life, and I wanted to see what the other side of life was like. Back in high school, my friends and I were always talking about Freudian psychology, or about how much we hated our parents because we thought they were the cause of all our problems," Rhoda once wrote to her son.

Amid the blue notes and improvisation of the Harlem jazz scene, Rhoda found the other side. At eighteen years old, and against the wishes of her parents, Rhoda moved to California, then on to Florida, where, for a brief period, she worked at a nightclub that featured celebrity impersonators as entertainment. Mildred and Jack, as one might suspect, were concerned by their daughter's behavior. After a series of long and grueling negotiations, they finally talked their daughter into moving back to New York City and enrolling in beauty school. This career move would do little to temper Rhoda's love for Manhattan nightlife. On Thursday nights, she and her beauty school classmates would perfect their bouffant hairdos and go directly to Birdland. By the summer of 1952, Rhoda was back in Greenwich Village, working as a camera girl at the Village Vanguard.

While modern-day music fans likely think of the Vanguard as a premier destination for jazz, the twenty-two-year-old version of Rhoda Palestine had no such luck. When Rhoda worked at the club, folk music and beat poetry were the business model. Folk wasn't Rhoda's cup of tea, and apparently such was the case for the Village Vanguard patrons of the day as well. Business steadily declined, managerial positions changed hands, and Rhoda was laid off.

"That didn't bother me. We all belonged to the 'Fifty-Two/Twenty Club.' Twenty dollars' unemployment for fifty-two weeks," Rhoda once wrote.

Those unemployment checks were spent at Rhoda's favorite jazz joint, The French Quarters, located on West 46th Street in Manhattan. Back in Brooklyn, Mildred Palestine paced the floors, wringing her hands with worry. For Rhoda, it must have felt like a moral victory over fate itself. She had escaped the standardized life that had been so carefully planned for her in Brighton Beach. She'd escaped sameness. She'd escaped rules. She'd escaped rituals. She'd escaped prescribed ways of thinking, feeling, and believing. With no long-term career plan, no safety net to catch her tightrope walk, Rhoda Palestine was free to be any kind of person she wanted to be. She was free to slip. She was free to fall.

■ ■ ■

It was a balmy summer night. The French Quarters was filled with cigarette smoke, sweaty patrons, and the sound of jazz trumpet, a palpable kinetic energy in the air. The capacity crowd was there to hear the great Miles Davis. Wearing a sleek black dress and high heels, a twenty-dollar bill stuffed in her bra, Rhoda Palestine squeezed through the crowd, made her way to the bar, and ordered a Johnnie Walker Black Label with a glass of water on the side. She did not pay for the drink.

"The place was full, so I figured some guy would treat me. And before I ordered the next drink, me still listening to Miles, that's what happened," Rhoda recalled.

"You're the prettiest red rose I've ever seen. I'm buying you this drink."[6]

The smooth voice washed over her body, not unlike the beautiful music hanging above the crowd. Rhoda glanced over her shoulder, felt a shiver up her spine. Dressed in a pearl-gray jacket with a black button-up shirt and a white satin tie stood Drew Bundini Brown.

"I turned around and I saw these flashing eyes and a shining happy face with bright flashing teeth—a beautiful black handsome face," she remembered.

Rhoda Palestine's life would never be the same.

At twenty-four years old, Drew Brown Jr. was a clean-shaven, strapping young man. He was a sharp dresser who wore his hair in the popular conk style, perhaps the most popular hairstyle among Black men at the time. Made famous by celebrities such as Chuck Berry, Fats Domino, and Little Richard, the conk was the result of a chemical mixture that relaxed naturally "kinky" hair, allowing it to be styled in a variety of ways. Obtaining this hairstyle was something of a cultural badge of honor. The relaxer, composed of lye, eggs, and potatoes, often resulted in chemical burns if not applied correctly. Bundini's conk had come out so well that his local barber asked him to come back the next day and take a professional portrait. Until the barbershop closed some years later, Bundini's framed picture hung in the window as an example for future customers.

Aside from his clean-shaven face, warm smile, and stylish demeanor, Bundini also possessed the gift of gab. He could talk his way in or out of any situation. The English language was his artistic weapon, and when it came to painting verbal portraits, he was Leonardo da Vinci. After a few more Johnnie Walkers for Rhoda, and a few Chivas Regals for himself, Bundini left The French Quarters in the early hours of that warm summer morning with the beautiful Rhoda Palestine on his arm.

In a fit of passion, Rhoda spent the next three nights at Drew Bundini Brown's modest Harlem apartment. Despite the dirty socks and pawn tickets scattered about, she was fully enamored by her lover. Brighton Beach had been full of good Jewish boys who listened to their parents and spent their days planning for the future. Those boys were safe, careful in their approach to life and love. Rhoda could predict what they were going to say before they even said it. Boys like that embodied everything Rhoda hoped she would never become. She had, for some time, stopped thinking of them as men at all. Drew Bundini Brown, on the other hand, was the walking personification of jazz, each moment of his life a wild improvisation. He talked the language of the streets, lived his life according to no tradition or external code of conduct. Here was a man who had been around the world, both literally and figuratively. Despite his youthful face, his was the soul of a traveler. Here was a man who did what he wanted, when he wanted. Drew Brown was different. He was exciting, something forbidden. Rhoda was primarily attracted to him because she admired his freedom. All of the pragmatic reasons they would never work as a romantic couple, when turned inside out, told the story of her attraction.

Or maybe it was the other way around. Bundini had never met a woman like Rhoda May Palestine. He'd never met a woman who could talk Socrates just as easy as she could talk Duke Ellington. He'd never met a beautiful white woman who cared very little about being beautiful or white. Back in Sanford, talking to white women could be a death sentence for a Black man. Here, lying in his Harlem bed, was a beautiful white woman. She loved jazz. She loved life. In fact, life was Rhoda's religion. Live your life and enjoy your life and be good to others were Rhoda's only commandments. In Bundini's young mind, difference made their sexual attraction all the more magnetic. Rhoda's home life, her education, her opportunities were in direct opposition to the story of his own existence. Rhoda had every advantage that Bundini never had and was willing to throw it all away for him. The Black Prince, as Bundini was often called on the streets of Harlem, was all but certain he'd found his princess.

After three wild nights in Harlem, Rhoda returned home to Brighton Beach. The following day, however, Bundini showed up in Brooklyn, phoning the Palestine residence from the boardwalk. To put it lightly, Rhoda was caught off guard. "You can't come up here," she warned, fearing how her mother might react.

"If we are going to be together, I need to meet your parents," Bundini argued.

"This isn't Harlem or Birdland," Rhoda replied, perhaps learning something about herself that she did not like.

"Rosebud," Bundini called, referencing the nickname he'd bestowed upon her that first night in The French Quarters. "I love you. I just want to meet your family," he pleaded.

After ten minutes of back-and-forth conversation, Rhoda finally gave in, hung up the phone, and prepared her mother for the unexpected visitor.

From the minute Drew Bundini Brown entered the apartment, Mildred Palestine was putty in his hands. Never had Bundini's oratory skills been so necessary. He was polite, considerate, and, at times, had Mildred in tears from laughing. From Rhoda's vantage point, everything was going as well as one could possibly expect, given the circumstances of the visit. That was until Brown made his true intentions evident.

"I've come out here to ask for Rosebud's hand in marriage, Mrs. Palestine," Bundini said, grinning as if the answer could be nothing else but yes.

"*Oy vay*," Mildred said, gazing toward the heavens.

"My husband's already sick. And if he comes home, this will make him worse. He might just drop dead. When he arrives, please tell him you're the plumber," Mildred begged.

Bundini would have none of it. When Jack Palestine returned home from work later that evening, Bundini was waiting.

The conversation was calm and cordial. Jack sat down on the couch next to Bundini and talked to him man to man. He showed Bundini courtesy and respect, hearing him out with a patience most fathers would not have in such circumstances.

"I want your blessing, Mr. Palestine. I love Rosebud and I'll take care of her."

"God made red apples and green apples," Bundini continued, attempting to alleviate any concerns about the couple's racial differences.

Rhoda was now more in awe of her lover than was the case that first night at The French Quarters. In less than an hour, Bundini had charmed both parents. He talked circles around their worries and trepidations.

If Jack Palestine had only asked Bundini for the specifics of how he planned to provide for his daughter, the young lover would have been able to offer no suitable response. In fact, he might have had to fall back on Mildred's original plan, claiming his identity as the plumber.

During his early days in Harlem, Bundini did, on occasion, hold down a legitimate job. He worked at Shelton Oliver's Rib House on an on-again-off-again basis. He even sold carpet at a local furniture store. By the time he met his Rosebud, however, Bundini had already earned his reputation in the streets. In Harlem, he was known as the Black Prince, Fast Black, or Bundini Brown, a hustler who learned to read people rather than books. His confidants were pimps, players, and dealers.

"I met Bundini years before I met Ali," Gene Kilroy, Ali's longtime friend, once told me. "I remember it like it was yesterday. I was in Birdland, sitting next to the great entertainer Lloyd Price, and I hear this booming voice coming from the back, shouting 'The Black Prince is here . . . the Black Prince is here.' I almost spilled my drink."

"When I was a little kid in my stroller, Daddy would shout 'The Black Prince is here' as we made our way through the streets of Harlem," Drew Brown III recalled when I relayed Kilroy's story. "He would shout it so loud that it would make me cry."

Whether it was in the clubs or on the streets, you couldn't do business in Harlem without hearing, or hearing of, the Black Prince. Nobody messed with Bundini. He was connected with the right, or wrong, kind of people, depending on how one chooses to look at the situation.

As the months went by, Drew and Rhoda continued their romantic relationship. They would meet up in jazz joints and, on a more frequent basis, Rhoda began spending nights in Harlem. Discouraged, or perhaps awakened, by Mildred Palestine's concerns, the couple decided to forgo the conventions of marriage and accept their odd pairing for what it was. As the relationship continued, Rhoda spent more nights in Harlem than in Brighton Beach. Mildred gradually picked up on what was happening. Once she learned that her daughter was sharing a bed, and an apartment, with Bundini, she made it her business to get the two married. Shaped by the morals and principals of her orthodox Jewish background, Mildred was determined to turn her daughter's budding love affair into something more stable. The next time Bundini visited their Brighton Beach apartment, Mildred made sure the subject of marriage became a conversational centerpiece.

"We decided that we aren't going to get married," Bundini said, incorrectly guessing that Mildred would be delighted at such news. This infuriated Mildred even more than the idea of her daughter marrying a Black man.

Although the passion Drew Brown Jr. and Rhoda Palestine felt for each other was undeniably real, the marriage, one could argue, was doomed from the start. There would be no romantic honeymoon or religious ceremony honoring faith, family, and tradition. The original wedding ceremony was to take place in the most ironic of locations, Bundini's Harlem apartment.

When Rhoda and Mildred arrived, they found a Pentecostal preacher, dressed in long purple robes, sitting on the zebra-print sofa, Bundini nervously pacing back and forth. Mildred, quick to read the situation, could tell the groom was having second thoughts.

"Don't worry. This kind of marriage doesn't count," Mildred assured her soon-to-be son-in-law. "Get married a'ready," she added, nonchalantly.

Mildred's last-ditch efforts did little to tame Bundini's indecision. In fact, they had the opposite effect. When the preacher confirmed for Bundini that the marriage would indeed be legally binding, he became irate.

"I'm not getting married," he boldly contended, citing Mildred's lie as justification for his sudden change of heart.

Embarrassed by the calamity that was unfolding, Rhoda arrived at her breaking point. In a fit of rage, she tore the marriage certificate into as many pieces as she possibly could.

"So long," Rhoda shouted, storming out of the apartment, dragging her mother along the way.

The next day Rhoda returned to Harlem to collect her clothes and personal belongings. The relationship, she believed, was over. Mildred, hoping to avoid confrontation, waited outside in a cab. With hands shaky from trepidation, Rhoda slid the key into the lock and turned, an arrival met with silence. Bundini was nowhere to be found. Rhoda quickly made her way to the bedroom and began shoveling clothes into an empty suitcase. In less than a few minutes, she collected everything she needed. Her perfectly scripted getaway, however, was interrupted when something on the coffee table caught her eye. It was the marriage license, perfectly reconstructed with Scotch tape. Rhoda picked it up, felt the rough edges in her hands. Through the pain and disappointment, she found a place in her heart to marvel at Bundini's patchwork. Rhoda placed the damaged certificate where she found it and exited the apartment, more peacefully than had been the case less than twenty-four hours earlier.

And there he was, standing at the bottom of the stairway, Mildred Palestine by his side.

"Rosebud," Bundini called, tears forming at the corners of his eyes. "Rosebud, I was scared. I've never loved a woman."

On Wednesday, October 29, 1952, Drew Brown Jr. and Rhoda Palestine were legally united in marriage. The ceremony, conducted by Reverend Melvin Solomon, took place at 302 West 122nd Street in Manhattan. Mildred Palestine served as the witness. And, as family legend has it, Drew Bundini Brown fainted when the Reverend said the words, "I now pronounce you man and wife."

At twenty-four years old, Drew Brown knew nothing of the dynamics of a successful marriage. Simply put, he'd never seen a successful marriage up close. His own mother, Elizabeth, had left him when he was only a child, and in traumatic fashion no less. The abrupt separation, as is often the case with children impacted by divorce or the loss of a parent, intensified Brown's adolescent thirst for independence. He spent much of his young life relying on himself, perhaps harboring a deep-seated resentment and distrust toward women in general.

"I tell you, it was a major problem in his life. Not just his mother leaving him, but leaving him in a crazy situation, and for the rest of his life feeling abandoned. He didn't understand why she didn't fight harder to take him," Drew Brown III suggested to me on one of my visits to him, holding the wrinkled marriage certificate in his hands.

Taking on the responsibility of caring for another human being was a new and strange endeavor, a task that Bundini was utterly unprepared for. Rhoda's concept of marriage, on the other hand, was molded by her strict Orthodox upbringing. Despite her skepticism of the concept of marriage, she was impacted by the gender-specific pressures surrounding Jewish girls in Brighton Beach.

"Growing up, I really wanted to be a virgin for my husband—whoever he might be. All of us girls felt that way to some extent, but I was serious. I dreamed about that special thing where I would fall in love, right, and be a virgin . . . but when I saw married people who weren't really happy, I wanted to cut through all the crap," Rhoda recalled.

"I came to believe that a woman's role in life was a combination of, like a Jewish mother and a geisha girl," she added.

Both Harlem newlyweds were experiencing the same internal struggle. Bundini's childhood in Sanford had been just as confined as Rhoda's life in Brighton Beach. Blacks in Sanford were prisoners to invisible borders;

Jews in Brighton lived according to strict moral codes. The couple had long been at odds with the power structures that dictated appropriate behavior in their communities. Drew and Rhoda fancied themselves rule breakers, to put it mildly. Their marriage, controversial by the cultural standards of the early 1950s, could be anything they wanted it to be.

Married life, for the Browns, consisted of torrid nights at jazz joints, listening to Billie Holiday, Duke Ellington, and Miles Davis, drinking and smoking well into the morning. As the months went by, Bundini began to do his own thing, hanging out with friends and going about life per usual. Rhoda did the same. When they would reunite at their Harlem apartment, one or sometimes both partners returned after having too much to drink. When Bundini would turn up missing for more than a few days, Rhoda would phone her mother in Brighton Beach. Mildred Palestine, a small, heavyset Jewish woman, served as a one-woman search party, sometimes dragging Bundini out of local bars by the ear in front of the pimps, hustlers, and gangsters who were watching in shock, having never seen the Black Prince belittled publicly.

"You should have seen Bubba and Bundini. Here was this big, Black, strapping, handsome man, an intimidating figure. And Bubba, this short, heavyset Jewish woman, smacking him over the head with a dish towel, shouting 'You bastard, you bastard,'" Rhoda's cousin, Irwin Levowitz, told me.

Aside from the frequent clashes with Mildred, most of which were justified, Bundini slowly began to win over members of Rhoda's side of the family. Based on our conversations, Levowitz clearly fell into this category.

"After they got married, I didn't have contact with him for a couple of months. Then I had to have shoulder surgery. I was injured playing football on the beach, without pads or a helmet. I was in the hospital in Harlem, long before it was gentrified. I was in there for six straight weeks after surgery. I was in a semiprivate room. The nurses were all Black and they pretty much ignored me. Bundini, God bless him, came to visit. 'How ya doing, Cousin Irwin,' Bundini called. It was like a scene out of that movie *Twins*, with Arnold Schwarzenegger and Danny DeVito. You should have seen the nurses looking at us when he said that. I remember Bundini brought me some barbeque from this place I liked. I told him the nurses weren't paying much attention to me. So the nurse comes in. He says, 'I hear you aren't taking good care of my cousin. You better fix that in a hurry.' After that, you'd have thought I was a representative of the royal family, the treatment I got," Levowitz recalled.

At first, Drew and Rhoda's open marriage, bohemian by the standards of the day, was the ideal arrangement for both partners. "I was never jealous about [Bundini] being with other women," Rhoda recalled. "For his thirtieth birthday, I paid for a gal to be with him. And he wasn't jealous of me. We weren't like that," she added. Unlike her husband, Rhoda knew the trappings of conventional life. She was well versed in the rules and standards of Orthodox Jewish marriage. Her attraction to Bundini was physical, spiritual, and philosophical. Rhoda longed for the kind of freedom Bundini had found traveling the world, living life on his own. Bundini's open disregard for social standards, his lack of concern for money, status, and power, was a key component of the attraction. In her unconventional marriage, Rhoda found new ways of being. The price of this newfound freedom was poverty. Aside from the obvious disadvantage of being a Black man in pre-civil-rights America, Bundini's prospects were especially limited. He had quit school in the third grade and was functionally illiterate.

"My father couldn't read well enough to study a manual and learn a skill," Drew Brown III reflected. "He couldn't read a magazine with sufficient insight to see how other people lived and aspire to another kind of life for himself."

The other side of conventional life was all that Bundini had ever known. Survival skills were the only skills he possessed. When the money ran out, Bundini knew that he could hustle to get it back. By the end of their first year of marriage, the honeymoon, so to speak, had come to a dizzying crescendo, if not a crash. Unable to sustain their jazz-joint lifestyle, the couple no longer frequented Birdland, The French Quarters, or any of their old haunts. Living off next to nothing, they rarely left the Harlem neighborhood at all.

■ ■ ■

While times were hard for Drew and Rhoda, Harlem, on the other hand, was in the midst of an unlikely socioeconomic resurgence. Along a two-block strip on Harlem's Seventh Avenue (now Adam Clayton Powell Jr. Boulevard, between 123rd and 124th Streets), an array of unused property was bought, refurbished, and reopened. The man behind the Seventh Avenue makeover was none other than the former welterweight and middleweight champion of the world, Sugar Ray Robinson. For the budding entrepreneur, recently retired from the ring with a record of 132-3-2-1, the early 1950s was a time of great prosperity.[7]

"[Sugar Ray's] businesses were gaining momentum in concert with the building boom in low-cost housing in the community," journalist Herb Boyd writes, outlining the perfect storm of economic conditions.

Shoulder to shoulder, like something off the Las Vegas strip, were Sugar Ray's Golden Gloves Barber Shop, Sugar Ray's Quality Cleaners, Edna Mae's Lingerie Shop, Sugar Ray Robinson Enterprises, and the most sought-after location of all, Sugar Ray's, a restaurant and nightclub that regularly attracted the likes of Frank Sinatra, Jackie Gleason, Nat King Cole, Dorothy Dandridge, Eartha Kitt, as well as prominent sports figures such as Joe Louis and Jackie Robinson. At thirty-two years old, the beloved and world-renowned champion was at a transitional moment in his life. Along with his philanthropic efforts, Robinson sought a career in show business (singing and tap dancing, in particular). When Robinson's flamingo-pink Cadillac made its way through the neighborhood, Harlem's most famous proprietor was greeted with a king's welcome. Robinson's business dealings bolstered the morale of a downtrodden community and, more likely than not, saved the life of Drew Bundini Brown.

In 1953, Drew and Rhoda relocated to a one-bedroom apartment located directly above Sugar Ray Robinson's nightclub. At first, the move appeared to be a step toward self-destruction. The couple would no longer have to travel any distance whatsoever to find the temptations that plagued their young marriage. In Drew Brown III's 1991 book *You Gotta Believe!*, Rhoda Palestine reflects on her brief foray into the life on the streets: "When Drew said we had to hustle, I took it on as a role, and really as a learning experience. I didn't care to make that much money. Just enough. So I guess I said okay, because I believed that, one day, I could use the experience somewhere in my life. Maybe as an actress, or to write a book—who knows what you think when you are young? And I was young—twenty-two—so I believed that nothing could get in our way."

For Rhoda, who could be just as rhetorically savvy as her husband, the hustle could be likened to that of a marriage counselor or psychiatrist. In the Harlem streets, hotels, and nightclubs where such activity frequently took place, Rhoda learned how to spot an easy target. As she gained confidence in her new trade, Rhoda became adept at getting men to pay her for conversation, as opposed to sexual pleasure. Fully immersed in Harlem street culture, the couple survived day to day.

"You mustn't believe, son, that [your father] was the cause. He wasn't really. We had to eat to live," Rhoda would later write to her son, reflecting back on the darkest days of her marriage. "Even when Drew wasn't good to me, I could see a goodness in that man," she added.

Back in Brighton Beach, Rhoda's family feared they had lost Rhoda to the streets of Harlem. Jack and Mildred Palestine worried themselves sick. Mildred relentlessly lectured her son-in-law, warning him about his association with "the wrong kinds of people." Bundini, however, was a product of the Florida swamps; survival was his hustle.

"My father was a player on the streets of Harlem. During the early fifties, some players were pimps or drug dealers; others ran scams or con games. But since all the best players survived by their wits, my father was a natural," Drew Brown III said to me.

"Granddaddy Drew hadn't given him much of a childhood, but he had raised his son to be a survivor. Daddy was well prepared to hustle," Drew continued, handing over a photograph of Mildred Palestine, dressed in a floral print dress, standing next to the legendary Sugar Ray Robinson.

3

Honey and Sugar

Rogers Simon was king of the Harlem hairdressers, Sugar Ray's Golden Gloves Barber Shop his stylistic palace. *Jet* magazine credited Simon as being the creator of the "finger-wave," a processing technique of straightening and flattening kinky hair by greasing it down and shaping it into an S pattern, a hairstyle that quickly became popular among prominent Black celebrities of the day. In Harlem, Simon was best known as the personal barber of the reigning welterweight champion of the world, Sugar Ray Robinson, traveling with the champ and even fixing his hair in between rounds. Robinson's flamboyant style, one could argue, was as iconic as his blistering combinations. Aside from the barbershop's famous proprietor, the draw was Rogers Simon, whose clientele included music greats such as Duke Ellington and Nat King Cole. During the early 1950s, Sugar Ray's Golden Gloves Barber Shop was the premier destination for the latest styles, particularly among up-and-coming pugilists.

For the twenty-four-year-old Drew Bundini Brown, the appeal had nothing to do with boxing. It was the steady hum of clippers, vibrations competing for sonic space among quick snips from carbon steel scissors, the soothing sounds of water disappearing into drains of acrylic sink bowls, the steady ringing of a telephone, the ding of a small bell sounding the arrival of new customers. It was laughter and teasing, cursing and consolation, conversations centered on the troubles of the day. It was a living community, family. It was therapy, coded in hip street lingo, an escape from the chaos and unpredictability of daily life in Harlem. When Bundini had a little cash in his pocket, he'd make his way down to Sugar Ray's and visit one of Rogers Simon's young protegees. His conk, requiring a considerable amount of effort to maintain, called for repeated application of relaxers as new hair grew in. In the streets of Harlem, looking fresh was everything, and Rogers Simon was the wizard of style. Amid this unique cultural marketplace, a mix of shadowboxing and jive talking, the career of one of boxing's greatest showmen was born.

Sandwiched between chairs one and three, facing the oval mirror, his back to the entrance, a familiar voice caught Bundini's ears. His life was about to change.

"Bo-dini. That you?"[1]

The voice belonged to Norman Henry, Bundini's old pal from Philadelphia. The two had met while Bundini was stationed in Philly as a Merchant Marine. Henry was a man of the streets, to put it lightly, a fly dresser and a slick talker. When times were tough, Bundini had slept on Henry's pool table. The two men forged a genuine friendship in their brief time together.

"What you doing in Harlem?" Bundini called, extending his arm from underneath the barber's cape.

"In town with my main man. He's training for his next fight," Henry answered, gesturing toward his partner, a slender, baby-faced, light-skinned Black man standing five feet ten and around 147 pounds.

Because of the flashy colors, a perfectly matching ensemble, complete with gold on his wrists and around his neck, Bundini mistook the man for a pimp. He did not recognize the stranger.

"This is Johnny 'Honey Boy' Bratton," Henry said, waiting for a reaction he would never receive. Bundini, never one to hide his emotions, erupted in laughter.

"*Honey Boy?*" Bundini teased, his bright smile illuminating the room. A few of the young men seated by the window joined in on the laughter.

"Why you laughing, man?" asked Bratton, his thin mustache contorted, perhaps a little offended. To this Bundini offered no intelligible response, only laughter.

"Ain't you ever heard of me?" Bratton inquired.

"Never heard of no *Honey Boy*," Bundini replied, a consummate teaser.

"You're talking to the former welterweight champion of the world," Henry fired back. "This man been in there twice with Kid Gavilan. Just fought Rocky Castellani at Chicago Stadium," he added.

"Only fighters I ever heard of in my life is Sugar Ray Robinson and Joe Louis," replied Bundini, to which Bratton responded with laughter.

"You don't look like no fighter to me. Where's your scars at?" Bundini added, studying the former champion's unblemished face, a smooth profile not unlike that of the barbershop's namesake.

In some respects, Johnny "Honey Boy" Bratton was Chicago's answer to Harlem's Sugar Ray. He was handsome, charismatic, traveled with a large entourage, dressed with style, had a slew of famous friends (e.g., Miles Davis), and, like Robinson, served as a beacon of hope to his downtrodden community, a section of South Side Chicago commonly referred to as the "Black Belt."

"The sight of Bratton being chauffeured around in a white Cadillac, dressed in a $400 all-red suit, gave hope that the dream their families had chased migrating north could become a reality," journalist Corey Erdman once wrote, highlighting Bratton's symbolic importance to poor Blacks living in Chicago's South Side.

During the 1940s, the scene in Chicago was similar to that of Harlem, an estimated 30,000 Black families moved to the Windy City, most from rural southern states such as Mississippi and Arkansas. Johnny Bratton's family had migrated from Little Rock, hoping to find opportunity and escape racism. At first, what the cocky youngster found was trouble. In a pattern familiar to boxing lore, street fights and trouble with the law set Bratton down the path to boxing. Despite his spindly frame, the Honey Boy, nicknamed for his sweet style in the ring, was a natural. After winning the Chicago Golden Gloves, Bratton dropped out of DuSable High School and, at the age of fifteen, signed a contract with Howard Frazier, a notorious Chicago boxing manager with a reputation for gambling and moving his fighters along too quickly. Frazier's managerial style, one might argue, suited the way Bratton lived his life, in fast-forward. At seventeen, Bratton had a child and was already divorced. At twenty-five, Bratton's age when he first met Bundini at Sugar Ray's Golden Gloves Barber Shop, he had already compiled a professional record of 58-20-3. A former champion now relegated to journeyman status, he was the kind of stepping-stone opponent young prospects face to gauge their development in the ring, Bratton was no longer a box-office attraction.

Yet the flamboyant ex-champion fully expected to be recognized by the patrons of Sugar Ray's Golden Gloves Barber Shop. Anybody who knew boxing knew Honey Boy Bratton.

"Johnny is in New York training for his next fight," Norman Henry said, attempting to deflect the interrogation.

"Who *he* fighting?" Bundini responded, with a playful inflection in his voice.

"I'm fighting Danny Womber at the Forum in Montreal, Canada, next Saturday," Bratton replied, visibly irked by the question.

"Ain't heard of no Danny *Whoever* neither," Bundini teased, sensing he was getting underneath Bratton's skin.

"Norman, this man ain't no fighter," Bundini goaded, urging the rest of the barbershop patrons to join in. Bratton had reached his limit.

"Listen man, you come down to the gym with us tonight and I'll show you I'm a fighter," he said, his ego bruised.

More interested in reconnecting with his old friend Norman Henry than discovering whether the skinny Black man with the pencil-thin mustache could actually fight, Bundini accepted the invitation.

That night in the gym, Bratton ran through his sparing partners, employing fast combinations and slick ring generalship, looking like the young teenager who earned the nickname "Honey Boy." In between rounds, Bundini kept with the teasing. It didn't take him long to realize Bratton was a professional, but he kept tormenting him just the same. Norman Henry had never seen his friend look so good.

"Bundini, you need to come with us to Canada. Give Johnny energy," Henry requested. "Come on, go with us. Get him mad like that—he needs to win this next fight. You can motivate him," he pleaded.

"I ain't no boxing trainer," Bundini responded, impressed by Bratton's demonstration and intrigued by the offer.

"No. You'll be his motivator," Henry responded.

Bundini jumped at the offer. In a life guided by feeling rather than reason, Bundini had learned to follow his instincts.

On June 9, 1953, Drew Bundini Brown accompanied Norman Henry and Johnny Bratton to the Forum in Montreal, Canada. Bratton's opponent, Danny "Bang Bang" Womber, also from the streets of Chicago, was coming off an upset victory over Kid Gavilan. Bratton had twice squared off against Gavilan, losing a decision in the first fight and fighting to a draw in the rematch.

"I'm dedicating this one to you, Bundini. To prove I'm a fighter," Bratton said in the locker room, just before making his way to the ring.

In one of the last great performances of his career, Johnny Bratton defeated Danny Womber by unanimous decision, employing an uncharacteristically aggressive style to outclass his Windy City rival.

"Bratton put on one of the greatest fights I ever saw," Bundini once reflected, looking back on the fight.

On some level, Bratton was impressed by Bundini's ability to bring out the best in him. When Bratton faced off against Al Wilson in Baltimore, Maryland, on October 7, 1953, Bundini was, once again, part of the entourage. The pairing would result in another resounding unanimous decision victory.

Bratton's back-to-back wins propelled him into a third bout with future Hall of Famer Kid Gavilan, returning Honey Boy to the upper crust of the fight game. The rubber match between Gavilan and Bratton would take place at Chicago Stadium on November 13, 1953.

The third time around would not prove to be a charm. Plagued by brittle hands for much of his career, Bratton suffered a severely broken right-hand injury early in the bout, fighting valiantly but coming up on the losing end of a unanimous decision.

In an interview with *Sports Illustrated* eighteen years later, Bundini reflected on Gavilan–Bratton III, his first major event in the sport.

"Trouble with [Bratton] was, his hands was smaller than his wife's hands. They used to shoot Novocain into his hands and freeze 'em so when he broke 'em he wouldn't feel it. If he'd had hands wouldn't nobody in his class—Gavilan or nobody—could beat him. But he was like a cripple running a race," Bundini stated.

After the Gavilan bout, Bundini began hanging out with Bratton on a regular basis. As the two became closer, Bratton introduced Bundini to some of his connections in the fight game, most notably Sugar Ray Robinson. By all accounts, Harlem's boxing king paid little attention to the Honey Boy's loquacious sidekick during their initial meeting.

"Bratton introduced me to people, but Sugar Ray didn't pay no attention to me. As the champ, he was one, and I was one among many," Bundini said.

Boxing scholars have written that Sugar Ray famously snubbed the young Cassius Clay in similar fashion during their first encounter as well.

Although the Gavilan–Bratton fight served as Bundini's first taste of world-class professional boxing, it would not mark his first time seeing the sport up close.

"My father first caught the bug working with my uncle Elbert back in Florida," Drew Brown III told me. "That's when he really fell in love with the sport."

When Bundini returned from his brief stint in the Navy, he sought out his estranged mother and brother in West Palm Beach. During the initial reunion, Bundini discovered that his mother had passed away and his younger brother, Elbert, was now making a name for himself as an amateur boxer.

Hoping to rekindle their relationship, Elbert invited Bundini to serve as a cornerman for one of his upcoming bouts. Over the next few months, the brothers worked together for a handful of amateur fights, all of which took place in dingy armories scattered throughout central Florida. While the allure of boxing, a seed planted by Joe Louis's historic victory over Max Schmeling, was strong, Bundini had no intentions of becoming a fighter himself. By his own son's estimation, Bundini was no athlete.

"My father didn't have an athletic bone in his body," Drew Brown III said to me. "He couldn't dance. He couldn't hit a baseball. First time I saw him hold a baseball bat, he held it the wrong way. Only time I ever saw my father run was in *Shaft 2*. He loved boxing but he knew that boxing wasn't his talent."

Working as an amateur cornerman did, however, spur Bundini on toward other boxing ambitions. Before moving to Harlem, he rented a town hall in Sanford and promoted the town's first-ever amateur boxing card. Elbert Brown would, of course, headline the show. With the money Bundini made from the event, he bought the railway ticket he would use to move to New York City.

Just as the Merchant Marines had set him free from the life of hard labor in the citrus groves of Sanford, meeting Johnny Bratton propelled Bundini forward. For Bundini, there were no coincidences. Boxing had given him his happiest memory with his father. Boxing had helped forge a new bond with his estranged brother. Boxing had brought him to Harlem—the sport had literally paid for his ticket on the Atlantic Coast

Railway. And it was boxing's greatest champion who bought and remodeled a dilapidated building, transforming it into the most famous barbershop in Harlem, the location where a skinny kid from Arkansas, a transplant resident of Chicago's South Side, determined to prove he had fire to match his flash, showed Bundini the path to his new life.

"Boxing isn't just physical," Bratton had told Bundini after their first fight together.

"Boxing is mental as well." You gotta strengthen the body and the mind."

"You're going to be my motivator," Bratton told him.

■ ■ ■

On January 20, 1955, Drew Timothy Brown III was born at Sydenham Hospital in Harlem, New York. According to family legend, the child was conceived after hours, in Sugar Ray Robinson's bar. Ironically enough, Rhoda went into labor while her husband took in Sugar Ray's bout with Ralph "Tiger" Jones on *The Gillette Cavalcade of Sports* (January 19, 1955). Bundini, not yet a member of the Champ's entourage, watched from the vantage point of his zebra-print sofa.

"I think it's time, Drew. It's time," Rhoda called from the bathroom.[2]

"One more round, Rosebud . . . the fight's almost over," Bundini replied.

"I'm not joking. It's time!" Rhoda shouted.

Bundini would have to wait until the following day to learn that Jones pulled off the stunning upset, handing Harlem's boxing savant his fourth defeat in 140 bouts.

Arriving in a yellow Checker Cab the following morning, Jack and Mildred Palestine made their way to the maternity ward, eager to meet their first grandchild. Their relationship with Rhoda and her husband, despite their unconventional lifestyle, remained stable. They loved Bundini because Rhoda loved him.

Mildred pulled back the soft baby blanket, taking in her new grandson for the first time.

"A little baby powder and my first grandson'll be all fixed up!" Mildred teased, poking fun at herself. Of the two grandparents, Mildred had been most concerned with the idea of an interracial marriage. The bedside joke was Mildred's way of signaling to her daughter the issue of race no longer mattered.

"He's mine. He's mine and I love him," Mildred cried, holding the cooing child in her arms, Jack peering over her shoulder with an ear-to-ear grin.

"You were a wanted child. It was necessary for you to be born," Rhoda would later write to her son.

Feeling the indescribable mix of joy and responsibility that washes over all first-time parents, Rhoda and Bundini were, at least during the early days as parents, changed. Attempting to answer the call of fatherhood, Bundini took a job as a cashier at his friend Shelton Oliver's restaurant, Shelton's Rib House, located two doors down from Sugar Ray's club. When he wasn't in the gym with Bratton, he was working as a cashier. His days as a street hustler were over, he believed. The wild nights in Harlem's jazz joints were replaced with quiet evenings at home caring for the new baby, who Bundini affectionately nicknamed "Sneezer."

"Why do you call him Sneezer?" Rhoda laughed, noting that the child had no sinus problems.

"When someone sneezes, the reply is 'God bless you.' And all I want for Sneezer is to be blessed by God," Bundini smiled.

Becoming a father, as is often the case with young men, forced Bundini to revisit and reevaluate his own relationship with his father, the limitations of his own childhood.

"He's gonna be the best Drew," Bundini would brag to Rhoda, peering down into the baby's crib.

"He's gonna be the educated Drew. He's going to be smart like you. He's gonna be able to read good and write good like you, Rhoda," he'd say.

"Sneezer is going to *college*," Bundini would insist, placing a pitch and tone inflection on the word "college"—sometimes saying it at an octave so high that it startled the child and caused him to cry.

Brimming with pride, Bundini boasted about the birth of his son to all his friends. Johnny Bratton, with help from Bob Nelson and a few of his boxing confidants, put together the ultimate pugilistic gift for the Brown family: a set of miniature boxing gloves that hung as ornaments in the crib, autographed by Joe Louis, Sugar Ray Robinson, and Jack Dempsey, a gift that remains in the Brown family today.

The gloves dangling above the sleeping child were a sign of things to come.

■   ■   ■

The flamingo-pink Cadillac slowly pulled up to the curb and men climbed over each other, pushing and shoving, while women shouted and whistled through rouge-red lips. Dressed in an exotic zoot suit and accompanied by his beautiful wife, the great Sugar Ray Robinson entered Shelton's Rib House to a king's welcome. Signing autographs and waiting to be seated, the Champ spotted an elderly Black woman dining alone at a table by the window, her crutches resting in the opposite chair.

"Make sure that lady's meal is taken care of," Robinson instructed, tossing a five-dollar bill to the cashier.

"Champ, they'll be falling in the ring, and you won't know why they falling," the cashier replied, collecting the money. "Shorty is gonna take care of you," the cashier added.

To this Robinson flashed a look of confusion.

"Shorty?" Robinson inquired.

"Call him Shorty," the cashier answered, his eyes glancing toward the elderly woman. "Call him Shorty because he takes care of the little guy," he added.

"What the hell you talkin' about?" Robinson laughed.

"That lady over by the window, that's Shorty. That's Shorty checkin' in on you, testin' you," the cashier replied.

Robinson, perplexed by the homespun doctrine, offered no response.

"Tonight, you passed the test, Champ. I feel sorry for the next man face you," the cashier philosophized.

"What's your name, brother?" Robinson asked, unaware the two had previously met.

"Some call me Bundini. Others call me Fast Black," the cashier responded, unfazed by Robinson's celebrity.

"Well, you a strange nigger, Bundini. Very strange," Robinson smirked, grinning that million-dollar smile, extending a handshake.

"Give me the little ones," Bundini replied, gesturing toward Robinson's pinky finger, his thumb removed from the exchange. "The big ones can take care of themselves," he added.

In the private dining area, a few moments later, Robinson relayed the conversation to his brother-in-law, Bob Nelson. Nelson reminded Robinson of Bundini's work with Johnny Bratton, the gloves he had signed for his newborn child.

"See if he needs extra work. I'll put him to work," Robinson told his brother-in-law.

"From then on, I was not one among many to him, I was just me," Bundini would later reflect.

■ ■ ■

One of the great mysteries of Drew Bundini Brown's boxing career, perhaps the least documented aspect of his professional resumé, is his role within Sugar Ray Robinson's entourage. Such an exploration requires one to reexamine the term *entourage* itself. In many ways, our modern-day understanding of the term begins with Robinson. Long before "Iron" Mike Tyson and Floyd "Money" Mayweather, Sugar Ray Robinson crafted a public persona of supreme dominance and flamboyant extravagance, a shadow so brilliantly cast that even his lackeys gained some measure of fame. Robinson cared a great deal about maintaining this image. His entourage was a key component in crafting it. From the clothes to the cars, everything the Champ did was marked by over-the-top excess. When Robinson hit the road, for example, his crew typically consisted of Millie Robinson (his wife), Bob Nelson (his brother-in-law), George Gainford (his manager), Rogers Simon (his personal barber and cornerman), Harry Wiley (his trainer), other assistant trainers, a secretary, a professional golf instructor, and a dwarf nicknamed Arabian Knight (serving the role of court jester). Among the traveling crew were a collection of cronies Robinson referred to as "odd-job men." It is estimated Robinson's entourage carried "100 pieces of luggage among them, and cost about $3,000 a week" to support.[3] Rolling with the Champ, as one might assume, came with many of the perks of being the Champ. Robinson famously wined and dined members of his team.

Despite his brief apprenticeship with Johnny Bratton, Bundini, one can safely assume, began his tenure as a member of Team Robinson as an "odd-job man." Much of his work would have had nothing to do with boxing. Recalling his father's well-known history of philandering, Ray

Robinson II writes, "My father would take me with him to various places where he hung out. . . . He would drop me off with Bundini (Brown) at the Apollo or leave me in the lobby of the Theresa Hotel when Charlie Rangel was the desk clerk, while he went out and checked his 'traps,' his various female partners."

It appears that Bundini spent much of 1956 partaking in such menial duties, running errands, babysitting, and earning the Champ's trust. By the time Robinson faced Gene Fullmer at Madison Square Garden on January 2, 1957, however, Bundini's role in the entourage was fully solidified.

"It started with those Fullmer fights. I know for a fact that Bundini went to camp with Robinson for those fights. I remember him talking about those training camps," former heavyweight contender and future Bundini pupil James "Quick" Tillis told me.

The invitation to accompany Robinson to training camp ended Bundini's time as a cashier at Shelton's Rib House, effective immediately.

For much of the Champ's storied career, the village of Greenwood Lake, located just outside of Poughkeepsie, New York, served as the headquarters for his ring preparation. Fifty miles north of New York City, the lakeside community, known for boating, skiing, and hiking on the nearby Appalachian Trail, offered seclusion from the distractions of Manhattan nightlife. Rocky Marciano and Joe Louis also used the facilities throughout their careers. The fighters stayed in cabins, training facilities were erected amid the beautiful wilderness, and, on occasion, locals were invited to watch the champions train. Summers were picturesque and winters were brutal. The setup, one might argue, was a precursor to Muhammad Ali's Deer Lake training camp in Pennsylvania.

For the twenty-eight-year-old Bundini, the experience of total immersion into the daily life of a world-class fighter would have been nothing short of an education, the experience different in every way from his time working with Johnny Bratton in Harlem. Spokes in a wheel, each member of Team Robinson dedicated their time to creating an atmosphere where the Champ could best mentally and physically prepare himself for the rigors of fifteen-round prizefighting. Working for the Champ was an around-the-clock job.

In *Pound for Pound: A Biography of Sugar Ray Robinson*, Sugar Ray Robinson II and author Herb Boyd evoke a commonly known Bundini/

Robinson story, perhaps providing a window into his early days as a member of Robinson's team:

> There's an incident in Ali's autobiography related by Bundini Brown, who was a trainer with Sugar before he joined Ali's team. He writes about his sleeping with "a champ" who is the best fighter in the world, "pound for pound." "I was green," Bundini said. "First time I'd been with a champ. No woman had ever asked me to get in bed with her husband before, and I didn't know what to make of it." "Just lie in bed with him," she says. . . . He's lying there in bed and I get in and lie next to him, and he cuddles up with my arms around him and goes to sleep. . . . By all indications, the man Bundini is cuddling is Sugar.

It is quite possible that Millie Robinson did order Bundini to bunk with her husband; in those days abstaining from sex before a fight was a key precautionary measure. While research suggests Millie did often stay with Robinson in Greenwood Lake, it is likely that she did not sleep with him. Regardless, all signs indicate that Sugar Ray took to Bundini. In just a few quick years, Bundini went from being elated to hang a pair of autographed Sugar Ray gloves above his son's crib to actually sleeping in the same bed as the champion.

"I didn't know what I was doing then, but it was the same as it is now—a spirit thing. But, like George Gainford once told me, 'Wherever you are and whatever you are doing, make sure whenever you leave you are missed,'" Bundini once told *Sports Illustrated*.

After the first Fullmer fight, when it came time to pay Bundini for his services, Robinson did so in cash. A handshake was all Bundini required as a contract.

"Pay me whatever Champ thinks I'm worth," Bundini negotiated with Gainford, a flawed system that would carry over to Bundini's time with Muhammad Ali.

The money often disappeared as quickly as it came.

When Bundini officially joined the Sugar Ray Robinson payroll in 1957, the dynamics of his relationship with his wife, Rhoda, once again began to shift. The job required that he spend much of his time at Greenwood Lake and traveling with Robinson to fights. This is not to suggest Bundini's new life was without its perks. Rhoda, Drew Brown III, and her parents would, on occasion, get to travel to Greenwood Lake to watch Sugar Ray train.

"My most vivid memory is watching Uncle Ray on the speed bag," Drew Brown III recalled. "He would knock it off the hinges and it would go sprawling across the floor."

The occasional visits to Greenwood Lake, however, did little to mend what was becoming an increasingly fractured marriage. Rhoda, a dynamic and independent woman, simply was not "housewife material." She had, in many respects, lost her jazz-joint partner. She had lost the danger that lured her away from Brighton Beach. She was now a devoted mother and provider. Bundini, on the other hand, was swooped up into a new and exciting world, enjoying all of the attention and perks and temptations that went along with being a member of the Sugar Ray entourage. The atmosphere not only took him away from his family but transformed him from a Harlem celebrity to a national celebrity.

"I always believed that we could be a well-adjusted, happy family. I dreamed of having a good family. And I always knew that, one day, he would make it big, and be a success in some way. But I really thought that he would then share that success with me and you. That's what I wanted more than anything else in the world," Rhoda wrote to her son, looking back on the final year of her marriage to Drew Bundini Brown.

■ ■ ■

"Daddy, what are you doing?" Drew Brown III called, walking into his parents' bedroom, taking in the sight of his father slowly putting on and tying his alligator shoes. The three-year-old's eyes were drawn to the suitcases stacked behind his father. He sat next to his father on the bed.[4]

"Sneezer, it's time for me to go," Bundini replied, his voice soft and wavering.

"You going to see Uncle Ray?" the boy asked, wishfully thinking, perhaps.

Bundini shook his head in disagreement.

"When are you coming back?" the boy asked, masking his trepidation.

"Sneezer, I'm leaving. But, I'll always be your Daddy," Bundini answered. "I won't be able to live here anymore. You'll be better off if I leave."

The young boy protested to no avail.

"I'll come visit you, from time to time," Bundini assured, tears forming in the corners of his eyes. "You'll have other fathers in your life."

The child violently protested. "No! You're my only Daddy. I only want you. When are you coming back?"

"I will always be your Daddy, I will always look out for you. I just can't live here anymore but I'll never leave you."

Rhoda Palestine and Drew Brown ended their six-year marriage in early 1958. The separation came as a result of the most explosive and turbulent period of their time together.

"Once Daddy started making it, he changed, towards my mommy," Drew Brown III told me. "They had been equals. Now that he started to see the possibility of prosperity, he wanted to be in charge. He wanted to be the man. He wanted my mother to give in to his every wish. She was not one of those 'stand by your man regardless' type of women. She was not subservient."

Because of the constant demands of Sugar Ray's busy schedule—Robinson was one of the busiest fighters of any generation—Bundini was rarely home. His new life also impacted Rhoda's newfound unwillingness to accept her husband's promiscuity. Rhoda, as one might imagine, was envious of the privileges her husband now enjoyed. While Bundini traveled, Rhoda was left home with their child, living off of government assistance. Two stubborn and unyielding personalities, neither partner would back down or relent to the other. Bundini, adept at talking his way out of any situation, had met his rhetorical match. As the arguments became increasingly volatile, Rhoda and Bundini came to the mutual realization that their marriage was no longer worth saving.

"The divorce divided not much money in half—zero divided by zero is still zero—so we all suffered financially," Drew III reflected.

When Bundini wasn't traveling with Sugar Ray, he stayed at a small apartment on West 86th Street, a space he shared with a revolving door of new girlfriends. Rhoda and her son lived at the Carver House, a government-subsidized housing project at 60 East 102nd Street, between Park and Madison. The mother and son moved into apartment 11-F.

A fifty-five-cent cab ride away in Spanish Harlem, in an eleventh-floor two-bedroom unit, Rhoda and her son began a new phase in their lives.

Just as Rhoda and Bundini approached marriage in an unconventional fashion, so did the couple embrace the concept of divorce with their own unique style. Even after the separation, Bundini would often stay at the apartment with his ex-wife and son. These visits sometimes extended to weeks at a time. When the arguments picked back up, Bundini would disappear. The unpredictability of Bundini's visitation schedule took a heavy toll on his son, who, as the years passed, obsessively worked to reunite his parents. Christmas soon became the only time of the year when differences were put aside.

"No matter how bad things got, there was always a holiday truce from fighting in our house. Both of my parents celebrated Christmas, not in a religious sense, but in a festive one," Drew III recalled.

"Daddy always came through on Christmas. It might be midnight before he arrived, but he never failed to show up, laughing, joking, and brandishing an armload of packages," he added.

On occasion, Bundini's famous employer would play Santa Claus to the young boy, providing a Christmas bonus that would allow him to purchase toy six-shooters, punching bags, or whatever else the boy wanted.

On the road, meeting celebrities and tending to the needs of boxing's most celebrated champion, every day must have felt like Christmas for Bundini. As a member of Team Robinson, he partook in headlining events at Madison Square Garden and the Convention Center in Las Vegas and experienced the nightlife of cities such as Los Angeles, Detroit, Miami, and even Honolulu. And just as he had earned a reputation as the Black Prince of Manhattan's jazz clubs, Bundini gradually became known in boxing circles. With this notoriety came famous friendships with Joe Louis, James Baldwin, Norman Mailer, and Lloyd Price. For a brief period, Bundini had an affair with up-and-coming R&B singer Ruth Brown. As his bond with Robinson grew, Bundini became a chief presence in the entourage, assuming the motivational duties Norman Henry had originally imagined him fulfilling for Johnny Bratton.

At the Greenwood Lake training facility, Bundini oversaw every aspect of Robinson's preparation. For seven straight years, he fulfilled the role of Sugar Ray's personal motivator, leaning over the ropes during sparring sessions, cheering him on as he worked the double-end bag, urging him to victory from ringside. Robinson, who often referred to Bundini as "Boone," fed off this energy, responded to it, and eventually came to rely on it.

"We worked together for seven years. I am proud of my association with Bundini. I extremely admire him. He is the best motivator I know in the fight game," Robinson once wrote.

During his apprenticeship Bundini discovered the psychological side of prizefighting, developing and sharpening his skills as a motivator. His unique ability to read personalities and tailor his oratory to the needs of the individual undoubtedly served him well. Just as he had done at the counter of Shelton's Rib House, Bundini captured his boss's imagination, motivated him to action. Working his way up to the title of assistant trainer of the great Sugar Ray, even for an ultimate optimist like Drew Bundini Brown, had to feel like the accomplishment of a lifetime. He couldn't have possibly foreseen that Robinson would not be his most famous business partner. Drew Bundini Brown's career in boxing was, in many respects, just beginning.

■   ■   ■

On March 12, 1963, a twenty-one-year-old heavyweight named Cassius Marcellus Clay sat on a small couch in his hotel room, on the eve of his headlining debut at Madison Square Garden, waiting for guests to arrive. As an amateur, Clay had won six Kentucky Golden Gloves titles, two National Golden Gloves titles, and the Light Heavyweight Gold Medal in the 1960 Summer Olympics in Rome, Italy, compiling a record of one hundred wins to only five losses. As a professional, he had compiled a record of seventeen wins with no defeats. His opponent, a tough New York City brawler named Doug Jones (21-3-1), was considered by many boxing experts to be something of a litmus test for the young contender who, in the months leading up to the fight, had been clamoring incessantly for a fight with the reigning heavyweight champion of the world, Charles "Sonny" Liston.

Despite all of Clay's accolades as an amateur, he was not without his detractors. Some speculated the youngster didn't pack enough dynamite in his fists to hurt top-tier heavyweights. Others claimed Clay's bad habit of holding his hands below his waist and his tendency to pull straight back from incoming combinations were technical flaws that would eventually lead to defeat as the quality of opposition increased. Many were simply rooting for the boastful challenger to be humbled.

Dubbed "The Louisville Lip" by supporters and detractors alike, Clay was rapidly becoming a controversial figure in the sport of boxing. Just one month earlier, on February 4, 1963, the New York State Assembly had held a special hearing where a special subcommittee, headed by state assemblyman Hayward Plumadore, introduced a bill that would, in effect, outlaw the sport of boxing. The controversial young challenger, known for correctly predicting the rounds in which he would vanquish his opponents, figured heavily in the investigation.

"You have been giving some predictions about which round you will win in. Don't you think these predictions, and the fact that these last few fights have happened to end in the exact round that you say, have given a bad image of the sport of boxing to the general public?" assemblyman Plumadore had pressed the young Cassius Clay, dressed in a black suit and matching bow tie, eager to respond.[5]

"It is on record that I predicted eight rounds on Archie Moore. He talked and talked so I cut it to four," Clay calmly replied.

"I have eleven fights, eleven of them I predicted what would happen. Would you say all of these people are crooks? All of the promoters are crooks? I say I'm the greatest and if he falls in five and he falls in five, that just makes me that much greater," Clay added, as onlookers in the courtroom erupted in laughter.

"Will it be a fix when Doug Jones falls in six?" Clay rhymed, his poetic flair unlike anything sport had ever seen.

Leading up to the Doug Jones bout, some members of the media were put off by Clay's cocky behavior.

"Cassius, during the past few weeks you've been centering your interest around squabbles you've been having with Sonny Liston down here. You've got a fight with Doug Jones. He's a pretty good fighter. Don't you think it's time you start concentrating on him?" a reporter asked Clay.

"I'm not concentrating on Doug Jones, he's nothing but a bum. Liston is the man I want. I'm not thinking about Doug Jones. He will fall in six and I might cut it to three," the young challenger bragged.

■ ■ ■

There was a knock at the door. Clay rose from the couch and answered it. Earlier in the week, when he arrived in New York City to promote his fight with Doug Jones, the controversial young challenger was given the opportunity to meet with one of his boxing idols, Sugar Ray Robinson.

"I saw [him] on television reciting poetry in Greenwich Village—that was no way to train for a fight," Robinson reflected, recounting his meeting with Clay.[6]

"I told [Cassius] he needed somebody to watch over him, somebody to keep him happy and relaxed. I had just the guy for him," Robinson stated.

"Man, who are you talking about?" Clay allegedly questioned.

"You need to go see the Black Prince. All you need is some spiritual motivation," Robinson replied.

Clay opened the door and was greeted by Bob Nelson, whom he affectionally called Bobby.

"You think you can talk, Cassius?" Nelson joked upon entering the hotel room. "You must hear this man," he added, gesturing toward his accomplice, a tall, thin Black man dressed in a tight red shirt and blue jeans.

Clay took in the stranger's conk hairstyle, the long cigar dangling from his mouth.

"This is Drew Bundini Brown. We call him Fast Black, the Black Prince of Harlem," Nelson stated, introducing Clay to the "spiritual motivator" Sugar Ray Robinson had told him about earlier in the week.

"Hey, man," Clay responded in his trademark southern drawl.

"You can't predict no rounds!" Bundini tersely responded, his eyebrows drawn in an accusatory fashion.

"You fixin' em! You a phony!" he added.

"You out of your mind, man?" Clay responded, shocked by his visitor's tone of voice.

"You can't be predictin' all them rounds," Bundini argued, his cigar moving up and down with each new accusatory remark. "Tell me the truth. Y'all got together and fix them fights, don't you?" he implored.

Clay did a double take, trying to figure if Nelson was somehow playing a prank on him.

"I'm no phony," Clay assured.

Bundini's time in the streets of Harlem had taught him to spot a con artist. Never in his tenure with Johnny Bratton or the great Sugar Ray Robinson had he heard of a fighter correctly predicting the round in which he would knock out his opponent. Bundini's strategy was to press the youngster, reading his facial expressions and body language when aggressively confronted.

"You gotta be fixin' 'em, or else you couldn't tell Archie Moore when he was fallin'," Bundini argued, studying the young heavyweight's clean-shaven face, waiting to uncover even the slightest hint of trepidation.

Clay, never at a loss for words, continued his protest. This didn't stop Bundini.

"You either a phony or Shorty's in your corner," Bundini finally conceded, placing a pillow from the couch on the floor, seating himself on the pillow with his legs crossed Indian style.

"Tell me the truth," Bundini urged, puffing from the cigar.

"You know what the truth is?" Clay finally responded, seating himself next to Bundini. "The truth is, every time I go into the ring I'm scared to death," Clay admitted.

To this, Bundini flashed a look of pure shock. He'd expected bravado from the cocky young heavyweight. Tears began to flow down Bundini's cheeks—by all indications he was quick to cry, never one to mask or hide his emotions.

"I knew Shorty was with you. Shorty had to be with you," he cried, pulling Clay in for a firm hug and kiss on the jaw.

"All that poppin' off, all that predicting, all those people wanting to see me get whipped, I know I'm in trouble. If I lose, they'll be ready to run me out of the country," Clay admitted. "I'm scared to death. Now that's a fact that only you and me know."

"You and me and Shorty," Bundini replied.

The following night Clay's prediction to knock out Doug Jones in six rounds would not come true. Rather, Clay would be awarded a close but unanimous ten-round decision. Jones proved to be Clay's stiffest challenger to date. The victory would do little to quell the critics, who argued that Clay didn't have the stuff of champions.

"If you get that shot at Sonny Liston, you need me in your corner," Bundini told Clay before the fight.

"Why you want to be in my corner?" Clay asked.

"'Cause you got the power and I got the spirit," Bundini argued.

"All right. You be in my corner if you want to be," Clay answered.

The title shot would have to wait. The razor-thin decision over Doug Jones led Clay's team to take a more cautious approach, opting instead for a tune-up fight before challenging Liston. Three months later, Clay would travel to Wembley Stadium in London, England, to face the tough journeyman Henry Cooper. In the bout, Clay would, once again, flirt with disaster. A leaping left hook from Cooper would send Clay crumbling to the canvas at the close of the fourth round. Although Clay would recover, winning the bout via technical knockout in the following round, the back-to-back difficult contests had exposed Clay's technical vulnerabilities, many critics argued.

Very few, if any, boxing experts felt that Clay could last more than a few rounds with the menacing Liston.

"You a heavyweight Sugar Ray. You'll beat Sonny Liston, all right," Bundini said to Clay, phoning him after the Cooper fight.

"Am I in your corner?" Bundini asked.

Sanford, Florida, 1942: A thirteen-year-old Drew
Bundini Brown signs up for duty at Naval Air
Station Sanford. *Courtesy of Drew Brown III*

Before Drew Brown met Sugar Ray Robinson, a photograph of his conk hairstyle was displayed at Sugar Ray's Golden Gloves Barber Shop in Harlem. *Courtesy of Drew Brown III*

Harlem, New York, 1955: Rhoda Palestine and Drew Bundini Brown with their newborn son, Drew Brown III. *Courtesy of Drew Brown III*

Sugar Ray Robinson leaning on his 1950 pink Cadillac convertible in front of his businesses in Harlem. Bundini and his wife Rhoda lived directly above Robinson's nightclub, Sugar Ray's. *Getty Images*

Harlem, New York, 1955: Drew Bundini Brown kisses his mother-in-law, Mildred "Bubba" Palestine. *Courtesy of Drew Brown III*

Sugar Ray Robinson and Mildred "Bubba" Palestine at Robinson's training camp in Greenwood Lake, New York. *Courtesy of Drew Brown III*

Mildred "Bubba" Palestine, Muhammad Ali, and Drew Brown III at P.S. 171 in Manhattan in 1964. Clay and Bundini attend Drew Brown III's school play. *Courtesy of Drew Brown III*

Dear Drew Brown JR.
I am getting Ready for the Big & Ugly Bear Sonny Liston. Tell all of your friends I said Hello. I will see you after I am the World Champion. So be Good. Your best friend Cassius Clay

POST CARD
ADDRESS
Mr. Drew T. Brown III
APT. 11-F
60 East 102 Street
New York City, N.Y.

Famous luxury hotels in Miami Beach, Florida

AIR MAIL

U.S. AIR MAIL

While training for his first bout with Sonny Liston, Muhammad Ali sends a postcard to Drew Brown III back in Harlem. Ali predicts his victory. *Courtesy of Drew Brown III*

I was out of shape so I'm shooting a double header the Next Champ and I will be in shape for the Greatest Sport Event Ever assembled Season's Greetings Drew Brown

G-9—GULF STREAM CARD & DISTRIBUTING CO., MIAMI, FLORIDA

MIAMI, FLA. 3 00 PM DEC 1963

4610-N-W-15-E Miami, FLa.

"CURTEICHCOLOR" REPRODUCTION FROM KODACHROME ORIGINAL

POST CARD

Mr. Mrs. J. Palestine
3121. BRighton. 5. St.
Bklyn 35 N.Y. #4K

Cassius Clay

LUXURIOUS HOTELS ALONG COLLINS AVE.
LOOKING FROM INDIAN CREEK
MIAMI BEACH, FLORIDA

During their training camps at the 5th Street Gym
in Miami, Florida, Drew Bundini Brown and
Muhammad Ali often sent postcards to the
Palestine family. *Courtesy of Drew Brown III*

Muhammad Ali, Liberace, Ali's brother Rahman, and Drew Brown III.
Courtesy of Drew Brown III

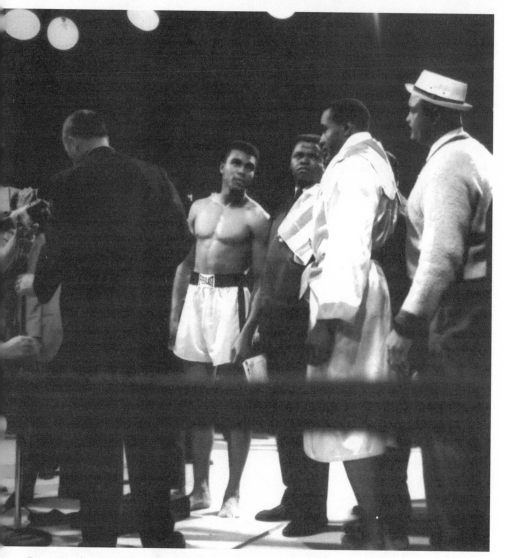

Drew Bundini Brown and Muhammad Ali glower
at "The Big Ugly Bear," Sonny Liston. *Courtesy of
Drew Brown III*

Muhammad Ali yells with Bundini during a press conference before his first fight with Sonny Liston at the Convention Center in Miami Beach on February 25, 1964. Ali won the world heavyweight championship when Liston quit on his stool at the end of round six. *Stanley Weston/Getty Images*

Drew Bundini Brown and Sonji Roi exit Muhammad Ali's training-camp bus before the rematch with Sonny Liston. *Courtesy of Drew Brown III*

4

Metamorphosis

The symbolism was easy to decipher. As Muhammad Ali opened the side door of the New London Theatre, he was blinded by the spotlight, crepuscular rays pouring down from above. Startled by the applause erupting from the studio audience, Ali momentarily looked as if he might retreat in the other direction. Like a scene from a Renaissance painting, Saint Peter at the Pearly Gates, television host Eamonn Andrews emerged from the shadows, one hand extended in a friendly greeting, the other clutching an oversized red leather-bound book with gold lettering. Had the cheers not been so deafening, Ali might have actually heard Andrews deliver the program's famous introductory line: "Muhammad Ali, *This Is Your Life*."

In keeping with the tradition of the 1952 American show of the same title, the British reincarnation of *This Is Your Life* relied heavily on the surprise element. This was documentary film meets hidden camera prank show, a precursor to reality television. Guests were led to the studio under false pretenses and were surprised by a cavalcade of individuals from their past. On Tuesday, December 19, 1978, Muhammad Ali was brought to the "studio" under the guise of an interview with ITV boxing commentator Reg Gutteridge. Months of planning and thousands of miles of travel went into the BBC sucker punch, a ratings bonanza for London-based Thames Television Network. Less than three months earlier, Ali had defeated Leon Spinks in their rematch at the Superdome in New Orleans, becoming the first man in the history of boxing to win the heavyweight championship three times over. After the bout, Ali announced his retirement from the sport.

The beauty of *This Is Your Life* was the producers' ability to highlight "fork in the road" moments in the lives of guests; chronology factored heavily in the narrative structure. Ali's parents, Odessa and Cassius, although separated at the time, appeared together, relaying stories of Ali's childhood. Gladius Carter, Ali's third-grade teacher, told stories of the Champ's elementary school years. Ali's first amateur boxing coach, Joe Martin, the police officer to whom a twelve-year-old Ali reported his stolen red bike, discussed the twelve-year-old's ring debut on his locally syndicated program *Tomorrow's Champions*. When asked if Louisville police had any leads on the missing red bike, Martin joked, "Not yet, but it'll turn up."

In one of the true surprises of the night, Ronnie O'Keef, Ali's first amateur opponent, stood face-to-face with "The Greatest" for a staredown twenty-four years in the making. Even Zbigniew "Ziggy" Pietrzykowski, the Polish Olympian Ali defeated to win the gold medal in 1960, was in attendance. Because of the language barrier, the two men could not converse but Ali clearly enjoyed the surprise nonetheless.

Next came Ali's legendary trainer Angelo Dundee, who relayed the story of his first time conversing with the cocky young fighter who correctly predicted he would one day become heavyweight champion of the world. At the close of Dundee's comments, producers cut to black-and-white footage of the pandemonium that ensued after Muhammad Ali, then Cassius Clay, dethroned Sonny Liston on February 25, 1964. For the first time that night, the smile was missing from Ali's face. Watching the footage of Liston perched upon his stool, arms resting on his knees, looking downward in defeat, the newly retired champion became stoic, contemplative.

"Well, Muhammad, that inimitable style of yours has challenged the descriptive talents of writers and commentators the world over. But a phrase that you will always be remembered by came from an unexpected source," Andrews said after the highlight reel ended, cueing the sound system.[1]

"I still say it to this day, Champ," a voice bellowing from the heavens spoke. "Float like a butterfly, sting like a bee," the voice beckoned.

The smile once again returned to Ali's face.

"He's been in your corner for fourteen years and forty-four fights, floating in from New York, Drew Bundini Brown," Andrews called, the golden *This Is Your Life* stage doors slowly parting. Dressed in a black and gray pinstriped suit, Drew Bundini Brown arrived on the set. Ali instantly leapt from his seat.

"Old Drew," Ali called, playfully pawing over Bundini's tailored suit, looking it over and opening the jacket to inspect the vest underneath.

"You bought it," Bundini teased.

"I've never saw him so dressed in my life . . . and he's sober," Ali replied, Bundini shrugging his shoulders and grinning.

"Drew Bundini, what was the moment that inspired that famous phrase that became so famous it even became a song?" Andrews inquired, referring to Johnny Wakelin's 1975 song "Black Superman," which borrows Bundini's famous phrase in the chorus.

"To love God is to love people. And, I must love Muhammad because he loves God. And, all great fighters had nicknames. Like 'The Brown Bomber,' Joe Louis. Rocky Marciano, 'The Rock.' Sugar Ray Robinson, 'Sugar,'" Bundini said.

A look of confusion washed over Andrews's face as he was visibly taken aback by the philosophical response.

"He was doing roadwork and I was talking to God, as I do. Not with my mouth but with my mind. And I was asking God what was his nickname. And a feeling came to me: *Call it the way it is. Float like a butterfly and sting like a bee*," Bundini proclaimed, the audience erupting with applause.

Producers of *This Is Your Life* were correct in signaling Ali's partnership with Drew Bundini Brown as a key moment in the career of the boxing legend. In some ways, Bundini was the final ingredient, the missing piece to the puzzle. This is not to suggest that he should be credited for teaching the Champ how to fight; this foundation was laid by amateur trainers Joe Martin and Fred Stoner, Ali's U.S. Olympic coaches (most notably Julius Menendez and Ben Becker), and, of course, the great Angelo Dundee. What Bundini brought to the table cannot be measured by punches.

"Drew charged Muhammad's batteries. He knew Muhammad. He was great for Muhammad," Dundee famously stated.

"Bundini was, no joke, the reason Muhammad won a lot of bouts that he otherwise might have lost: he pushed him to the limit, both in training and in the championship rounds," Rahman Ali, Muhammad Ali's brother, wrote in his 2019 autobiography.[2]

"Bundini was a poet of the streets, a source of energy that Ali fed off of constantly; someone who put words together in a way that connoted exactly what he meant and Ali could understand," Ali cornerman and personal physician Ferdie Pacheco argued.

"Bundini was a great man for Ali. There was a bond between them, something really good. Nobody else could deal with Ali like Bundini . . . he gave him spirit and got him to work," said Wali "Youngblood" Muhammad, an assistant trainer who would join Ali's team during the second phase of the champion's career.

While the chemistry between Ali and Bundini has been documented, serious attention has yet to be paid to Bundini's rhetorical message or pedagogical approach. Aside from his coining the famous "float like a butterfly" tagline, outlining the specifics of Drew Bundini Brown's role in Muhammad Ali's camp is no easy task.

In my personal conversations with some of the individuals who knew Ali best, it became abundantly clear that Bundini's contributions are more appropriately described in the metaphysical sense.

"I think Bundini was the source of Muhammad Ali's spirit. I wouldn't even call him a trainer or cornerman—he was more important than a trainer. Ali had an unmeasurable determination and he got it from Bundini," two-time heavyweight champion George Foreman said to me.

"When you talk about Bundini, you are talking about the mouth of Muhammad Ali, an extension of Muhammad Ali's spirit. There would never have been a Muhammad Ali without Drew Bundini Brown," Khalilah Camacho-Ali, the Champ's second wife, suggested, echoing Foreman's comments.

"He was Ali's spirit man. A motivator. I can't explain it. It was a feeling thing. He fed the soul, he fed the spirit," James "Quick" Tillis reminisced.

"In training camp, Bundini kept everything going. Kept everything lively. Bundini gave Ali his entire heart," former heavyweight champion Larry Holmes said to me, looking back on his five years working for Ali as a sparring partner.

"Bundini played a very important part in Ali's career. He was Ali's right-hand man. He knew exactly how to motivate him. He was the one guy who could really get him up to train and get him ready to fight," former Ali opponent and Deer Lake stablemate Earnie Shavers told me.

"Bundini made Ali do more than he could do. The sound of his voice motivated Ali. He was an asset to Ali. A lot of boxers try to find a Bundini but they never going to find one like him. Boxers need trainers and motivators. Bundini was a one of a kind, you will never see another one like him," two-time heavyweight champion Tim Witherspoon suggested.

"I remember Bundini always telling Ali, 'I'm not your trainer, I'm your spirit,'" Gene Kilroy, Ali's longtime business manager, remembered.

To truly recognize the importance of Bundini's services, be they poetic or spiritual, one must start with the beginning of his working relationship with Muhammad Ali. Facing the formidable challenge of Sonny Liston, who like Mike Tyson a few decades later defeated opponents before they stepped into the ring, the young challenger was never in more need of a spiritual or psychological boost.

When looking back on Cassius Clay's first nineteen bouts as a professional, it becomes clear that the young fighter had yet to fully come into his own. In Clay's professional debut, he went the six-round distance with a part-time boxer and full-time police chief from Fayetteville, West Virginia. In Clay's eleventh professional bout, he was dropped by youngster Sonny Banks in the second round, a hard left hook that firmly planted the Louisville Lip on his backside. Clay had even flirted with defeat in his bout with Doug Jones. Judges Frank Forbes and Artie Aidala scored the fight 5-4-1 in Clay's favor, but referee Joe LoScalzo maintained a much wider margin of victory for Clay. In the fight leading up to Liston, the young challenger was leveled by a left hook from British journeyman Henry Cooper, hit by a punch that he later joked was so hard "his ancestors in Africa felt it." Because of Clay's back-to-back shaky performances, there was reason to believe he was in over his head against Liston. "The Big Ugly Bear," as he was dubbed by the young challenger, was coming off two consecutive first-round knockout wins against the great Floyd Patterson, erasing all doubt that Liston was the true heavyweight champion.

With his surly temperament, piston jab, dynamite right hand, lengthy criminal record, and ties to notorious mob figures such as Joseph "Pep" Barone, a front man for mobsters Frankie Carbo and Frank "Blinky" Palermo, Liston was the walking personification of intimidation. In hindsight, it is clear why oddsmakers had made Clay a 7-1 underdog in the fight. None of Clay's first nineteen opponents were anywhere near the talent level of the seemingly unbeatable Liston. What the oddsmakers and pundits couldn't have possibly known, however, was that Clay was about to tap into a deeper layer of his spiritual psyche, find new levels of courage and determination. When Drew Bundini Brown joined Clay's entourage, something changed. When the opening bell finally sounded, ending months of publicity stunts, trash talk, and prefight hype, the world would see a new version of Cassius Clay. Together, the duo would do nothing short of shake up the world.

■ ■ ■

True to the hotel-room promise he made the night before his bout with Doug Jones, Cassius Clay hired Drew Bundini Brown shortly after being granted the opportunity to face Sonny Liston. Unlike Sugar Ray Robinson, who primarily employed Bundini as a motivator in training camp, Clay invited Bundini to take on the responsibilities of an assistant trainer, serving as both a presence in camp and in the corner. To this point in his boxing career, Bundini had never worked a professional corner. The fact that Bundini replaced Clay's younger brother Rudy (later Rahman) as one of his cornermen for the Liston fight is telling. The young fighter clearly wanted what Bundini was giving him in the gym during the fight and in between rounds, a decision that would prove crucial to the outcome. While it had taken Bundini five years to gradually climb the ladder in Sugar Ray's entourage, he instantly found a key spot on Clay's team. Why Clay was willing to take on a relatively unknown boxing figure before the biggest fight of his life has, for some time, been the subject of speculation among historians.

"I heard this from his friends. Ali always felt like a bit of a faker when it came to the boxing world. The other boxers were hardcore city guys from the ghetto who had real street cred. He didn't. He was more middle class. He was only one of two kids from a solid two-parent family. Very early in his career he gets the help of this white police officer, and this white group of super-wealthy businessmen, all southerners. Bundini was like his alter ego. He had an authenticity that was missing from his persona. He knew that he could make some of that his own," Ali biographer Jonathan Eig suggested to me.

When Bundini arrived at the 5th Street Gym in Miami, Florida, in late 1963, Clay's entourage, as it is known by boxing fans today, was just beginning to take shape. The search for the trainer who would guide Clay's championship ambitions, in the early stages of his professional career, had proved difficult. After capturing Olympic gold in Italy, Clay worked with his original amateur mentor, Fred Stoner, for his ring debut. Concerned that Stoner did not have the experience to guide Clay to the highest levels of the professional ranks, Clay's backers sought out a big name. The first offer went out to Sugar Ray Robinson. Aging but not yet retired, Robinson declined.

Next came light-heavyweight champion Archie Moore, who also was still an active fighter. By all accounts, Clay and Moore were oil and water; their personalities simply did not jibe. The partnership would last only one fight, a second-round knockout against Herb Siler. When Clay returned to Louisville, his sponsoring group made a second pitch to Sugar Ray Robinson, before ultimately phoning Harry Markson, president of Madison Square Garden Boxing, for recommendations. Markson recommended Angelo Dundee, the chief second to a light heavyweight named Willie Pastrano. By the time Bundini joined the team, Clay and Dundee had worked together for just under four years, seventeen fights in total.

When Clay hired Dundee to be his head trainer, the leading voice in his corner, on December 19, 1960, the 5th Street Gym in Miami instantly became his official training headquarters. Run by Angelo Dundee and his brother Chris (a Miami-based fight promoter), the old-school, no frills boxing gym featured its own cast of colorful characters.

One of the most prominent figures in the 5th Street Gym was Ferdie Pacheco, a local doctor who worked in a downtrodden clinic in the area. Long before his career as a boxing analyst on NBC and Showtime, "the fight doctor," as Pacheco would come to be known, served as the official physician to Chris and Angelo Dundee's boxers, thus earning his place in Clay's inner circle.

Another Dundee associate was Cuban boxer Luis Sarria, dubbed by Ferdie Pacheco as "the dean of masseurs, the guru of fitness." As was the case with Pacheco, Clay quickly took a liking to Sarria, who worked for Dundee as a conditioning coach, cutman, and masseur.

The boisterous young challenger, of course, brought his own set of followers to the mix. First and foremost was Clay's younger brother, Rudy, also a professional boxer. Throughout Clay's career, Rudy served as his sidekick, sparring partner, errand runner, and occasional cornerman.

Then there was Clay's business manager, Gene Kilroy, a marketing executive for Metro Goldwin Mayer and later the Philadelphia Eagles, whom Clay had befriended during his Olympic experience in Rome. Kilroy was known as "the facilitator" in Clay's entourage. If Clay wanted a Cadillac, as journalist Gary Smith once wrote, it was "Kilroy's job to facilitate it."

Next to join the team was "Captain" Sam Saxon, later known as Abdul Rahman, a Muslim street minister from Miami. During Clay's early days at the 5th Street Gym, Saxon played religious adviser to Clay's budding interest in the Nation of Islam, which had begun prior to Bundini joining the entourage. In the summer of 1962, Clay struck up a friendship with Malcolm X, the Nation of Islam's most famous and fiery rhetorician. Clay and his brother Rudy had met Malcolm X at a luncheonette located next to a Detroit mosque.

"Cassius came up and pumped my hand. . . . He acted as if I was supposed to know who he was. So I acted as though I did. Up to that moment, though, I had never heard of him. Ours were two entirely different worlds. In fact, Elijah Muhammad instructed Muslims against all forms of sports," Malcolm X later reflected.

After the chance encounter, Clay and his brother began regularly attending Nation of Islam events with "Captain" Sam, many of which featured Malcolm X as the keynote speaker. Clay was fully enchanted by the power and eloquence of Malcolm X's rhetoric. Never in his life had Clay seen a Black man demonstrate so much power, eloquence, and outright defiance toward the injustices of White America.

In 1962, Clay also befriended *Los Angeles Sentinel* photographer Howard Bingham, the man who would serve as the Champ's official photographer throughout his career. Sharing an almost childlike playfulness in their approach to life, made evident in the "secret language" the two men developed over the years, Bingham and Clay were, in many ways, best friends. Clay would ask Bingham to serve as the best man in his wedding; Bingham would bestow the same honor upon the Champ.

When Drew Bundini Brown joined the team in late 1963, serving as Clay's chief motivator and poet laureate, the Cassius Clay entourage was finally complete.

In returning to Florida for the Clay–Liston training camp, Bundini's life had, in many ways, come full circle. It was fitting that the biggest moment of Bundini's boxing career would take place in his home state of Florida. Bundini had emerged from the swamps of Florida to travel the world, take on New York City, and befriend the most celebrated fighter of a generation, Sugar Ray Robinson. Bundini's time with Robinson, in hindsight, can be seen as something of a seven-year apprenticeship, the fight game's answer to a college and graduate-school education. As a trainer to the most promising and controversial prospect in the sport, front and center in the media coverage, Bundini would no longer linger in the shadows. The Liston bout would make or break the careers of both Clay and Bundini.

Back in Sanford, Bundini's family members, as one might suspect, were proud of their vicarious connection to the fight everyone was talking about.

"Drew always kept in contact with the family, even when he was in New York. That's one thing I always admired about him," Claudia Brown, Bundini's niece, told me.

"At that time, he didn't really know how big he was back in Sanford. He'd been off in New York with Sugar Ray all those years. But with this fight, everyone in Sanford was starting to realize the impact he was having in the fight world. All of a sudden, Drew was *big*," Claudia added.

While the town of Sanford, particularly the Georgetown section of the city, was buzzing over Bundini's homecoming, this excitement was not visibly expressed by Drew Brown Sr. Even in old age, Drew Sr. remained stern, unemotional. He was not the type of father who would tell his son "good job" or "I'm proud of you." This form of validation would elude Bundini for much of his life.

Back in Harlem, Drew Brown III, now nine years old, was beginning to realize that his father was someone special in the boxing world. Leading up to the fight, Drew III began to see his father on television, his picture in national newspapers. The child's enthusiasm was not shared by his mother, Rhoda, who was struggling to find her way after the divorce.

Reflecting on the year that made his father world famous, Drew Brown III remembers 1964 as a dark year for his mother: "She had married a Greek guy from Brighton who was an alcoholic and unemployed mechanic. He moved into the projects with us but his drinking only drained our finances more. She was attempting to get the marriage annulled when, one night, he died of a heart attack on the Boardwalk. After that, nothing seemed to work in her life. She went from one bookkeeping job, back to unemployment, then on to another bookkeeping job just long enough to draw more unemployment. But to her credit, I never knew as a child that she was unemployed. Momma got up every morning and dressed for office work, then saw me off to school—even if she had nothing more to do that day than collect welfare and unemployment checks, or look for a new job. Looking back, I realize that in remarrying, then in her second husband's death, and even in the drinking that followed, Momma was struggling."

While Drew III's life in the Carver housing projects was anything but posh, his father's new job was not without its perks. Before leaving for Florida, Bundini arranged for a meeting between Cassius Clay and his son.

"Uncle Ray and my older brother Cassius were famous but that didn't make me love them any more than I did my other Harlem family," Drew III told me. "I remember just being happy that Daddy had a job," Drew added.

Not yet married and without children of his own, Cassius Clay instantly took a liking to his new cornerman's son, playfully nicknaming the boy "Lil' nappy-headed Jew." In the coming months, the two would become pen pals of sorts. After their first meeting, a postcard from Miami Beach arrived in the mail. The postcard reads as follows:

> Mr. Drew Brown III,
> I am getting ready for the Big Ugly Bear Sonny Liston. Tell all of your
> friends I said hello. I will see you when I am World Champion so
> be good.
> Your best friend,
> Cassius Clay

While boxing experts gave Clay almost no chance of pulling off the upset, Drew Brown III, full of boyish admiration for his father, remained confident that his daddy would be able to give the challenger the same magic he lent to Sugar Ray Robinson. Cassius Clay, rallying his own courage via an increasingly exuberant public bravado, was perhaps hoping the very same thing. Clay's admiration for Sugar Ray, demonstrated by his team's repeated attempts to coax the middleweight champion into joining the fray, is key to understanding his willingness to listen and follow the instructions of his new cornerman. Bundini's credibility was clearly bolstered by his vicarious connection to the pound-for-pound legend, perhaps the fighter Clay admired most.

■ ■ ■

To understand Drew Bundini Brown's approach to motivation, one must first come to understand his views on spirituality. Bundini believed that truly great fighters were chosen by Shorty rather than cultivated by truly great trainers.

"Working with these champions, I know they are born, not made in a gym. If you could make 'em in a gym, they'd turn 'em out like a bakery turns out cookies," Bundini once said. "Sugar Ray was a true champ, like [Cassius Clay] is a true champ. They don't need no teaching. Worst thing for a fighter is to be trained by a fighter. An ex-fighter tries to make the fighter like the old fighter was. I couldn't teach the champ to deliver a blow. No man could do that. But I can talk to him about other things."

Considering this philosophy, it is next to impossible to imagine Angelo Dundee felt no trepidation whatsoever when asked to coexist with the new addition to Clay's corner. By most accounts, Dundee was a relatively mild-mannered, x's-and-o's-style boxing trainer. In an interview with *Sports Illustrated*, Dundee reflected on the day he found out that Bundini was joining the team: "I met [Bundini] just before our Doug Jones fight. He was talking about the planets. Like to drove me up the wall. While we were getting ready for our first fight with Liston, the Champ says, 'Angelo, guess who's coming down?' I said, 'Oh no, don't tell me!' But there's no friction between Bundini and me. There's no crossing of roles. I like him. The trick is, if you try to understand him, he'll drive you crazy. So I don't try."

While Dundee now had competition for Clay's ear space, he quickly recognized that Bundini could bring out the best in Clay with respect to energy and effort. Dundee was smart enough to recognize that whatever was good for Clay was good for business. To appease the future champion, he and Bundini would quickly learn to coexist. The degree to which Dundee and Bundini were able to do so has been the subject of much speculation.

"The funny thing was the war of space. The two of them would basically race up the ring steps. Dad wanted the stool in there immediately," Jim Dundee, Angelo's son, said to me. "He wanted to be up there first. Drew loved Muhammad so he wanted to be up there first. It was a race. Dad would always laugh about it. He genuinely loved Drew. I can promise you that. My dad always confided in me, throughout life, and I don't remember him ever being mad at Drew. Sure, there were times when Dad didn't like the crying. Dad wasn't emotional and Drew would cry at the drop of a hat. But, let me tell you this, they became good friends. Drew took Dad to the Cotton Club one time. He was so excited that Drew did that. Going to Harlem, back in those days, was the most incredible thing to my dad."

By Angelo's son's estimation, Bundini gave Ali something that his own father, despite all of his experience working with fighters such as Carmen Basilio and Willie Pastrano, could not. Dundee's job was to cultivate Clay's boxing IQ; heart, determination, and spiritual strength became Bundini's territory.

"Listen, Dad was fairly emotionless," Jim Dundee told me. "When it came to work, Dad, at that point, worked very quietly in the corner, with a few exceptions. Muhammad loved Drew's emotion. My dad got a kick out of it too. I remember them all sitting around together, Muhammad and Drew, doing the rhymes. My dad would jump in and give it a try as well."

Each day began with Bundini waking the challenger for early morning roadwork, a process he referred to as "getting the gas" (filling up one's metaphorical gas tank). For Bundini, the day was won or lost by the manner in which a fighter woke up, showed up, and paid attention. A successful day of training was based on a fighter's ability to take responsibility of his actions and be in tune with his emotions. This component of Bundini philosophy was dubbed "the circle theory." He firmly believed in a what-goes-around-comes-around approach to preparing one's mind and body to do battle. The *work* had to be done because Shorty, the proprietor of one's natural gifts, was watching. "Shorty is watching," Bundini would shout. Every sit-up had to be conducted with complete focus. Each stroke of the speed bag had to be as important as the last. Bundini's motivational approach could be defined as the gospel of total awareness. *Feeling*, an idea closely linked to the Buddhist concept of mindfulness, was Bundini's end goal.

"Plug in your television. Thirteen channels are here in this room, but you can't see 'em unless you are plugged in. On the radio, 150 stations are coming in, but you can't hear 'em unless you turn it on," Bundini once preached, highlighting the importance of acknowledging and embracing feeling, especially fear.

"A blind man live, a deaf and dumb man live, but when you lose your feelings you're dead," Bundini told the young Cassius Clay.

For Bundini, fear was fuel. It could be used as a weapon to propel humans beyond their limitations. During sparring sessions, one of Bundini's key phrases was "Be free, Champ." To accept pain, fatigue, and fear was to be free. The ability to think clearly in uncomfortable spaces made a great fighter that much greater, Bundini figured. Be it hitting the heavy bag or skipping rope, he preached the gospel of freedom, absolute focus, the process of embracing the pain, holding it closely, acknowledging its power, and accepting it.

"You gotta get up and get the gas," Bundini would say each morning.

"Be free, Champ . . . ain't nothing better than free," he would shout as he leaned over the ropes during sparring sessions.

While Clay and his new trainer were bound by their gift of gab and poetic sensibilities, the two were, in many ways, an odd couple. Clay, at this point in his life, was still shy around women. Bundini was Clay's polar opposite in this regard. While Clay lived a completely clean life in regard to drugs and alcohol, Bundini was known as a heavy drinker and a recreational marijuana user. The primary difference between the two, however, centered on their views regarding race and religion. At the time, Clay was fully enamored with the teachings of the Honorable Elijah Muhammad, leader of the Nation of Islam. All but an official member of the organization, Clay, at first, was advised by his handlers to temporarily conceal his religious beliefs, in fear that proclaiming his support for the Nation of Islam would tank his chances at being granted a title shot. A converted Jew, but only in the loose sense of the term, Bundini had learned a thing or two about the teachings of Elijah Muhammad during his time in Harlem. To put it mildly, Bundini was not a fan. By all accounts, he did not coddle his new boss in this regard. He was aware that Elijah Muhammad was teaching that the "White Man" was the devil, a message that touched a nerve with Bundini because of the bicultural makeup of his own son.

"That mean my son is half devil?" he would ponder to Clay.

Bundini was aware that Clay had instantly taken a liking to his son. Thus, Drew III would serve as Bundini's primary evidence in his repeated attempts to debunk the teachings of Elijah Muhammad.

In *Ali: A Life*, Jonathan Eig reminds readers of the ideological disparities between Clay and Bundini: "The men seemed mismatched in many ways . . . [Bundini] talked about a God who encompassed all religions, and he described race as a misguided human concept, not a heavenly or natural one. . . . Brown challenged Clay like no one else, telling him Elijah Muhammad was wrong, that white people were not devils, that God didn't care a thing about a person's color."

As the training camp progressed, Bundini relayed his philosophies on both boxing and life to the young contender. Clay did not accept all of Bundini's viewpoints with open arms. When the subject turned to the topic of race, arguments often ensued, neither man giving a rhetorical inch.

"When you can appreciate a human being and respect him for his good and try to help him for his wrongness, you've found God's law," Bundini lectured.

The two would argue, laugh, and often argue some more.

"Trouble is, people become robots, mechanical, puppets. But that's not the real thing," Bundini preached. "Life ain't for robots. Life is a *feeling*," he would argue.

Despite their differing worldviews, a strong bond quickly formed. Clay was attracted to Bundini's street vocabulary, his verbal gymnastics, inspired by the idea of an omnipresent God from which human beings can gain strength.

Aside from the motivational speeches and religious debates, "Brown served another, more specific role in the Clay camp: he helped boost and improve the boxer's poetic output, which to that point had been confined to short lyrics ending in the numbers one through ten," Jonathan Eig writes.

Early into their time together, the two began rehearsing the "butterfly" routine that would soon become famous. One week before the fight, CBS sports broadcaster Bob Halloran and a group of local and national media visited the 5th Street Gym to profile the loquacious underdog's training camp, providing the duo with the perfect opportunity to unveil their new battle cry to the sports world. When the camera crews arrived, Clay's notorious bravado, inspired by professional wrestler Gorgeous George, was on full display. Visibly amused by Clay's antics but still searching for actual sports content, Halloran made several unsuccessful attempts at steering the interview back to the subject of boxing.

"You're going around saying you're not going to reveal your strategy . . . can't you tell us a little bit about what you're going to do in the fight?" Halloran pleaded, attempting to divert the conversation away from the topic of Clay's greatness.[3]

To this question, the young Clay rose to his feet as if Halloran had given him the cue he had been waiting for.

"You know how great I am. I don't have to tell you about my strategy. I'll let my trainer tell you . . . Bo-dini, come here," Clay called, motioning Drew Bundini Brown into the camera shot.

Dressed in a nylon mesh polo shirt and matching cap, a towel draped over his shoulder, Bundini stepped into the American spotlight.

"Bo-dini," Clay shouted, "Tell 'em what we are gonna do."

In perfect rhythmic timing, Bundini launched into the routine that would make him famous the world over.

"We're gonna float like a butterfly and sting like a bee," Bundini called, followed by a collective "Ahhhhh . . . Ahhhhh, Rumble, young man, rumble."

"That's what we're gonna do, you heard it, that's my trainer, he'll tell ya," Clay insisted. The performance, which would be picked up by newspapers and sports broadcasts around the country, foreshadowed a new chapter in boxing history. The theatrics of professional sports would never be the same.

■ ■ ■

While modern boxing fans likely think of weigh-ins as a key component of the promotional buildup to any pay-per-view attraction, such was not the case before Liston–Clay. Staredowns, shoving matches, and hyperbolic trash talk had yet to become an audience expectation for a prefight ceremony that, in those days, took place the morning of a fight.

"Before Clay's fight against Sonny Liston, championship bout weigh-ins had been fairly standard and boring. But Muhammad Ali reinvented the rituals of boxing, and after the show he put on in Miami Beach, weigh-ins would never be the same," Ali biographer Thomas Hauser writes.[4]

Dressed in a blue denim jacket with the words "Bear Huntin" inscribed on the back, Cassius Clay, accompanied by Angelo Dundee, Bundini, and Sugar Ray Robinson—who had flown down to Miami to be part of the entourage (per Clay's request)—set the tone for what would be one of the most talked about prefight spectacles in boxing history. Bursting through the double doors of the room where the weigh-in was to be held, Clay and Bundini shouted at the top of their lungs: "Float like a butterfly, sting like a bee: rumble, young man, rumble."

As Clay made his way through the room of officials, pundits, and reporters, his rhetoric reached a fever pitch. "Alarmed by what they'd seen so far, representatives of the Miami Beach Boxing Commission followed [Clay] and warned of a fine if his behavior didn't change," Hauser writes. When Liston's team entered the room, some twenty minutes later, the routine, once again, picked back up.

"I'm ready to rumble now . . . I can beat you anytime, chump! You ain't no giant! I'm gonna eat you alive! Tonight, I predict somebody is gonna die at ringside from shock!" Clay shouted at anyone who would listen.

Throughout the hysterics, Dundee and Robinson took turns holding Clay back. The challenger, who was unable to stay in one place for more than a few seconds, seemed completely out of control. The consensus in the room was that Clay had come unraveled. As the wild theatrics continued, Morris Klein (chairman of the Miami Boxing Commission) took to the microphone to announce that Clay would be fined $2,500 for his behavior. The announcement did little to deter Clay's antics.

Earlier in the morning, before the weigh-in, Angelo Dundee and Sugar Ray Robinson had all but begged Clay to abandon his psychological game plan. In *Muhammad Ali: His Life and Times*, Ferdie Pacheco reflects on Dundee and Robinson's cautionary advice: "God, what a show Cassius put on that morning. In the dressing room, Angelo and Sugar Ray gave him a lecture. They said, 'Look, this is a weigh-in for the heavyweight championship of the world. Hundreds of members of the press are here. It's not for craziness.' And to be honest, I didn't think he'd have the nerve to pull it off. I mean, here's a twenty-two-year-old kid in front of the entire news media. And even though he'd talked about psychological warfare before the fight, I just didn't think what happened would happen."

Bundini, Clay's accomplice in the theatrics, firmly believed the only way to gain a psychological edge over Liston was to convince the champion he was in the ring with a crazy man. While the cameras were rolling, Bundini encouraged his pupil's fury. Just when it appeared Clay was beginning to settle, Bundini would stoke the fire by repeating the "butterfly" refrain. Regardless of whether the routine had any effect on Liston, Clay and Bundini succeeded in convincing members of the media that they were indeed crazy.

"It looked to me like Clay was having a seizure," journalist Mort Sharnik recalled.

"At the weigh-in, Clay sure as hell fooled me," boxing writer Jerry Izenberg remembered. "I was covering the fight for the *Newark Star Ledger*, and I couldn't begin to get a handle on it all. He behaved like an absolute lunatic."

"Dad was worried they were going to call off the fight because of Muhammad's blood pressure," Jim Dundee remembered. "Ferdie was too. But there was Drew, lighting the fire. That's what he did best. He always lit Muhammad's fire. That was Drew's job."

For those who believed Clay was more concerned with selling the fight than actually winning it, the weigh-in served as evidence of Clay's internal panic. The real shock would come later that night in Convention Hall.

■ ■ ■

Dressed in khaki pants, a cardigan sweater, and a matching bow tie, an outfit paying homage to his days as a steward in the Navy, Bundini straddled the bottom rope, one long leg resting on the ring apron, the other resting inside the squared circle, a television camera over his shoulder.

"I can't see, cut 'em off! I can't see, cut off the gloves!" Clay shouted, his eyes blinking, face contorting in pain.

Much to the surprise of the capacity crowd at Convention Hall in Miami, and for the millions watching around the world, the young challenger had dominated the first four rounds of the fight, demonstrating superior speed, reflexes, and defensive skill. Gliding around the ring as if he were on skates, Clay slipped and countered Liston's every offensive move, firing back with whiplash combinations. On his way back to the corner at the conclusion of the fourth round, however, Clay instantly became unsteady on his feet, running his right glove along the top rope to guide himself back to the corner. Blinking profusely, Clay began to shout in pain. The challenger was temporarily blinded.

One of the great mysteries of boxing history, never completely proved, suggests that Sonny Liston, when faced with the reality that he was clearly outmatched by the young Cassius Clay, asked his cornerman Joe Pollino to "juice the gloves." Some have speculated that Pollino applied a mint-like oil of wintergreen to his fighter's gloves, instructing him to rub the gloves near Clay's eyes during a clinch. Others have suggested the gloves were doused in ferric chloride, a substance that trainers often use to tend to open wounds.

In *King of the World: Muhammad Ali and the Rise of the American Hero,* David Remnick's best-selling Ali biography, Jack McKinney of the *Philadelphia Daily* (who was close with both Liston and Pollino) supports conspiracy theories that suggest Liston contaminated his gloves with an illegal substance in a Hail Mary attempt to salvage the fight: "Immediately after the fight, Joe, who was very close to me, unburdened himself to me. He told me Sonny had told him to juice the gloves, and he went ahead and did it. Not only that, he said that they always were ready to do that in case of danger, and that they'd done it in fights against Eddie Machen and Cleveland Williams. . . . Pollino told me that he put the stuff on the gloves at Sonny's express instructions and then threw the stuff under the ring apron as far as he could. . . . Joe himself felt so conflicted over this. He'd been sucked into it, but he knew if he ever came clean he would never work again."

Regardless of whether Liston's gloves were actually tainted, there is no disputing that Clay begged his trainers to stop the fight in between rounds four and five. Clay did not *attempt* to quit, he did quit. Dundee and Bundini, on the other hand, simply wouldn't allow their fighter to do so.

In hindsight, there was more at stake than the heavyweight championship of the world; the history of boxing was hanging in the balance. If Clay had quit on the stool after the fourth round, boxing pundits and sportscasters—especially those who did not care for Clay's braggadocio ways—would have enjoyed giving the twenty-two-year-old fighter his comeuppance. Liston, who'd been thoroughly outboxed in the first four rounds, would have likely been hesitant to give his rival a rematch. The surly champion felt a genuine disdain for Clay. Had the young challenger committed boxing's cardinal sin, there would have been plenty of fans who would have argued Clay had taken the coward's way out. Perhaps never before in the history of the sport had a team of cornermen been given a more difficult situation to navigate. Their fighter, who just moments earlier had been pulling off one of the biggest upsets in the history of the heavyweight championship, was now claiming that he could not see and wanted the fight stopped.

"This is the big one, daddy," Dundee calmly reminded Clay, taking a wet sponge and attempting to squeeze water into Clay's eyes to wash them out.

"Cut the bullshit—we're not quitting now," Dundee repeated, as he ran the sponge over Clay's forehead.

Writhing in pain, Clay attempted to get up from his stool, in hopes of alerting the referee to Liston's tactics. Bundini, now fully in the ring, blocked Clay's path. Clay flung his arms in the air in desperation as Dundee ushered the fighter back to the corner, guiding him by the waist. "Remember Elijah Muhammad, remember all those people you fighting for. If you quit there'll be children in Harlem crying tonight!" Bundini shouted in Clay's ear.

Unlike Dundee, Bundini rarely kept a calm tongue in the corner. Practicing what he preached, in terms of being connected to emotion, Bundini would often be moved to tears during bouts. This would be the first of many such occasions.

As Liston made his way toward Clay at the beginning of round five, both Dundee and Bundini were still in the ring, hastily exiting as the fighting continued.

"Go out there and run!" Dundee shouted into one ear.

"Shorty is watching you!" Bundini shouted into the other.

Despite his own opposition to the Nation of Islam, Bundini understood what motivated Clay. Like any good rhetorician, Bundini knew the importance of audience awareness.

"My father would carry a small picture of Elijah Muhammad in his pocket and he would use to it remind the Champ of what he was fighting for," Drew III told me.

When the bout continued, Dundee and Bundini remained standing. "Run—get on your bicycle!" Dundee shouted from the ring apron.

"Yardstick 'em," Bundini called, making his way down the ring steps, signaling his homespun code word for Clay's long left jab.

Instantly recognizing that his opponent was blinded, Liston charged, hammering Clay with lethal left and right hooks to the rib cage. Suddenly,

Liston returned to form. As Clay blinked and attempted to clinch, Liston unleashed an onslaught of power punches.

On unsteady legs, Clay attempted to dance around the ring, using his left arm as a measuring device to gauge his opponent's distance.

"Yardstick 'em!" Bundini screamed at the top of his lungs. As Liston dove in with leaping left hooks, the yardstick method of self-preservation proved key.

"Clay's corner is complaining that something has got onto those gloves and into his eyes," the broadcast team said as Liston pounded Clay against the ropes.

"He's just pushing his left arm into Liston's face," the announcers repeated as Liston attempted to finish his weakened opponent.

By the final minute, however, Liston appeared to have punched himself out, having spent all of his energy in the early moments of the round. Clay's yardstick defense saved him from being caught flush on the chin; many of Liston's sweeping hooks to the head had missed by only inches. When the bell sounded, Clay returned to his corner, still blinking. Dundee and Bundini both entered the ring, their heads pressed together as they nervously inspected their fighter.

When the fighters returned to the center of the ring for the sixth round, Clay's vision was now clear, as made evident by the challenger's crisp jab. Throughout the round, Clay repeatedly snapped Liston's head back with sharp combinations. Flat-footed for the first time in the fight, Clay began to sit down on his punches and deliver them with power. The Liston rally was over. The challenger dominated the fight at the center of the ring, just as he had done in the first four rounds. The playground bully had met his match in the so-called Louisville Lip, who was on his way to becoming the heavyweight champion of the world not because of his superior speed, defense, and ring generalship but because he possessed the mental strength, the spiritual wherewithal, to endure going temporarily blind in the ring. The true difference between Liston and Clay, at least for that one night, was mental strength. When the bell sounded for the start of the seventh round, Liston remained on his stool.

Sensing what was about to happen, Clay began his famous shuffle, his arms raised to the heavens. Bundini must have sensed it as well because he skipped his way to the center of the ring, draped his long, ropey arms around Clay's waist in celebration, and awkwardly lifted the lanky fighter from the canvas. As the referee attempted to raise Clay's hand in victory, the new champion charged toward the ropes, Bundini still clinging to his waist.

"I am the king of the world! I am the king! I am the king of the world! Eat your words, eat your words!" Clay shouted into the crowd.

As Clay made his way around the ring, Bundini refused to relinquish his celebratory grip, tears streaming down his face. When the new champion finally made his way through the crowded ring for the postfight interview, Bundini was still firmly hugging his young pupil.

"I must be the greatest . . . I told the world, I talk to God every day. If God is with me, can't nobody be against me!" Clay shouted into the microphone.

Liston, who had cited a shoulder injury as his reason for stopping the fight, was taken to St. Francis Hospital. Clay, who would carry his theatrics from the ring into the pressroom, continued to provide great copy for the media.

"The next morning, I saw my daddy on every front page of papers at every newsstand in Harlem," Drew Brown III remembered.

The postfight headlines marked the beginning of what would become one of the most controversial and unpredictable title reigns in the history of the sport.

■ ■ ■

Muhammad Ali's first year as heavyweight champion can best be described as controlled chaos. The new champ wasted no time in making sociopolitical waves. The following morning, at a press conference in the Veterans Room of Convention Hall, the youngest heavyweight to lift the title from a reigning champion ended the persistent speculation regarding his religious beliefs. Heightened by Malcolm X's ringside presence at the fight, many of the questions directed at Clay had nothing to do with boxing.

"I believe in Allah and in peace. I don't try to move into white neighborhoods. I don't try to marry a white woman. I was baptized when I was twelve, but I didn't know what I was doing. I'm not a Christian anymore. I know where I'm going and I know the truth, and I don't have to be what you want me to be. I'm free to be what I want," Clay told reporters.[5]

Soon after the press conference, the young champion announced that he had changed his name to Cassius X, informing the media that he was abandoning the slave name of Clay.

Less than a month later, on March 6, 1964, Elijah Muhammad announced in a radio address that Cassius Marcellus Clay was now a follower of the Nation of Islam and would receive the full Muslim name of Muhammad Ali, an unprecedented honor for a new member of the organization.

While Ali continued making headlines, highlighted by a celebratory trip to Africa and the Middle East, his enigmatic boxing rival was also in the news. Arrested on March 12, 1964, Sonny Liston was charged with speeding, reckless driving, driving without an operator's license, and for carrying a concealed weapon, a loaded .22-caliber pistol. From his shadowy opponent to his impromptu marriage to Sonji Roi, a cocktail waitress, every aspect of Muhammad Ali's personal life, it appeared, was newsworthy. Ali and Roi had instantly fallen in love and were married one month after their first date, on August 14, 1964.

When the Ali–Liston rematch was officially announced, shortly after the young champion's marriage, many within the media were skeptical of the bout. Much of this skepticism was connected to the fact that investigative journalists had uncovered that Liston's team had negotiated a rematch clause in conjunction with the original contract. The World Boxing Association, at that time, did not allow for rematch clauses in championship bouts. Those who were simply unable to grasp Ali's stunning upset believed Liston had either taken a dive for the mob or had simply realized that he had more to gain financially by losing the match. Because of the negative publicity surrounding both combatants, prominent state boxing commissions, most notably New York, California, and Nevada, refused to host the bout. Originally scheduled for the Boston Garden on November 16, 1964, a swarm of unexpected plot twists fueled the increasingly popular notion that the Ali–Liston rematch was more farce than fight, nothing more than a public spectacle.

Back in Harlem, Drew Brown III was also in for *the* public spectacle of his young life. Dressed in a white wig, playing the role of an English Bürgermeister, the young boy took the stage to recite the brief speech he had memorized for his first school play. Upon taking his position at center stage, Drew III spotted his grandparents, Mildred and Jack Palestine, in the crowd; his mother, Rhoda, was in attendance as well. As the boy began to deliver the opening lines of his speech, the auditorium doors burst open, accompanied by a collective gasp from the fourth, fifth, and sixth graders in attendance. Dressed in a tailored black suit, Muhammad Ali entered the room, accompanied by Drew's father. Unsure of whether he should continue with his lines, Drew III froze. Ali and Bundini made their way toward a pair of empty seats, collectively nodding and motioning for the English statesman to continue with his lines. The young boy stumbled through his speech, providing the audience with his best rendition of a British accent. When the curtain closed, the principal announced Ali's presence and the Champ took the stage for a brief motivational speech.

"My popularity with the kids at P.S. 171 in Manhattan received a huge boost," Drew III remembered. "As Ali got up, I looked from the wings of the stage and saw my daddy's gaze connect with mine. 'See, son, I told you,' his happy eyes seemed to say. 'I'll never let you down. I'll always come through for you.' In response, I stuck my little finger in the air, as a gesture to symbolize my daddy's [give me the little ones] handshake," Drew III remembered, harkening back to the day Ali delivered on his promise to visit the boy after becoming champion of the world.

The Hallmark family moment, one of the few in Drew III's young life, would soon be swept away by the storm of controversy that loomed ominously on the horizon for his father and Ali. The controversy surrounding the Ali–Liston rematch was brought to new heights when, only three days prior to the fight, it was announced that Ali had been taken to a local hospital in need of emergency surgery because of a hernia that he had suffered in training. The unofficial public relations man to the Champ, a somber Drew Bundini Brown, broke the news to the media outside the hospital.

Surrounded by cameras and microphones, an uncharacteristically timid Bundini would state the following: "Well, we were having dinner. Spinach, steak and potatoes, a tossed salad, and hot tea. A regular fighter's dinner. And after dinner, we were watching a movie, *Lil' Caesar*. And he vomited. And the pain came on. And he said, 'Man, I'm really hurting.' And we brought him on here. We wanted to take him to a private doctor but he kept saying, 'Man, I'm in bad shape.' The doctor said he was glad we brought him on over here because he was getting in bad shape," Bundini said.

Liston, who had trained diligently for the rematch, was both dejected and enraged. "That son-of-a-bitch, I'll never get in shape like this again," Liston allegedly told his advisers.

As the new date for the rematch, May 25, 1965, approached, Liston was involved with a second arrest, prompting Boston Garden officials to back out of the fight. Just a few months prior to Liston's second prefight arrest, February 21, 1965, Malcolm X had been assassinated at the Audubon Ballroom in Manhattan. Rumors circulated that the Nation of Islam was behind the attack and that a retaliatory incident of violence was to occur at Muhammad Ali's bout, adding an additional layer of danger and controversy to the promotion.

Desperate for a new fight location, and with little time to find a venue of comparable size, promoters focused on salvaging closed-circuit and television revenue. If the bout were to be postponed again it might never take place, both camps feared. In a plot twist that not even Nostradamus could have predicted, the Central Maine Youth Center, a junior league hockey rink located in the mill town of Lewiston, Maine, was announced as the replacement venue. To this day, the Ali–Liston rematch remains the only heavyweight championship fight ever to take place in the state of Maine. The actual fight, like the odd set of circumstances leading up to the opening bell, would prove to be equally tumultuous.

Because of the remote location of the venue and rumors of violence surrounding the promotion, Muhammad Ali's first title defense would take place in front of the smallest crowd ever to witness a heavyweight championship bout. Those who chose to stay home didn't miss much. Liston fell to the canvas one minute and forty-four seconds into the first round, hit by a right hand that Ali would later dub "the anchor punch." After crumbling to the canvas, Liston rolled onto his back, then flopped onto his belly, all before making it to one knee and rolling onto his back for a second time.

When Liston finally made it to his feet, Ali was leaping with joy and parading around the ring in celebration, winding up his right hand in a comical gesture. Referee Jersey Joe Walcott, who was visibly distracted by Ali's refusal to go to a neutral corner, lost track of the count. As the fight continued, Ali bombarding Liston with combinations, Walcott was notified by Nat Fleischer that Liston had been counted out during the knockdown. Bundini, once again, was first into the ring to lift Ali in a celebratory embrace. The moment of triumph was short lived.

Like the vanquished Sonny Liston, Drew Bundini Brown would soon find himself sprawling on the canvas, searching for the answer to how it all slipped away so quickly.

5

**Blue Eyes and
Brown Eyes,
See Grass Green**

The story of Muhammad Ali's missing heavyweight championship belt is a key piece of Drew Bundini Brown's boxing mythology, a dark cloud that looms over all that Bundini accomplished in the sport. There have been multiple versions, each crafted with self-serving intentions.

"Bundini Brown, isn't that the guy who stole Muhammad Ali's championship belt? He sold it for drug money, right?" a colleague asked when learning of my participation in this project.

This version of the story, a revisionist history promoted in Columbia/Tristar's 2001 biopic *Ali*, positions Bundini as a fringe member of the Ali entourage, a hanger-on, a disloyal companion to the trusting and good-natured Champ. For those who label Bundini as such, it is a story that likely figures into their reasoning.

Michael Mann's *Ali* provides moviegoers with a larger-than-life, Paul Bunyan–style version of boxing's most celebrated champion. In many ways, Mann does so at the expense of Drew Bundini Brown. The dramatic tension of the film, bookended by Muhammad Ali's stunning upsets over Sonny Liston (1964) and George Foreman (1974), centers on the Champ's years as a civil rights martyr and his landmark victory over the U.S. government. The apex of the conflict occurs in what is perhaps the most talked about scene in the movie, where Ali, played by Academy Award winner Will Smith, discovers that his cornerman, played by fellow Academy Award winner Jamie Foxx, has sold his championship belt to a Harlem barber. Mann's dramatic rendering of the events signifies a low point in Ali's life. Unjustly stripped of his heavyweight title, exiled from boxing, targeted and persecuted for his religious beliefs, Ali is both unable to make a living in his home country and unable to leave it. As Ali's prospects dwindle, his most trusted friends and advisers show their true colors. This is Muhammad Ali at his rock bottom, a man who has lost both his mythical title and its symbolic representation.

The buildup to the filmic confrontation between Ali and Bundini takes place in the previous scene, where Ali and his personal photographer, Howard Bingham, played by Jeffrey Wright, take in Joe Frazier's victory over Jimmy Ellis. Watching from the comfort of Ali's modest living-room sofa, Bingham interrupts the fisticuffs, nodding to Ali between sips of coffee.

"I saw Bundini when I was in New York . . . he's bad, in bad shape, you'd better get your belt back," Bingham warns.[1]

The context in which these lines are delivered is key to understanding Mann's approach. Later in the scene, Ali's wife Khalilah, played by Nona Gaye, echoes Bingham's ominous warning by suggesting that Ali should "put some new people" around him if he ever wants to return to the ring.

"Where are Herbert [Muhammad] and them when we need them? Gene Kilroy is dropping off groceries like charity . . . they are all over you when you got it but they just drop off you when you die," Khalilah adds, dramatic violin strings accompanying her cautionary advice.

At the close of the scene, Mann makes a swift cut to Ali and Bingham rushing up the dilapidated corridor of a rickety staircase, a disheveled motel clerk leading the way.

"He gave me your number when he checked in . . . normally he's up there making a lot of noise," the clerk frantically shouts, her shrill voice echoing in the narrow stairway.

Inside the filthy motel room, Ali violently draws the curtains, pouring light into the room, dust filling the air as Bundini awakens from the shadows.

"That's called sunlight," Bingham smirks.

Jolted to consciousness, Bundini scurries along the bed like a cockroach, eyes squinting. Ali wears his disappointment like a mask, smashing a half-empty liquor bottle against the wall as a violent expression of his disgust. A sleuth searching for clues, Ali grasps at Bundini's tattered cardigan sleeves, attempting to locate the needle tracks that signify intravenous drug use. Bundini resists the search but Ali finds what he is looking for.

"Why you killing yourself . . . why you shaming yourself . . . why you doing that to yourself . . . why you disrespecting yourself?" Ali shouts.

Unable to contain his emotion, biting his lip and clinching his fists, Ali turns from the bed and directs his scowl toward the window. Bundini, now fully aware of the situation, attempts to save face by spouting off some of his most famous rhymes, to which Ali coldly replies, "Those rhymes are old . . . you need to get some new ones."

As the crescendo builds, the camera focuses on Ali's outward gaze; Bundini can be seen from the reflection of a dirty mirror.

"I sold your belt," Bundini finally mutters, his voice shaky and wavering. "I sold your belt to a barber for $500 . . . I couldn't help it . . . I got a crazy mind . . . I took that $500 and put it in my arm," he whimpers. "Take me back, Boss . . . I can get the belt back."

Michael Mann's version of the story is more symbolic than factual. First, there was never a sofa-side conversation with Ali and Bingham. Mann portrays the conversation in this fashion to highlight that Ali was low on money during his exile, out of the limelight as the boxing world moved on. Ali was ringside the night Joe Frazier and Jimmy Ellis faced off at Madison Square Garden. He was seated next to his friend Drew Bundini Brown. Second, Ali never confronted Bundini about the missing belt in a rundown Harlem motel. Nor did he ever find Bundini strung out on drugs. Mann's portrayal is designed to highlight Ali's willingness to forgive those who have betrayed him during his darkest days. The goal of Mann's scene is to position Ali as betrayed, by both his entourage and his country. Two scenes later, for example, after Ali is finally granted a boxing license, Bundini shows up at the 5th Street Gym, once again begging for his job back. Ali demonstrates his compassion. The reunion is sealed with a stoic rendition of "Float like a butterfly, sting like a bee."

Despite the film's box office success, *Ali* was not without its critics. Some members of the Ali entourage were taken aback by Michael Mann's portrayal of Bundini, particularly the suggestion that he was a heroin user.

"I was very upset by how Bundini was portrayed in the movie," Gene Kilroy, Ali's longtime business manager, told me. "All of us were upset about it."

"Jamie Foxx played Bundini as a crackhead. He was never on hard drugs. Bundini would smoke pot. He liked to drink," Kilroy added.

Ali's second wife, Khalilah Camacho-Ali, expressed a similar brand of disapproval: "It was wrong of them to portray Bundini as strung out on heroin. He was never falling around like that. It hurt me to see that. I was mad as hell. I know drug addicts. You can't hide that. It comes out. We knew Bundini liked to drink, he would smoke his little marijuana. But he never did any of that around Ali. All of this stuff in the movie about him being strung out isn't true. He was never like that around us. Ali never once saw him like that."

Former heavyweight champion Larry Holmes, who worked closely with Bundini during his five years as Ali's sparring partner in Deer Lake, Pennsylvania, also felt that Mann's characterization of Bundini was unfair: "When you've seen the real thing, the movie just doesn't look right. Bundini liked to drink wine, he liked to go out to the club. He liked to socialize. But he wasn't on drugs like that. He was a good guy. I felt bad for how they did him," Holmes said.

The disappointment was greatest for Drew Brown III, who was so upset at Mann's characterization of his father that he stood up in the movie theater and screamed, "That's a lie!!!"

"If they had said my father spent the money on booze, I wouldn't have had a problem. I wouldn't have liked it but I would have understood what they were going for. But he wasn't a heroin addict. They lied about my father to make the story more interesting," Drew told me.

While Bundini's alcoholism has been well documented, no published historical accounts of his life have suggested he was addicted to heroin. Stories of Bundini's recreational drug use fall into murkier territory, however, the most recent example coming in Rahman Ali's biography, where the Champ's brother suggests Bundini "wasn't averse to the harder stuff," when discussing the prominence of cocaine in the 1970s.

Perhaps more important to the story than Bundini's alleged drug use is the assertion that he stole the championship belt, a notion that is, once again, disputed by key members of the Ali entourage.

"The movie made it look like Bundini stole the belt. Ali gave it. Ali didn't give a shit about the belt," Gene Kilroy argued.

Khalilah Camacho-Ali supported Kilroy's version of the story in a separate interview: "Bundini didn't take nothing unless Ali gave it to him. He never stole nothing in his life. He wasn't that kind of person. Ali is not a person that cares about material stuff. He would just give things away. I bought Ali a Louis Vuitton briefcase one time and he gave it away to somebody that he didn't even know and it broke my heart. He didn't value material stuff. He was not materialistic. Bundini had the belt because Ali gave it to him."

Drew Brown III, who discussed the incident multiple times with his father during the course of his life, felt the creative liberties exercised in *Ali* were designed to divert audiences from the true nature of the circumstances surrounding the fallout between his father and Ali. "Anybody that thinks my father stole Ali's belt doesn't know the true story. Champ gave the belt to my father and didn't expect it back. My father didn't sell the belt. He took a hammer and knocked out some of the precious stones. He did that because the Black Muslims withheld his pay. What makes me most upset is that the movie completely ignores the reason my father did that in the first place."

There is no disputing the fact that a public fallout between Ali and Bundini did occur; the championship belt certainly factored into the bitter disappointment each man felt for the other. This aspect of the story has long been common knowledge, at least for hardcore boxing fans. Highlighting the true nature of the rift between Ali and Bundini requires a detailed exploration into some of the more controversial teachings of the Honorable Elijah Muhammad and the Nation of Islam during the early 1960s. Pairing Ali with these specific attitudes would likely complicate his reputation as a civil rights figure for contemporary audiences. Mann, like many biographers, aims to construct a specific version of Ali, one that will resonate with the attitudes, values, and beliefs of his target demographic.

Mann's dramatic rendering of the incident, inaccurate on multiple levels, is largely based on a story featured in Ali's 1975 autobiography *The Greatest: My Own Story*, written in collaboration with Richard Durham, who at the time of the book's release was the chief editor of the Nation of Islam's official newspaper, *Muhammad Speaks*. Durham was, as one might suspect, handpicked for the job by Herbert Muhammad, son of Elijah Muhammad. Durham's charge, as brilliantly spelled out in David Remnick's *King of the World*, was "to do for Ali what Parson Weems had done for George Washington." The book deal, arranged and negotiated by Elijah Muhammad's lieutenants, was designed to serve as something of an Eden story for the Nation of Islam, crafting an Ali that best served their agenda.

"Just as Weems had described a mythical Washington chopping down cherry trees and hurling them across the Potomac to highlight moral purity and awesome physicality, Durham made Ali out to be a champion fueled almost solely by anger and racial injustice," Remnick writes.

The story of the pawned heavyweight championship belt presented in Durham's book, which does not include the details of Bundini being addicted to heroin, conveniently excuses the Nation of Islam of their role in the chain reaction of events.

As is the case in Mann's 2001 film, *The Greatest* suggests Brown sold the belt to a Harlem barber during Ali's exile years. Calling the validity of this story into question requires one to first consider its placement in the book. It should be noted that Durham's version is told in conjunction with the single most controversial tall tale found in the book, the story of Muhammad Ali's gold medal.

It is perhaps the best of all the Ali fables. The story begins with Ali, back in his hometown of Louisville, Kentucky, being denied service at a segregated restaurant, harassed by a white biker gang afterward. This scene shows up in the 1977 film version of Durham's book as well (*The Greatest*, Columbia Pictures). Fed up by the racial injustice he is forced to endure in the segregated South, despite the celebrity afforded to him by his Olympic victory, Ali walks to the Second Street Bridge in Louisville and tosses his most prized possession into the Ohio River. The gesture is both tragic and symbolic, a bold statement designed to highlight the hypocrisy of American racism. Durham's gold medal story serves as a lead-in to the story of Drew Bundini Brown hocking Ali's championship belt to a Harlem barber. Ali tosses his Olympic medal into the Ohio River because it means nothing if he is not truly a free man in the country he won it for. The moral of the story is that Ali doesn't need a medal or a belt to be the champion. Both narratives remind readers that Ali's fight is outside the ring. This is why Durham chooses to tell the stories back-to-back, despite the alleged incidents occurring eight years apart.

Today, most boxing insiders recognize that Ali was, at best, indirectly involved in the writing of his 1975 biography. In *Muhammad Ali: His Life and Times*, a collection of first-person interviews seen by most boxing scholars as the most comprehensive look into Ali's legacy, Thomas Hauser, in collaboration with Muhammad Ali, fully exposes the controversy surrounding Durham's biography.

"Ali was uninterested in the project and spent relatively little time with Durham. Indeed, he never read his biography until after it was published," Hauser writes.

While Hauser argues that Durham's text is more accurate than not, he acknowledges that certain creative liberties were taken to craft a very specific Ali persona. In these instances, the truth is more than stretched.

The exaggerations found in *The Greatest* did not go unnoticed by Ali insiders. For example, in *Muhammad Ali: A View from the Corner*, Ferdie Pacheco expresses his disapproval for the book's folklore approach: "[Durham] hung around, stirring up phony scenarios with racial themes, trying to write pathetic revisionist history, making Ali a cross between Martin Luther King, Dred Scott, and Joan of Arc. The book he finally delivered had to be heavily edited by its publisher and does not present the Muhammad Ali I know," Pacheco writes.

The most famous example of "revisionist history" found in Durham's book is the story of the gold medal, a fable that carries with it a sort of pseudo-truth, one that is firmly attached to Ali's legacy. There was "never any white motorcycle gang incident, and [Ali] did not throw away his medal, he lost it," David Remnick writes in *King of the World*. For Remnick, the story is crafted as a symbolic gesture, one that places both Ali and the Nation of Islam on the correct side of history. While the hypocrisy of American racism is true, the actual events are not.

"If you drained the Ohio River, you'd be more likely to find a mermaid than a 1960 gold medal," boxing writer, and longtime Ali friend, Jerry Izenberg argues in *Muhammad Ali: The Whole Story*.

The most credible literary voices to speak out against the book's validity were those closest to the project: James Silberman, editor in chief at Random House at the time of the book's publication, and Pulitzer Prize–winning author Toni Morrison, who worked on the project as an editor.

"The story of the Olympic medal wasn't true, but we had to take in on faith . . . after some time, as happens with people, Ali came to believe it . . . when he was young he took everything with a wink, even the facts of his own life," Silberman confesses to David Remnick.

"My anxiety on the Ali project was always Herbert [Muhammad], who threatened at every moment to do something awful," Toni Morrison adds. "As for the gold medal story, Ali came to deny it was true when the book came out. I think it was at a press conference where he was asked about the medal and he said, 'I don't remember where I put that.' He also said he hadn't read the book. So [Ali], in a sense, discredited the book in a way that was unfair to the stories he had told Richard [Durham] in the first place or to the stories Richard may have invented to make a point."

Today, most boxing scholars view Ali's gold medal story as purely myth. Few have called into question the validity of the second half of Durham's two-part fable. Upon closer inspection, the story of Bundini selling Ali's heavyweight championship belt to a Harlem barber, as it is presented in the book, appears to be equally suspect.

"I thought about how you dropped the Olympic medal in the Ohio. I should have dropped the belt in the Hudson," Durham's version of Bundini tells Ali, referencing an incident that we now know to be an invention of the author's imagination.

Critiquing the historical inconsistencies and outright untruths found in Durham's so-called autobiography, or Mann's film for that matter, does not require that we strip Muhammad Ali of his social and political significance. Ali's importance as a humanitarian and civil rights figure is rightly cemented in history. Nor does such a critique require that we excuse Bundini of any wrongdoing. Regardless of which narrative you choose to believe, Ali's championship belt winds up either missing, smashed, or pawned.

To truly understand the circumstances that led to the initial breakup between Ali and Bundini, one must first reject the timeline of events given to us by these agendas: blatant reconstructions of history that often ignore observable facts. Drew Bundini Brown did not sell the heavyweight championship belt during Ali's exile years. The missing championship belt is referenced by color commentators during a handful of Ali's pre-exile bouts, particularly the Zora Folley fight. Video and audio evidence proves as much. The split between Ali and Bundini occurred during the summer of 1965, shortly after Ali's rematch with Liston. Bundini's exile from the Ali camp lasted for seven fights. It is the story of a broken symbol, its cracks and ridges the appropriate metaphor for the pain and disappointment of a splintered friendship.

■ ■ ■

On June 23, 1965, twenty-nine days after his controversial first-round knockout of Sonny Liston, Muhammad Ali filed a complaint in Dade

County, Florida, Circuit Court, seeking an annulment of his marriage to Sonji Roi. By all accounts, Roi was hardly the ideal Muslim wife. She was a former cocktail waitress with a free spirit and a taste for nightlife. Her devotion was to Muhammad Ali, not the Islamic faith. From the outset, Ali's spiritual handlers viewed the marriage as a conundrum. After the news broke, rumors circulated that the divorce was a top-down mandate from the Nation of Islam.

"When Elijah was alive, he made the rules and Herbert carried them out. And I think Herbert made some of the rules himself. Herbert is very smart, very cunning. He has his ways; he gets what he wants. The last word on anything Muhammad Ali did depended on Herbert," Roi once told Ali biographer Thomas Hauser.

"Someone else made the decision—I'm sure of it—and it hurt me," she maintained.

This rationale, audacious as it might seem, is in line with what scholars have uncovered regarding the relationship between Ali and his spiritual companion Malcolm X, their breakup occurring the previous year. Like Roi, Malcolm X was banished from Muhammad Ali's life.

Less than a month after Ali's initial victory over Sonny Liston, Elijah Muhammad announced in a radio address that Cassius Marcellus Clay was now a follower of the Nation of Islam and would receive a full Muslim name. Malcolm X, who was suspended from the Nation of Islam and then proceeded to form his own organization, Muslim Mosque, Inc., saw the proverbial writing on the wall when the announcement was made.

For Muslims throughout the country, the choice, as Ali biographer Jonathan Eig eloquently points out, was either Elijah Muhammad or Malcolm X—the teacher or the disciple. Elijah Muhammad, embattled by a public sex scandal, could not risk the newly crowned heavyweight siding with Malcolm X's budding organization. There was much at stake for the Nation of Islam. Ali's back-to-back victories over Liston had made him the most famous Muslim athlete in American sports, providing the Nation of Islam with an effective recruiting tool for the organization. They had gifted Ali his name, a new identity, and with that name and identity came a certain image that needed to be upheld. His example, both inside and outside the ring, was of grave importance to an organization that was increasingly becoming fractured and embattled by scandal. During those early chapters of Ali's championship reign, the Nation of Islam instructed Ali both spiritually and professionally. Ali followed their instructions unwaveringly. He obeyed Elijah Muhammad's orders and severed all ties with his friend Malcolm X. Sonji Roi was the next to go. And, in the summer of 1965, Drew Bundini Brown was uncoincidentally fired from Ali's team.

"When Muhammad Ali split up with his first wife, Sonji, on grounds that she did not behave as a proper Muslim woman should, there were renewed, more insistent demands that Bundini should also be expelled from the champion's life if he did not become a Muslim," journalist Erwin Sharke writes.

The friction between Bundini and members of the Nation of Islam was anything but a secret to the journalists and sportswriters of the day.

"[Bundini] was of no mind to become a Muslim," writer George Plimpton contends in *Shadow Box*, detailing his time with Ali and Bundini during their second Liston training camp. But, "the Muslims certainly tried," Plimpton argues.

"The Black Muslims were always messing with Daddy and, at one point, they even offered him a large sum of money to convert to Islam," Drew Brown III insisted to me. "They didn't like that Daddy would challenge the teachings of Elijah Muhammad so they drove a wedge between my dad and Ali."

"Yes. There was a little bit of stuff going on during the Muslim situation, early on," Jim Dundee reflected. "Initially they wanted a Black guy in there to replace Dad as well. [Bundini] had issues because he wouldn't convert. He had no interest. I don't know why they bothered him. Obviously, they couldn't do that with Dad."

For a number of reasons, Bundini's presence in Ali's corner was concerning for leaders of the Nation of Islam. Bundini's lifestyle was, in many ways, in direct opposition to the teachings of the organization. Not only was he a heavy drinker, he had married Rhoda Palestine, a white Jewish woman—and they had a biracial son who was nine years old. For both Liston fights, Bundini had worn a gold Star of David medallion around his neck. He was a Black Jew who had earned a public reputation as having an affinity for white women, an Ali confidant who spoke openly on his views regarding race and religion, often engaging in debate with the twenty-two-year-old Champ.

As a father, Bundini was particularly sensitive to comments regarding his son's biracial identity. "Show me the part in the Koran that says white people are devils, read it to me," Bundini would argue. "My son is proof they wrong, Champ. My son ain't no devil."

Bundini, fourteen years older than Ali, viewed himself as more street savvy than his younger counterpart. He, unlike other members of the Ali camp, would directly contest Ali's budding religious views. His years traveling the world as a Merchant Marine shaped his understanding of racial identity. He was baffled by the concept of racism and skeptical of anyone who to another. "Blue eyes and brown eyes, see grass green," was one of his favorite and most often-quoted sayings.

Drew Brown III recalled a childhood incident in which his grandfather, Drew Brown Sr., traveled from Sanford, Florida, to visit the family in Harlem. Moments into the visit, Drew Sr. made an off-handed comment about his "light-skinned grandson." Bundini was so angered by the comment he and his father almost came to blows. The visit would last less than an hour.

"I remember Grandaddy Drew lugging one of those big trunk suitcases back down the staircase, leaving before he'd even arrived," Drew III told me.

Humankind is made up of only one race: the human race. This notion is key to understanding Drew Bundini Brown's personal philosophy. The world, for Bundini, was made up of two kinds of people: *good* people and *bad* people.

"And it don't take long to figure out which is which," he would often say.

This philosophical attitude would get Bundini into trouble with both his Black and white friends—he had plenty of each.

"My father didn't like being called African American. Mankind started in Africa. We all are African Americans, who live in this country. The idea of racial pride was even kind of ridiculous to him," Drew III told me.

Despite being born into a society where skin pigmentation served as a key barrier to access and privilege, Bundini refused to follow the racial statutes of his day. He continuously ignored these restrictions, often paying the price for his defiance. Once, in Houston, Texas, for example, Bundini and a white companion attempted to patronize a Mexican tavern. The waitress instantly ordered them to get out. When Bundini and his friend returned to the coffee shop in their hotel, he rehashed the incident for a waitress.

"Which one [of us] was it them Mexicans wouldn't sell a beer to?" Bundini asked. "This Texas, I tell you, it's as confusing as real life."

Bundini's hardheaded approach to integration was unquestionably a point of contention between he and the young Ali. One of the more famous Ali/Bundini stories, brought to life in George Plimpton's *Shadow Box*, centers on a bus trip where Ali and Bundini leave their Miami headquarters, Ali at the wheel, heading north for the Liston rematch. Plimpton's story begins with the bus making a pit stop at a small diner/ gas station located in rural Georgia. Patronizing the diner, according to Plimpton, is Bundini's idea. Hesitant to push their luck, Ali and some of the other sparring partners remain near the gas pumps. As Bundini enters the restaurant, Plimpton and a few others by his side, he is greeted with unwelcoming glares from customers. Bundini takes a seat at the counter and waits to be served.

The manager, attempting to avoid a confrontation, softly replies, "I'm sorry . . . we have a place out back . . . separate facilities . . . food's just the same." Bundini persists to no avail and the manager finally warns, "In this county—Nassau County—there'd be a riot."

Bundini spins around in the stool, a sudden and defiant gesture, and rises to his feet. "The heavyweight champion of the world, and he can't get nothing to eat here," Bundini announces before exiting.

Out in the parking lot, Ali is enraged by Bundini's actions, launching into a vicious tirade. "I tol' you to be a Muslim. Then you don' go places where you're not wanted. You clear out of this place, nigger; you ain't wanted here, can't you see. They don' want you, nigger," Ali shouts.

The lecture continues for miles down the road. Bundini, according to Plimpton, is almost brought to tears by the prolonged scolding.

"Uncle Tom! Tom! Tom! Tom!" Ali continuously repeats, leaning over his seat and forcing Bundini's head down.

"Bow your head, Bundini," Ali orders.

Unable to endure the taunting, Bundini begins to fight back, verbally, outlining his rationale in the process.

"My head don' belong between my knees. It's up in the stars. I'm free. I keep trying. If I find a waterhole is dry, I go on and find another," Bundini responds.

"That man . . . that manager . . . he'll sleep on it. . . . He may be no better, but he'll think on it, and he'll be ashamed. . . . I dropped a little medicine in that place," Bundini theorizes.

From Plimpton's vantage point, Bundini's willingness to exchange with Ali does him no favors. The Champ refuses to concede his argument or drop the conversation.

"What's the matter with you—you damn fool! You got showed! You belong to your white master!" Ali shouts.

As the lecture persists, tensions rise. According to Plimpton, the conversation becomes increasingly theoretical.

"I'm a free man . . . God made me . . . I'll be what I was, what I always been. . . . In my heart I'm a free man . . . no slave chains around my heart," Bundini argues.

Plimpton's story ends with the bus stopping a little further down the road. Bundini, Plimpton, and a few of the others enter a packed restaurant, tempting fate. Ali and the Muslim members of the team once again remain outside. This time around, Bundini is greeted with both hospitality and a menu. Bundini's giddy excitement is highlighted by a request to be seated at the head of the table. Grinning and waving out the window like a child, he tells Plimpton, "I'm going to eat three steaks standing up so's they can see."

After a while, Ali eventually strides into the restaurant.

"What you doin' here?" Bundini calls to Ali, teasing. "This place only for integrators."

"The best example of Bundini standing up to Muhammad is that bus scene, the one when they are driving up from Florida on their way to Boston, the one where Ali calls Bundini a Jackie Robinson, in a derogatory way," Ali biographer Jonathan Eig said to me. "Bundini is the one that is right. They can use their fame and power to go in there and demand to be served. Ali wouldn't do it. Nobody on that bus would have challenged Ali that way. Deep down, Ali probably recognized that the Nation of Islam's ideas toward integration were hypocritical. Three quarters of the people on Ali's bus were white."

In another well-known Bundini story, fight doctor Ferdie Pacheco tells of Bundini attempting to marry an unnamed white woman during his first training camp at Angelo Dundee's 5th Street Gym in Miami.[2] The story begins with Brown and the woman showing up at Pacheco's medical office, asking for a blood test. Pacheco chooses to label the woman as a "crazy lady, living in a sleazy hotel," a castoff from a wealthy Florida family. Before administering the test, Pacheco attempts to talk Bundini out of the marriage. It is unclear whether Pacheco does so because of the woman's character or because she is white, or both.

"Bundini had decided he was going to marry her . . . no amount of talking could convince him otherwise, including Florida's miscegenation laws," Pacheco writes.

After Pacheco administers the blood tests, the couple makes their way to the Dade County Courthouse. Upon entering the building, they ask a police officer where the Bureau is located. The policeman directs them to the third floor. After patiently waiting in line, they approach the front desk clerk, requesting a license. To this the clerk replies, "fishing or hunting?" The police officer, it turns out, has directed them to the wrong floor.

"He couldn't imagine that a black guy and a white woman would be coming to the Dade County Courthouse to get married," Pacheco speculates.

Angered by the clerk's question, Bundini allegedly replies, "A fucking license."

Tensions escalate and Bundini and his lover are thrown out of the courthouse.

"I tried to warn you that was going to happen," Pacheco scolds Bundini when he returns to the 5th Street Gym the next day, perhaps signaling that his trepidation had more to do with the woman's race than her moral character.

It should be noted, however, that Bundini was no stranger to the area. He was born in West Palm Beach and raised in Sanford, Florida. Just as is the case in Plimpton's Georgia diner story, Bundini is anything but naïve. His defiance does not stem from ignorance.

"He was very upset. He was crying, and let's face it, the mores of the South were wrong," Pacheco reflects.

By today's standards, the freethinking Bundini was far more ahead of his time than his pugilistic counterpart. During Ali's time as a college lecturer, he continuously spoke out against interracial marriage. The separatist politics of the Nation of Islam were the politics of the young Ali. In the HBO documentary *Ali–Frazier: One Nation Divisible*, Ali claims to have spoken at a Ku Klux Klan rally to voice his opposition to miscegenation.

"I told them . . . blue birds with blue birds, red birds with red birds, pigeons with pigeons," Ali states.[3] "They told me, *go teach the rest of them niggers that*," Ali adds, laughing and mocking the southern accent of a Klan member.

These quotes do not easily transfer to contemporary Hollywood films. The culture industries have sanitized the young Ali, stripping him of his radical beliefs, turning him into a Hallmark ornament. It is far easier to paint Bundini as a heroin addict than to remind audiences of the Champ's 1965 worldview.

That said, it would be overly simplistic to suggest that Bundini was simply removed from the team because he would not convert to Islam. Bob Arum, Genre Kilroy, and Angelo Dundee, white men who were far from Muslim, were permitted to stay. Harold Bingham, a Christian, was never asked to leave the entourage. Bundini's stubborn defiance, his insistence on speaking and living his own *truth*, is what cost him his job. In Edwin Shrake's cornerstone *Sports Illustrated* article, Elijah Muhammad is quoted as saying that he would rather "convert Bundini than 12,000 ordinary men." George Plimpton indirectly quotes Elijah Muhammad as saying Bundini would be "worth ten battalions of ministers to the movement."

As these passages demonstrate, Bundini was hardly a yes-man. He was not dismissed from the Ali corner for pawning his championship belt. Rather, Ali "sent his friend packing, albeit temporarily, because Bundini had upset Muslim leadership," Jonathon Eig writes.

When attempts to coax Bundini into joining the organization failed, the decision was made to remove him from the team.

■　■　■

On November 22, 1965, Ali returned to the ring to square off against former two-time heavyweight champion Floyd Patterson. The bout, which took place at the Convention Center in Las Vegas, would serve as Ali's second title defense. His championship belt and outspoken trainer were noticeably absent from the ring. Instead, the proverbial elephant in the room was seated ringside, next to Plimpton.

"Bundini flew out to Las Vegas to watch Ali fight Patterson. [He] went as hired assistant to George Plimpton, supposedly to furnish expertise for a magazine story on how Patterson could beat the champion," Edwin Shrake writes, outlining Bundini's ringside encouragement for Patterson.

From the first bell until the final blow, there was no mistaking Bundini's rooting interests. His sonorous voice could be heard ringside, shouting words of inspiration to the challenger. It had indeed been an ugly breakup.

"I remember Bundini calling before the fight and saying 'Shorty is going to get you. You'll be sorry. Shorty is gonna get you for doing this to me,'" Gene Kilroy recalls.

That night in Vegas, Bundini would not be alone in rooting for the soft-spoken Patterson. Ali was feverishly booed on his way to the ring. The buildup to the fight, as was often the case in Ali's career, centered on issues of politics, race, and religion, polarizing boxing fans and sports pundits alike. Even prominent Black sports figures, such as Joe Louis and Sugar Ray Robinson, began to publicly distance themselves from Ali. This trend was further exacerbated by Patterson's insistent claims that he was going to return the heavyweight championship to "all of America, not just the Black Muslims."

For those who were hoping to see Ali get his comeuppance, Bundini included, it would be a night of disappointment. Ali masterfully picked apart the aging challenger, systematically breaking Patterson down with whiplash combinations. The bout was mercifully called to a halt in the twelfth round.

"I would like to thank my leader, the honorable Elijah Muhammad, for the prayers he just gave me, all praises due to Allah for giving me the strength to overtake a crowd booing against me," Ali said in his postfight interview, moments after the bout was stopped.

Leading up to the Ali–Patterson fight, there had been rumors that Patterson's camp had offered to bring Bundini aboard as an assistant trainer. It is unclear whether Patterson's trainer was looking to get strategic insight from Bundini or simply play mind games. Patterson, who made the final decision to nix the idea, worried that Bundini, in the end, would prove loyal to Ali. This was a risk that Ali's next opponent, a rough and rugged brawler from north of the border, was willing to take.

An abundance of controversies surrounded the promotion. First and foremost was the U.S. Armed Forces' decision to lower draft standards, a move that would reclassify Ali's draft status as 1-A. This new classification meant that Ali was now eligible to be drafted and inducted into the Army. Ali's public opposition to the war in Vietnam, and to his reclassification, added to his growing list of detractors. Then came news that the World Boxing Association was planning to strip Ali of his title because of his management team's inability to make a match with Ernie Terrell, the WBA's number-one contender. While Ali still held claim to his WBC belt, splintering the unified titles was hardly a popular move. When the Terrell negotiations fell through, the bout, which had originally been scheduled for Madison Square Garden, was moved to Maple Leaf Gardens in Toronto. One can easily imagine how this news was received in U.S. sports circles.

Next came the controversy surrounding Terrell's replacement. There was an almost instant backlash from U.S. sportswriters when Canadian George Chuvalo was announced as Ali's opponent. Bob Arum, Ali's promoter, was clearly banking on the Canadian's local following. As a professional, Chuvalo had fought twenty-seven times in his home city of Toronto. This is not to suggest Chuvalo was merely a local fighter. He was a known commodity in the boxing world, having fought bravely against top heavyweights such as Floyd Patterson and Zora Folley. However, Chuvalo's recent loss to the number-one contender Terrell made the bout a hard sell to boxing fans who were clamoring for an Ali–Terrell matchup. Chuvalo's lack of defensive skills and straightforward brawling style, perfectly designed for a master boxer like Ali, along with his journeyman's record of 34-11-2, led most experts to view the bout as a total mismatch.

Outside the negative headlines, the Ali–Chuvalo matchup lacked a dynamic narrative. When Chuvalo announced that Bundini was joining his team, sports journalists finally had their story. Before the Chuvalo bout, rumors of turmoil in the Ali camp had begun to surface.

"The Muslims won't let [Ali] drive his Cadillac anymore. His chauffeur and valet seem to have been excommunicated or something—the chauffeur for allegedly trying to peddle Elijah Muhammad's book in the ring after the Patterson fight, the valet for allegedly messing around," journalist Gilbert Rogin reported for *Sports Illustrated*.

The juiciest story to emerge would involve the newest member of team Chuvalo. When reports surfaced that Bundini had "hocked Ali's championship belt," some viewed the subplot as something of a publicity stunt, one designed to drum up interest in a bout that nobody wanted to see.

While Bundini worked with Chuvalo in the gym during his brief training camp, he did not serve as a cornerman on the night of the fight. The prefight weigh-in would be the closest Bundini would get to Ali. Although the hawkeyed glares between Ali and his former cornerman were anything but staged, most sportswriters viewed Bundini's presence in the Chuvalo camp as an inconsequential promotional footnote. Little did they know, Ali was in for a fight.

From the outset, two things became apparent to all who were watching. First, Ali's speed and agility were too much for the plodding Canadian slugger. Second, Chuvalo wasn't going anywhere. Plowing through Ali's rapid-fire combinations, digging to the body and occasionally landing wild hooks to the head, Chuvalo's grit stole the show. By the end of the fifth round, the Canadian challenger had disproven those suggesting the bout would be a one-sided affair. Chuvalo was taking his fair share of punishment, but he was also dishing it out. Ali, at times, appeared exhausted. The champion would be tagged by more power punches in this fight than both Liston fights and the Patterson fight combined. The loudest cheers came from Chuvalo's newest fan.

In *Sting Like a Bee: The Muhammad Ali Story,* former champion Jose Torres and legendary boxing writer Bert Randolph Sugar note Bundini's vibrant ringside presence. "Think of yo' babies . . . think of yo' babies," Bundini called to Chuvalo, a father of four, between rounds.

While it is next to impossible to gauge Bundini's impact on his training camp, there is no doubt that Chuvalo earned his place in boxing history that night in Toronto. This was a different George Chuvalo than the one who lost to Patterson and Folley. Ali clearly won the majority of the rounds, but the gritty Canadian was the first to take the young champion to the fifteen-round distance. His gutty performance was the story of the night.

"He's the toughest guy I ever fought," Ali famously stated in the postfight interview.

"Bundini was a great help as an adviser to our camp as we attempted to dethrone Muhammad Ali. Bundini added spiritual and emotional stimulation," Irving Ungerman, Chuvalo's trainer and manager, later wrote.

After Ali's hard-fought victory over Chuvalo, public interest in the Ali/Bundini rivalry gradually began to wane. This was partly because Ali's next three title defenses would take place overseas. None of Ali's European challengers were remotely interested in bringing Drew Bundini Brown into the fold. For Bundini, these were days filled with anger, disappointment, and eventually depression. Back in Harlem, Rhoda was also faced with a crossroads decision. As her own financial situation began to worsen, she began to wonder whether her son would be better off living with her parents. She feared for the day he would come of age in Carver Housing Authority, a location that had become visibly infested with cocaine and heroin abuse. The courtyard that separated the two large project buildings was littered with pimps, drug dealers, and junkies. Rhoda began to worry that her son would one day partake in the temptations that so noticeably surrounded their life in Harlem. Unfortunately, there was little Bundini could do to provide solace. Never one to properly manage his money, Bundini's prospects were, at the time, no better than hers.

On November 14, 1966, Ali would return to the United States to face journeyman Cleveland Williams at the Astrodome in Houston. Two months later, Ali would return to the Astrodome to finally take on Ernie Terrell, who, in the buildup to the fight, repeatedly insisted on calling the champion by his former name. "What's my name? What's my name?" Ali shouted throughout the fight, taunting his opponent as he administered a hellish beating. Eight fights into Ali's title reign, he had run out of dragons to slay. He had beaten all of the top contenders. Ali's only real challenge, it would appear, would come in the form of the U.S. Armed Forces. The tempest surrounding Ali's tumultuous life was more present outside the ring than inside the ropes of the squared circle.

And then one day, seemingly out of nowhere, Gene Kilroy received a phone call that would forever change the course of boxing history.

"Bundini called me up on the phone, he was crying," Kilroy told me. "'I'm doing bad. Bring me back. I'm doing bad.'"

This was all that Bundini could muster beyond the tears. He had hit rock bottom and saw no way to reconcile his life than to beg for Ali's sympathy. It would have been easy for Kilroy to tell Bundini what he wanted to hear, hang up the phone, and never pay the request any mind. But Kilroy, like other members of the Ali team, recognized the larger problems that were mounting on the horizon. Despite all of the bad blood surrounding Ali and Bundini, Kilroy felt obligated to bring the request to the Champ.

"I'd seen Ali in the gym with Bundini and seen him in the gym without Bundini," Kilroy said to me. "Ali was better when Bundini was around," he added.

In our interview, Kilroy specifically outlined his strategy: "I waited for a day when Ali was in a good mood. I said something like, 'It's sure quiet around here without Bundini, don't you think? Maybe we should bring him back? Ali, he's a good guy. He may stumble but he doesn't fall.'"

Much to Kilroy's surprise, the proposition was not a hard sell. Perhaps time and distance had healed the wounds. Maybe Ali, somewhere underneath the surface, missed his old friend. Pausing for a moment to think, Ali finally nodded.

"You bring him back," Ali said, his voice stern. "But you are responsible," he warned.

One month later, when Ali returned to the ring to face Texas native Zora Folley on March 22, 1967, at Madison Square Garden, Drew Bundini Brown, dressed in his trademark bow tie and cardigan, was, once again, by his side. Ali would knock out Folley in the seventh round. Bundini's exile from the Ali camp lasted seven fights—fourteen months to be exact. He would be present in Ali's corner for each of the final twenty-five bouts of the Champ's historic career.

"Ali could be vain and unpredictable. At twenty-two, he was still a boy in many ways, and still growing, too," Drew III once wrote.

"My father believed that all men were created equal, while Ali held just as resolutely to Black Muslim beliefs of Black separation and liberation," he reflected, thinking back to the summer that almost ended his father's relationship with the Champ.

Repurposing the story of the missing championship belt does Muhammad Ali no favors. Rather, exploring the true nature of the fallout between Ali and Bundini allows us to better understand the diverse perspectives of Black men in America during a turbulent time in our country's history.

"Blue eyes and brown eyes, see grass green." It was a simple slogan that demonstrates how one man chose to view the chaos. Bundini stood up for his beliefs and paid the price. Ali, on a far grander scale, was about to do the same. Their friendship, strong enough to endure disappointment and betrayal, would prove more important than ever in the dark days ahead.

.

6

Bundini's World

From 10 a.m. to 10 p.m., the building played home to the Old Spaghetti Factory restaurant, located on St. Charles Avenue in downtown New Orleans. Open seven days a week, the business enjoyed a steady flow of traffic. On Friday and Saturday nights, however, from midnight until dawn, like a pumpkin turned carriage, the facilities were transformed into one of the most talked about party spots in the Big Easy. At Bundini's—a club Drew Brown III opened in November of 1979—Cinderella's ball did not have to end at midnight. Adorned with oriental rugs, Tiffany lamps, beautiful wall tapestries, and antiques from around the world, the club exuded high-end mystique. The entire staff was uniformed. Men wore white tuxedo jackets, black dress pants, and matching black bow ties. The women wore tuxedo jackets with tails and fishnet pantyhose on their legs. Female patrons were given a single rose upon entering the club and were treated to sparkling champagne. Outside, lines of partygoers hoping to get in, hoping to spot one of the many celebrities who mingled at the club, wrapped around the city block.

When Bundini's opened, the disco era was in full bloom. Two DJs kept the music pumping well into the early morning. During those wild New Orleans nights, Drew Brown III played master of ceremonies to the reincarnation of what was once his father's vision, a failed Manhattan nightclub aptly titled Bundini's World.

Hiding behind the glitz and glamor, bow ties, and shot glasses was a pain not unlike his father's. Despite the outward appearance of success, at twenty-four years old, Drew Brown III was a troubled young man. The victories of his life would be over opponents his father would never fully be able to defeat, yet their demons were much the same. Buddy Drew, as he came to be known by family members, fulfilled his father's crib-side prophecy. With no financial assistance from his family whatsoever, he had become "the educated Drew," earning a basketball scholarship at Southern University at New Orleans, graduating with a bachelor's degree in business in 1977. Post-graduation, Drew III took a job that required him to live and work out of Caesars Palace in Las Vegas, securing advertisements for fight programs produced by a Texas-based publication firm. His first magazine placement was for Roberto Duran's title defense against Esteban De Jesus. In hindsight, the proverbial leap from college to Sin City had been too great. The first-generation college graduate traded in his dorm room for a comped luxury suite with a Jacuzzi, twenty-four-hour room service, and access to any of the Palace's clubs, bars, and restaurants. Like his father, Drew III was drawn to the nightlife.

"Work in Las Vegas is a party, and partying is work. Alcohol was such a normal tool of my business that I considered it no more harmful than the telephone," Drew III remembered.

Las Vegas would prove to be dangerous ground for the young husband and father who was, perhaps subconsciously, chasing the thorny legacy of his namesake.

■   ■   ■

During his senior year at Southern University of New Orleans, Drew Brown III was elected captain of the basketball team. One unofficial duty that came with the title of captain was scouting the area competition on off-nights. This meant frequent visits to the campus of SUNO's crosstown rival, the University of New Orleans. Drew and his teammate, Cornell, hadn't been in the gymnasium fifteen minutes before they began scouting Laurie Guimont, a stunningly beautiful creole girl with fair skin and dark hair, seated on the opposite side of the court.

"You see that girl? Who is she?" Drew commented to Cornell during a lull in the action. "I'm gonna marry that girl," he added, before play resumed.

Drew spent the entire game attempting to find out where the fetching New Orleans girl worked and lived. Ironically, Laurie's boyfriend played for the rival UNO Privateers. A few days later, Drew casually strolled into D. H. Holmes Department Store, where Laurie worked the register in the women's clothing department. After exchanging numbers, Drew waited for the perfect time to call. Like his father, Drew understood the power of theatrics. When a powerful storm hit the Gulf Coast, Drew seized the opportunity to phone Laurie, playing up the story of his being a New York boy who knew nothing about hurricanes. "I'm a little scared—can you give me some information on what I should do? I thought maybe you could help," Drew said. The two conversed throughout the entire eight-hour storm.

As a couple, Drew Brown III and Laurie Guimont were mismatched in many ways. Drew was an only child, Laurie one of seven children. His parents came from different races, religions, and socioeconomic backgrounds. Her parents, Lynne and Lawrence Guimont, were both creoles, born and raised in the same New Orleans parish. Drew's life had been a roller coaster of financial and familial instability. Laurie had a somewhat conservative Catholic upbringing, her father was a steady provider who had worked for the U.S. Postal Service since graduating high school. Drew's parents divorced when he was a small child yet maintained a sporadic on-again-off-again way of being. Laurie's parents maintained a rock-solid marriage; family was the center of their universe. Drew fancied himself just as savvy with women as his father. At nineteen years old, Laurie was a virgin, had never traveled much beyond the Louisiana area—hadn't even tried Chinese food. Drew had grown up referring to Sugar Ray Robinson as "Uncle Ray" and thinking of Muhammad Ali as a big brother. Laurie had never met a celebrity.

Despite Laurie's somewhat sheltered background, she had always dreamed of traveling the world. As a young girl, she would pretend to have a French or Spanish accent and had spent hours in her bedroom studying world maps. New Orleans felt small to the bashful Louisiana girl with big ambitions. In Drew III, Laurie found mystery, the man with whom she could share her cosmopolitan dreams.

"Drew was so outside of the box and so fun," Laurie confided to me. "He'd been all over the world and had such an interesting viewpoint on everything. I saw him as an international person. And I wanted a bigger life. My sisters, brother, and I just loved him."

A few months into their relationship, Drew III was equally convinced he had found the one. Eager to show off his new love, Drew and Laurie flew to New York to meet his father.

In retrospect, Laurie expressed fond memories of that first meeting with her future father-in-law: "Bundini booked us a room at Marriott Essex Hotel on the Upper West Side of Manhattan. It was the most gorgeous thing I had ever seen in my life. I was a young girl from New Orleans. I hadn't much exposure at that point. Immediately upon meeting me, Bundini nicknamed me Angel. I guess because I was blushing a lot. I was a young, naïve girl. So, I was Angel from that point forward. That's how Bundini was. He sized you up immediately. He was a sharp guy. That's what he would do."

In December of 1976, an unplanned pregnancy quickened the pace of Drew and Laurie's courtship, instantly shifting the dynamic of the relationship. The wedding was planned in haste and was held at an Episcopal church in New Orleans in March of 1977. One of Drew's SUNO professors presided over the ceremonies. The reception, held at Laurie's parents' home, was brought to a resounding crescendo, a clash of cultures so to speak, by the drunken antics of Drew Bundini Brown, who celebrated a little harder than members of the Guimont family were perhaps accustomed to.

Five months after the wedding, Drew and Laurie's first child, a beautiful, bright-eyed baby girl named Taryn Christine Brown, was born. In becoming a father, Drew III felt an extraordinary responsibility to be a provider for his wife and daughter. Bundini, despite all of the fame and success, was repeatedly held back by his limited education, inability to properly manage money, and struggles with alcohol. He was never able to be what many would consider a good financial provider. As a boy, Drew had longed for a *Brady Bunch* family existence. He'd convinced himself that he would one day attain this lifestyle via his own family. In becoming a father and husband, Drew set out to right the wrongs of his childhood. But in aiming to become everything his father wasn't, Drew inadvertently gravitated toward the darker side of who Bundini was. As was the case for the Drews who preceded him, the disease of alcoholism was firmly ingrained into Drew Brown III's genetic profile. His formal education and his drive to rectify the mistakes of the past were no match for the temptations of Las Vegas. In Sin City, the young college graduate quickly became known as "Boo-dano."

In a relatively short amount of time, Drew supplied the fight programs for twenty-eight championship fights, drawing from contacts such as

Muhammad Ali and LeRoy Neiman to edge out the competition. He soon became a fixture in the Las Vegas boxing scene. With success came temptation, the siren's call of Vegas nightlife. Chasing money, status, and fame, Drew reopened old familial wounds. He soon found himself surrounded by drug dealers, pimps, gamblers, hustlers, and high-class hookers who had much less to lose than him. Laurie, who lived separately with little Taryn while her husband commuted from Vegas, could sense the coming danger. Her husband was changing and everyone who loved him began to notice.

One night, after visiting his son, Bundini phoned Laurie, expressing his concern. "Angel, what's wrong with my boy?" Bundini asked, his voice full of emotion.

"I don't know what it is. He's just having a time of it. He shouldn't be where he is," Laurie responded.

Sobbing like a child, Bundini launched into a lengthy sermon on the dangers of drugs and alcohol. Laurie, who had seen the private, ugly side of Bundini, was baffled by the lecture.

After hanging up the phone, Laurie thought to herself, "What kind of man is Bundini Brown? He says all the right things, but he doesn't even live what he talks. So how is he going to persuade his son to do anything different?"

The following day, Bundini did just that. He phoned his son, demanding that he leave Las Vegas and return to his family. Bundini's words were harsh and direct.

"You know what, son? I don't care how many championship fights you work. You're a bum. You're a bum because you're doing the same thing I did. You're hustling. But you, boy—you got a college education. So don't bullshit a pro. You're not a real Drew, boy, because a real Drew would use his education. Don't hurt your family like I did. The most important thing in life is family, Buddy Drew," Bundini urged.

Drew Brown III listened to his father's advice and quit his job later that day, leaving Las Vegas and never looking back.

In the spirit of his father's entrepreneurial legacy, Drew III returned to the familiarity of Laurie's hometown of New Orleans and opened a nightclub bearing Bundini's name. On the surface, it was a more stable proposition than remaining at Caesars Palace. Yet despite Drew's enthusiasm, Laurie had mixed emotions about the business venture. On the one hand, Laurie was happy to be reunited as a family and to be financially stable. On the other, she felt cheated. Part of Laurie resented remaining in New Orleans, despite having family nearby.

"But of all things, Drew, why the bar business?" Laurie argued when her husband first pitched the idea of opening the club.

At first, Bundini's appeared to be a resounding achievement. The business grew at a phenomenal pace. Frequent appearances by Bundini and other celebrities like Muhammad Ali brought media attention and free publicity to the club. With the sudden influx of money came a resurgence of temptation. Drew III once again lost sight of his goals.

In looking back on some of the darkest days of his marriage, he said the following: "I began to lose myself in New Orleans nights. I somehow hoped that my hurt would disappear in the alcohol that I consumed, side by side with the patrons in my bar. And when I wasn't there, I hit the other night spots in New Orleans. My excuse was that I had to keep up with the competition. But I was actually staying out night after night, and heading toward the kind of alcoholism that I had so abhorred in my parents' lives. I lost a business because of ignorance and alcohol—the same mistake that had sunk my parents' bar business in Manhattan more than a dozen years earlier."

As the sons of great men often do, Drew Brown III failed to learn from mistakes of the past, both his father's and his own. He failed to correctly identify the moral of his father's most frequent rhetorical construct: "Don't do what I do. Do better than I do," Bundini would often say.

Drew's errors in New Orleans were the same mistakes that had sent his life spiraling out of control in Las Vegas. When Bundini's was forced to close its doors, just over a year after the grand opening, Drew found himself riddled with disappointment, plunging into a deep depression. At twenty-five years old, blinded by pain and frustration, drowning his sorrow in alcohol, the young husband and father began to view himself as not being so special.

"Drew would transform back into a little boy when he was around Bundini. I always felt like Drew was chasing his father, trying to make him proud," Laurie said to me.

In retrospect, Bundini's, and to a lesser extent Las Vegas, had been part of an ongoing sparring match, both figurative and literal, that began back at apartment 11-F in Harlem.

The thick, green metal door slammed. The twelve-year-old version of Drew Brown III eagerly scampered from the apartment kitchen to meet his father. Dressed in a brand-new leather coat, the smell of the leather hanging about him like an aura, Drew Bundini Brown greeted his son with a tight hug.

"Come on, Daddy. Let's box," Drew III called, breaking into Cassius Clay's signature defensive posture.

Bundini's mouth became tight, lower jaw thrust forward, eyes glaring with disappointment. He said nothing. Sensing his actions were getting underneath his father's skin, Drew, full of boyish orneriness, began to jab and dance around his father, doing Clay's famous shuffle.

"Betcha can't stop me, I'm so fast," the boy teased, his punches increasing in power.

"Boy! I don't want you to be no fighter," Bundini responded, his voice booming with anger.

"C'mon, Daddy. Let's box," Drew repeated, lightly punching his father as he attempted to make his way through the apartment.

As the onslaught continued, Bundini finally squared up, his large shoulders hunched forward in an awkward boxing stance. Bundini began punching his son lightly. Frustrated by the ease with which his father was able to connect, Drew began to throw his tiny fists with all of his might. He wanted to show his father that he was a man. Bundini's return blows became harder and harder, his voice and punches thundering with ferocity.

"You're going to college, boy," Bundini repeated after each connect.

The young boy finally collapsed in his father's arms, crying, "Stop Daddy, stop Daddy."

"This ain't your heart. Don't you ever lie to yourself, boy. Don't ever lie to Shorty. He made you to be the educated Drew," Bundini said, tears in his eyes.

After losing his New Orleans nightclub, Drew III began the process of redirecting his life, for the first time perhaps, moving toward the destiny of his own greatness, a painful lesson not unlike a hard right hand.

■　■　■

Like the spark of a flame instantly vanquished by a sudden gust of wind, the Madison Square Garden reunion between Muhammad Ali and Drew

Bundini Brown ended before it could truly begin. Less than a month after landing the lead right hand that sent Zora Folley crumbling face-first to the canvas, Muhammad Ali found a far greater adversary awaiting him at the U.S. Armed Forces Examining and Entrance Station in Houston. On April 28, 1967, at one o'clock in the afternoon, Ali was brought into the "ceremony room" to be inducted into the Armed Forces. Bundini accompanied him to the facilities.

When the name "Cassius Marcellus Clay" was called by Lieutenant Clarence Hartman, Ali refused to step forward. "Refusal to accept a lawful induction order constitutes a felony under the Universal Military Training and Service Act, punishable by up to five years' imprisonment and a five-thousand-dollar fine," Lieutenant Hartman cautioned, as it became evident the Champ was not going to comply with the symbolic gesture. Ali was then taken to a private room where the consequences of his actions were once again explained to him.

Unwavering in his stance, Ali produced the following, written for Hartman: "I refuse to be inducted into the armed forces of the United States because I claim to be exempt as a minister of the religion of Islam."

On May 8, 1967, ten days after refusing induction, Ali was indicted by a federal grand jury on charges of draft evasion. As a result of the indictment, Ali was stripped of his title and passport and was denied a boxing license in every state in the country. With Sugar Ray Robinson officially retired from the sport, for almost two years at this point, and Muhammad Ali exiled from the ring, the joy Drew Bundini Brown felt in being reunited with the Champ at Madison Square Garden was now replaced by uncertainty.

As the ensuing media controversy surrounding Ali's conviction gained momentum, Bundini returned to Harlem and Ali to Chicago. Both would continue to make headlines. On August 17, 1967, Ali married seventeen-year-old Belinda Boyd (now Khalilah Camacho-Ali), a young Muslim girl who he'd had his eye on for some time. The two first met in 1961 when Ali made an appearance at the University of Islam, headquarters for the Muslim school structure in Chicago. As legend has it, Ali nicknamed the ten-year-old Khalilah "little Indian girl" because of the long braids she wore in her hair. Khalilah's parents were members of the Nation of Islam, her mother, Aminah, a close friend of the Honorable Elijah Muhammad's wife. "Man, you scribble; you can't even write. You ought to go back to school and study how to read and write until you do it better," the ten-year-old Khalilah, then Belinda, said to Ali, upon laying eyes on the autograph. Ali never forgot the exchange.

As a teenager, Khalilah worked at her family's bakery in Chicago, a location where she and Ali would eventually reconnect. Just under six feet tall, with a vibrant smile, beautiful bright eyes, and an outgoing tomboyish spirit to match, Khalilah quickly captured Ali's attention. After Ali joined the Nation of Islam, he and Khalilah became close friends, sometimes conversing on the phone for hours at a time.

Unlike Ali's first wife, Sonji, Khalilah was raised in the Muslim tradition and was devout in her faith. From her physical beauty to her moral character, Khalilah seemed like the perfect candidate for the Champ's second attempt at marriage. Her parents, because of their ties to the Nation of Islam and conscientious objection to the Vietnam War, were supportive of the union. Only seventeen years old and raised in a somewhat sheltered Muslim background, Khaliah, at this point in her life, couldn't have possibly understood the world she was about to enter.

In October of 1967, Khalilah accompanied Muhammad Ali to New York City, where she met her husband's famous best friend, Drew Bundini Brown, for the first time. In a personal interview, Khalilah reflected on the meeting, an introduction to the circus that was to come: "When we were first married, we were a young couple. Ali told me all about Bundini. We'd been married a few months and then we finally had to go to New York one day. As a matter of fact, I think we were going there to do an interview with Dick Schaap, the great sports journalist. We were at the hotel and he said, 'I want you to meet some of my boys.' One of the people that came to the hotel was Bundini."

Waiting on Bundini's arrival at the hotel, Khalilah became nervous and began to press her husband for more information.

"He'd told me beforehand, Bundini refers to God as Shorty. 'Shorty is watching you. Shorty is looking out for you.' Stuff like that. Ali told me Bundini was a down-to-earth person. If he loves you, he loves you until you are dead," Khalilah remembered.

In the middle of Ali's explanation, Bundini arrived at the hotel, dressed in a white polo shirt and matching white pants.

"This is my cornerman, Bo-dini. He loves me. He takes care of me. And, he's the one that came up with 'float like a butterfly, sting like a bee,'" Ali said to his new bride.

Khalilah, who had followed her husband's career since she was ten years old, was somewhat starstruck. She, like much of the American sports public, viewed Bundini as a key component of Ali's poetic persona. Until meeting Bundini, Khalilah had not truly experienced the boxing side of her husband's life.

Perhaps Khalilah had expected a rendition of "float like a butterfly, sting like a bee." Maybe she was waiting for Bundini to illuminate another side of her husband. Much to Khalilah's surprise, she found Bundini to be withdrawn, lost in the crowd, so to speak. It wasn't until later in the evening, after eavesdropping on one of Bundini's side conversations with another member of the entourage, that Khalilah caught on to the reason behind his sheepish behavior:

"That day, Bundini tried to hide it from me that he had married a white woman. I'd hear him talk about his son, but he tried to hide him from me, too. Because back in those days it was taboo. Controversial. It was a marry-your-own-kind type of thing. Then I heard him telling someone not to tell me because I was a Muslim."

Hardly an introvert, Khalilah made her way through the crowded hotel room and toward Bundini.

"Don't tell me what? What you talking about?" Khalilah pressed, unwilling to drop the conversation until Bundini came clean.

"When I found out about it, I said, 'I don't care what color she is! It doesn't matter if she Black or White. If you and your ex-wife love your son, that's all that matters! It's none of my business.' And, instantly, I could see that made him feel more comfortable," Khalilah remembered.

Tears began to form in the corners of his eyes. "Thank you," Bundini whimpered, hugging Khalilah as tight as he possibly could.

"Shorty really loves you. Shorty is going to be kind to you," Bundini said after the embrace.

Curious about the exchange, Ali made his way toward his wife and cornerman.

"Champ, she's the one!" Bundini called, his trademark smile returned, a renewed vigor in his voice.

Muhammad and Khalila's marriage would last just over ten years, during which time the couple had four children: Maryum, twins Jamillah and Rasheda, and Muhammad Ali Jr. During the early portion of their relationship, Khalilah served as one of the few stable forces in Ali's life.

Vilified by the mainstream media as a "radical Muslim" and "draft dodger," death threats became a regular occurrence and FBI surveillance became an everyday part of their life. During these difficult times, Khalilah also formed a strong bond with Bundini.

"He was loyal to Ali [during exile]," Khalilah told me. "You ask Bundini to do something, he would stay right where you asked him, wouldn't budge. Bundini would protect us. What he called protecting. We'd be out somewhere and Ali would say, 'Bundini, watch over my wife. Stay here in the car and watch my wife.' He'd do it. And most of the time it was us sitting and talking about Shorty. And, as the years went by, Bundini did turn out to be a really good friend. I liked him because he was sincere. I mean, I know he would milk Ali for money but you know he had every right to because he was one of the only ones that was loyal. You couldn't pay Bundini enough for that loyalty."

During her ten-year marriage to Muhammad Ali, Khalilah also formed a strong bond with Drew Brown III. Their relationship grew so strong that Muhammad Ali would, at times, express jealously.

"Ali was jealous about me being around young Drew [Brown III] when he was a teenager. He was jealous because the boy was so pretty and so young. I couldn't understand that," Khalilah told me. "I said, 'Ali, I treat that boy like he was one of my own.' Ali said, 'I was pretty and young once too,'" Khalilah added.

When word of Ali's jealousy made its way back to the teenage boy, he couldn't help but feel some measure of pride. "I was fifteen and sixteen years old and the Champ was jealous of me. I was proud," Drew III chuckled.

Ali's jealousy was perhaps a product of his own guilt. Throughout his marriage to Khalilah, the Champ took part in a variety of illicit extramarital relationships, fathering children outside the marriage, and eventually leaving his wife for Veronica Porché, a relationship that began while Ali was in Africa preparing for his epic bout with George Foreman.

During the early days of the marriage, the young husband and wife would find little comfort or certainty. Khalilah had married a man who was on the brink of disaster. With no future fights on the horizon, Ali was forced to reinvent himself. The United States, one could argue, was in the process of reinvention. By January of 1968, 19,560 American soldiers had died in the Vietnam War and another 16,502 would die by year's end. The peace movement, no longer merely composed of academic scholars, college students, and anti-establishment hippies, gained increasing visibility with the participation of the American civil rights movement, second wave feminism, and Chicano Movement, as well as support from key figures within sectors of organized labor.

Opposition to the war was no longer relegated to the pages of beatnik poems or bullhorn diatribes of student protests occurring along the cobblestone walkways of college campuses across the nation. Gallup polls documented the growing civil unrest, indicating that the majority of Americans found the U.S. involvement in the war a mistake. With increased media attention came decreasing support as opposition grew. The Vietnam War had firmly polarized the country, splintering and dividing it, as wars often do. Seven months into Ali's exile from professional boxing, each of the key members of the Champ's entourage found themselves, like much of the nation, splintered and divided. The success and prosperity the team had enjoyed from 1963 to 1967 had come to an abrupt halt; each man was now forced to move in new directions. The conversation shifted from when or if Ali would return to the sport of boxing to whether Ali would eventually be sent to prison for refusing induction into the Army. It was Ali, of course, who had the most to lose.

With the arrival of 1968, the Champ found himself a twenty-six-year-old newlywed with a child on the way, stripped of his heavyweight championship, denied a boxing license by a host of athletic commissions, and unable to leave the country. Out of jail on appeal, with no prospects of resuming his boxing career, Ali faced a daunting legal battle, as well as the hefty legal expenses that go with it. At first, Ali supplemented his income by making public appearances. Ali's handlers looked to capitalize on the growing anti-war sentiments among college students by arranging for Ali—the nation's most famous conscientious objector—to lecture at Temple University and Cheney University before pairing the Champ with Richard Fulton, Inc., a national speakers bureau. Embarking on a full-fledged college speaking tour, with stops ranging from Harvard University to the State University of New York at Albany, Ali hit the road spreading the Honorable Elijah Muhammad's message.

Next came Ali's failure in the restaurant industry. "Twice [Ali] lent his considerable renown to startups, one a would-be competitor to McDonald's, called ChampBurger," food critic Peter Romeo writes.

Founded in 1968, ChampBurger attempted to capitalize on the quick-serve McDonald's craze sweeping the nation. "Ali was reportedly paid $900,000 and promised 1 percent of revenues to affiliate himself" with the Miami-based restaurant, the deal stipulating that the menu could not violate Muslim dietary laws. In the end, it would prove to be a poor business decision.

The transition to life after Ali was perhaps easiest for promoter Bob Arum and trainer Angelo Dundee. In the wake of Ali's conviction, Sports Action, Inc., founded by Arum, Mike Malitz, Jim Brown, and Fred Hofheinz (whose father owned the Houston Astrodome), teamed up with the World Boxing Association and ABC television to promote an eight-man elimination tournament to determine an heir to Ali's vacant heavyweight throne. The announcement was understandably met with immediate skepticism from members of the boxing world. Joe Frazier, seen by many boxing experts as the deserving number-one contender, declined Arum's invitation to participate, choosing instead to fight Buster Mathis. Frazier's absence, coupled with the fact that half of the participants had previously been defeated by Ali, dampened expectations that Arum's brainchild would actually produce a legitimate heir.

Arum's tournament kicked off on August 5, 1967, at the Astrodome, a doubleheader that featured Ernie Terrell (39-5) vs. Thad Spencer (31-5). Spencer, an up-and-coming California-based heavyweight, pulled the upset over Terrell, a favorite to win the tournament in the eyes of many pundits. In the co-feature that night, Jimmy Ellis (23-5), Angelo Dundee's newest pupil (Dundee served as both trainer and manager to Ellis), defeated Leotis Martin (24-1) by a ninth-round technical knockout. Two months later, on December 12, 1967, in Jimmy Ellis's hometown of Louisville, Kentucky, Dundee's fighter easily defeated Oscar Bonavena by unanimous decision, advancing to the championship round. Less than a year after Ali was systematically banned from the sport of boxing, both Bob Arum and Angelo Dundee were poised to recapture the heavyweight championship of the world.

Bundini, noticeably absent from the 5th Street Gym posse, was not invited along for the ride. Bereft of opportunities in the fight game, Bundini reverted to what he knew best: New York City nightlife.

■ ■ ■

On January 25, 1968, Bundini's World, a bar located on Second Avenue and 81st Street in Manhattan, opened its doors to the public. The Champ was, of course, in attendance on opening night.

"What I remember most distinctly was that Daddy started carrying business cards that listed himself as the bar's president," Drew III remembered.

Bundini's celebrity, heightened by his key role in the Ali–Liston fights, provided new opportunities for the out-of-work cornerman. Of all the business pitches that came his way, owning a bar made the most sense. For better or worse, the venture soon became a family affair—Bundini's ex-wife, Rhoda, served as the bar's bookkeeper and was regularly in attendance. The renewed partnership held symbolic weight for Bundini and Rhoda, a recapturing of their wild Harlem nights perhaps. As a young married couple, they'd spent much of their time in the environment that now became their livelihood. Early on, Bundini's World was touted by lifestyle critics as an upscale version of Sugar Ray's, which was no longer in business. During her youthful days at the former middleweight champion's nightclub, Rhoda couldn't have possibly imagined that it would one day be her husband's name on the marquee.

When in New York, Ali and Khalilah made frequent appearances at the club, keeping Bundini's World in the society pages of New York City publications and the likes of *Jet* magazine. Aside from the Champ, Bundini had accrued his own set of famous friends, many of whom became patrons of the bar. Looking back on those visits, Khalilah positions Bundini as a man deeply connected to the Black entertainment world.

"That man knew a lot of people in Black entertainment," Khalilah told me. "All of these great famous authors, singers, and composers. All of them out of New York and Bundini introduced us to most all of them. Civil rights figures. Entertainers. All of these great revolutionaries in seclusion, running from the Feds. This man knew a lot of people. James Baldwin. William Marshall. I met these people under Bundini. He was a catalyst to the Black world. He took Ali to the Apollo Theater for the first time. He introduced Ali to everyone at the Hotel Teresa. Bundini introduced Ali to Baldwin. Later, he introduced us to Gordon Parks. Richard Roundtree. He introduced us to some of the greatest men in Black America. Nobody knows that. His everyday friends were people that are a part of history."

On a good night, patrons would be triple-parked outside the star-studded Manhattan club. Literary figures such as Norman Mailer and George Plimpton would mingle with entertainers such as Sam Cooke and Lloyd Price. LeRoy Neiman, the world-famous painter, crafted a brilliant rendering of Drew III's elementary school graduation picture, which proudly hung above the cash register at the bar. The young boy featured in Neiman's painting would, on occasion, accompany his parents to the bar. Filled with joy at the sight of his parents reunited, at least in a working capacity, Drew Brown III held out hope that Bundini's World could serve as the glue that would mend his broken family.

At first, the business venture did seem to heal old wounds for the formerly married couple. Shortly after the bar opened, Bundini and Rhoda began collaborating on a manuscript that would outline Bundini's philosophy on life and his keys to being a master motivator (a street-smart self-help book, so to speak). Bundini would philosophize and Rhoda would click away at her Underwood typewriter. The plan was to capitalize on his literary connections (e.g. Norman Mailer and George Plimpton) to shop the book to New York's top publishers. Working on the book was something positive the couple could do together, outside their time at the bar.

Conflicting reports suggest Bundini and Rhoda tried their hand at fiction writing as well. Willie Morris, editor in chief of *Harper's Magazine*, once claimed that Bundini tried to sell him a novel. "It was the story of a trip on a riverboat in Florida," Morris recalled. "There were plenty of hotdogs and Cokes for everybody, and everything worked out fine. It was very touching," Morris added.

While some boxing scholars have written that Bundini was a devoted reader who held tightly to his literary ambitions, the poetic cornerman was essentially illiterate. These characterizations likely stem from rumors of Bundini manuscripts that floated around during Ali's exile. Understandably so, many have assumed these texts were written by Bundini. They were not. Rhoda Palestine was the woman behind the typewriter keys. She was his key collaborator. Many of these thoughts, words, and ideas were completely hers.

As Bundini and Rhoda began to spend more time together, Drew Brown III's aspiration was to get his parents back together. This crusade became the young boy's purpose in life.

Aside from his parents' reconciliation, Drew was also drawn to the club by the revolving door of celebrities who frequented the Manhattan hot spot. Reflecting on his boyhood days in Bundini's World, Drew said the following:

> One day I walked in with Daddy. It was early, 6 p.m., I think, and there was this guy with a big white lambswool coat on. He had a large afro. He was talking to a beautiful white woman. I wanted to see his face so I walked around. I had to see who it was. And, the guy is holding up a cardboard black-and-white Marilyn Monroe mask on a stick. And he is talking to this woman through the mask. He didn't talk through the mask and put it down, like a joke. He literally held it over his face for their entire conversation. I ran and got my father. I said, "Daddy, there is a crazy person in here." He said, "Buddy Drew, leave him alone." It wasn't until later I realized it was Jimi Hendrix.

The neon lights, the cheers and laughter of the patrons, the beautiful women and dapper men held a spell over the young boy's imagination, just as it had done for his parents during their youthful nights in Harlem. *This is what success looks like, this is what living is all about,* Drew III figured. In the young boy's imagination, his father was the Black Prince, the most impressive man in all of New York.

Aside from the success of the bar, there were other reasons for Bundini and Rhoda to celebrate. Their only son was about to become a man.

On Saturday, February 17, 1968, Drew Timothy Brown III celebrated his bar mitzvah at Oceanview Jewish Center in Brighton Beach, New York.

"For the first time, all of my family was together," Drew III reflected. Drew Brown Sr. (Drew's grandfather), along with Brown family aunts, uncles, and cousins, made the journey from Sanford to Brooklyn. The mixing of cultures was a sight to behold. Bouncing on the knee of Drew Brown Sr., the surly Florida alligator hunter who, during his younger years, freely spoke of his hatred for crackers, was Rhoda Palestine's niece, Tracy. All men wore yarmulkes (skullcaps) and white tallit prayer shawls, including Drew Brown Sr., who had never attended any Jewish-sponsored event. The subtle grin that adorns his stern face in the bar mitzvah photographs demonstrates a certain measure of growth. A mixture of Black and white faces, the men and women smiled, laughed, mingled, hugged, posed for pictures, and exchanged stories. The Palestine family was, of course, heavily represented at the bar mitzvah. Mildred and Jack

Palestine paid for the ceremonies. Their daughter, ever the nonconformist, chose to wear a festive red and gold-leaf Indian sari made of silk. Bundini and his son wore matching suits.

To open the festivities, Drew Brown III said his Hebrew prayers in a tone that reminded Mildred of a cantor from the Holy Land. In an unconventional move, the boy read a speech (in English) written by his mother:

> In the Jewish calendar the year is 5728. In the Gregorian calendar the year is 1968. It is a time of chaos, confusion, and insecurity in the world. Today, on February 17, I stand here ready and willing to accept the first responsibilities of manhood. I sincerely give my gratitude with all my heart and soul to the people who made this day possible. My dearest mother, Rhoda. My great father, Drew Jr. My wonderful grandparents: Zeda Jack Palestine and Bubba Mildred Palestine, and all of my relatives and friends. I would like to give recognition also to my wonderful rabbis: Rabbi Lazar, and Rabbi Irving Fuller, who helped guide me spiritually to become a man who will respect all mankind, through understanding, love, and respect. My prayer to the world of today is that man should find peace and harmony within himself, in order that he may be able to get along with all mankind. GOD will not destroy the world! But man will, if he doesn't find peace, love, and understanding with his fellow man. The price of a free world is respect, love, and peace for each other! Shabot Shalom.[1]

Before Drew's seventh-grade year in school, Rhoda decided that it was best for her son to move in with his grandparents in Brighton Beach, enrolling in P.S. 43, James J. Reynolds Junior High in Sheepshead Bay, Brooklyn. With Jack and Mildred, Drew found the familial stability that had eluded his childhood in the projects of Harlem. His grandparents saw to it that their grandson was brought up within the Jewish tradition, instilled with the values, customs, and traditions of their ancestors. Before moving to Brooklyn, Drew had only attended synagogue on high holidays. During his visits, he had learned some Yiddish and a few words in Hebrew. Four months before his bar mitzvah, Drew enrolled in Hebrew school and began preparations for the ceremonies. Rabbi Lazar's first Black pupil, Drew impressed all in attendance with his linguistic fluency.

The only Black person Drew Brown III would ever meet in Brighton Beach was a homeless alcoholic on the corner who, ironically, went by the name "Shorty." Brighton Beach, all white and all Jewish, presented its own set of cultural obstacles for the young boy. During his visits to Sanford, Florida, Drew had no idea that he was staying in the Black section of town. Harlem had given the boy a multicultural array of experiences. His father had taught him that race, as it is understood by most, is a false concept. In Brighton Beach, the young boy simply could not understand why some of his new schoolmates were not allowed to play with him. "I never felt less than. But that was my introduction to the idea of racism," Drew recalled.

During those early days in Brighton, Drew began to recognize the various ways that race played a factor in how he was perceived by others, adopting a hair-trigger defensiveness.

"Bubba [Mildred Palestine] said I had a brown nose one day and I ran into the bathroom, locked myself in there, and cried. She beat on the door, saying, 'What's wrong with you?' I didn't know the meaning of the phrase and thought it had something to do with my skin color. She'd called me that because of how many times I sat at the window waiting for my father to come, being disappointed most of the time. She said I always had my nose up my father's butt," Drew recalled.

With both sides of his family under one roof, Drew finally began to grasp his father's views on race and family. Drew Brown III did not have two families. He had one. Aside from the birth of his children, Taryn and Drew IV, February 17, 1968, continues to be one of the greatest days of Drew Brown III's life.

The photographs in Drew's bar mitzvah book, images that visually juxtapose the seemingly conflicted worlds Bundini and Rhoda brought together by falling in love back in 1952, demonstrate a powerful racial, cultural, and religious harmony, cultivated by love for the boy. For one day, these contradictory worlds were in accord, unified by a family's love for the boy they called "Buddy Drew." The Browns of Sanford stand arm in arm with the Palestine family of Brooklyn. Bundini and Rhoda pose with their son, hands locked in embrace. Beaming with pride, smiles decorate their faces. The love in their eyes could easily convince any viewer the two were happily married. Jack and Mildred, doting grandparents unable to contain their joy, make frequent appearances.

"One of the most treasured moments was the picture-taking session. I took control of that," Drew told me. "For the first shot, I positioned my father and Poppa Jack—Black and white, with me in the middle—standing before the holy Torah. Next, I arranged the same shot, but with Black and white grandmothers on either side of me, and again before the Torah. I continued on with my aunts and uncles. I wanted all the pictures to show that it was finally okay that my family looked different."

Reviewing Drew's bar mitzvah book during my first visit to his Atlanta home, two pictures struck me as particularly telling. The first featured Bundini, Rhoda, Drew, and what appeared to be a young girl who bore the physical signifiers of Down syndrome. The young girl was seated with Bundini. According to Drew, his father sought out the young girl, a cousin on the Palestine side of the family, and insisted that she be included in the picture.

"This is the family picture. Let's include her in the group photo," the photographer had cautioned. Other family members quickly agreed. Neither Bundini nor his son had ever met the girl.

"She isn't the one who is mentally challenged. We are. Kids like that only seek joy and love and hugs," Bundini argued. "She has no damn clue how to hate or judge. She don't care about how you look or the way you think," he added.

Sensing he had struck a nerve, the photographer attempted to smooth over the situation.

"Oh, we should definitely include her in a picture. But, this is the big shot. It's the one you'll want to hang up in your living room. The family shot. We'll definitely make sure she gets her picture taken, Mr. Brown," he said.

Bundini glared at the photographer, pausing before delivering his final statement, "You telling me you're going to ask God to step out the picture?"

"Later on, I was told by her family that that was one of the greatest days of her life. She felt loved and felt like she belonged," Drew III told me.

Equally gripping, and perhaps the only foreboding image from the bar mitzvah book, is one in which Bundini and his son share a firm handshake, each with a shot glass of whiskey in their free hands. In the background, a white sign rests on a wooden table. The sign reads, "Today, you are now a man." Perhaps no two images more accurately represent the irony of Bundini's world, dual narratives of a father and son, lives both brilliant and flawed.

The peace and unity felt at the Ocean View Jewish Center would be short-lived. Despite the early wave of success, running the bar proved to be a poisonous environment for Bundini and Rhoda. Lost amid a party that didn't have to end, their drinking began to spiral out of control. As suggested by the club's name, patrons came from an odd mix of universes. Despite the upscale draw, the club attracted an array of pimps, players, and hustlers. Bundini found himself back with old people from his days in the streets. Rhoda fell back into bad habits.

One night, as Bundini was closing the bar, two armed men, one brandishing a pistol, the other yielding a switch blade, burst through the front door. As one of the criminals attempted to remove the LeRoy Neiman painting of Buddy Drew off the wall, Bundini grabbed him and was subsequently slashed in the face by the switchblade, resulting in a six-inch scar on his left cheek that he would wear for the rest of his life. With Bundini on the floor bleeding, the two men cleaned out the register and escaped with the painting.

A few days later, Bundini came to the projects to visit his son. Unaware of the robbery, the young boy found his father in the bathroom, placing a new bandage on his face. The old bandage rested on the sink, heavily stained with blood.

"Daddy, what happened?" the boy asked.

"Don't worry about it. Let Shorty do what he does," Bundini swiftly replied.

"No daddy, what happened?" Drew persisted.

Eventually, Bundini rehashed the story, to which his son angrily replied, "Daddy, let's go kill them."

Bundini placed his arm around his son.

"Don't worry. The circle theory will take care of them," Bundini instructed, carefully securing the new bandage to his face.

Two weeks later, Bundini's prophecy proved correct. The robbers were both killed in a botched holdup attempt. Full of teenage wisdom, Drew rejoiced in the news.

"Buddy Drew, don't you ever do that again. Don't you ever take joy in Shorty's payback. When people get what they deserve, you just keep moving on," Bundini lectured.

In many ways, Bundini's philosophy proved to be true again.

By the fall of 1970, Bundini's World closed its doors.

"We both made the same mistake. We were our own best customers," Drew said to me.

■   ■   ■

When Drew Brown III was just a child, living in the projects in Spanish Harlem, his parents told him a story that shifted as the years went by.

"The story was that a married couple who were Daddy's friends had been unable to have children. The husband was sterile, they said. My mother and father were so close with the couple, and they thought so much of Daddy, that they asked him to impregnate the man's wife. Momma said the child was born the day before I was born," Drew confided in me.

Drew dreamed of one day meeting his sibling and thought of the child as something of a missing twin. His parents fervently suggested that he could never meet the boy because he had his own life and family and had not been told about his biological father.

"All that Momma told me was that [his mother] was a famous jazz and blues singer and if anyone found out about this, it might hurt her career," Drew remembered.

In the March 24, 1955, edition of *Jet* magazine, the caption reads as follows: "Camera Debut for Singer's Son: Apparently testing his own vocal cords for his first published photo, Ronald David Jackson, seven-week-old son of blues singer Ruth Brown, reaches for a high note while steadied by his mother and saxophonist dad, Willis Jackson."

Lying stomach down on the floor, the celebrity couple smiles as they prop up the baby boy, his mouth agape as if he were belting out one of his mother's blues songs.

Drew Brown III spent his entire childhood believing he had a long-lost brother somewhere out there in the world. It was not until he was a full-grown man that he discovered that his half-brother was the son of famous singer, songwriter, and actress Ruth Brown.

To a certain degree, the story of Ruth Brown's life played out similarly to that of Drew Bundini Brown. She was a small-town Virginia girl who ventured off to New York City in search of promise, attempting to escape what must have felt like an inevitable fate in her hometown. The woman who would one day come to be known as the "Queen of R&B," the oldest of her seven siblings had originally found her gift in the pews of her father's church. Ruth Brown's father, a dockhand, was also the director of the local church choir at Emanuel African Methodist Episcopal Church.

Perhaps as a direct response to her conservative upbringing, Ruth Brown rebelled as a teenager. In 1945, she ran away from home at the age of seventeen, with her boyfriend and soon-to-be husband. The young lovers set their sights on New York City, sharpening their talents at USO shows and seedy nightclubs. As a young woman, Ruth Brown dreamed of becoming the next Billie Holiday or Dinah Washington. In New York, success would come quickly. By 1950, Ruth Brown had a hit record on the radio. With the release of "Teardrops from My Eyes," the young singer became a major industry player for Atlantic Records, earning the moniker "Miss Rhythm."

It was during the early days of Ruth Brown's swift rise to fame that she met and had a brief affair with Drew Bundini Brown who, at the time, was not yet a full member of Sugar Ray Robinson's entourage. He was, however, the Black Prince. The nightclubs and jazz joints of New York City were Bundini's playground.

After the birth of his own son, Drew Jacques Brown IV, his middle name in honor of Poppa Jack, in 1979, Drew Brown III became preoccupied with the idea of finding his long-lost brother. When Bundini came to New Orleans for the grand opening of his son's nightclub, Drew III asked his father about the boy—a conversation they had not revisited in many years.

"[I] might meet him soon," Bundini quickly responded, catching his son off guard. "I'm working on it. Soon, it may happen soon," Bundini told his son.

A few weeks later, Bundini would get the opportunity to see his long-lost son. The small jazz club was sold out, filled with cigarette smoke and nostalgic rhythm and blues fans. The band took their positions on stage, performed an opening number, and then a young black man appeared. Ronnie David Jackson was the opening act.

Seated in the center section of the crowd, a few rows back from the main stage, Bundini's eyes locked with those of the performer on stage. An incredible feeling overcame him. He instantly knew there was something special about this encounter. The more he watched, the more he came to the realization that this was his other son.

"He was shorter and darker-skinned than Daddy, but he was still my father's son. That was unmistakable. Daddy later told me that he was scared and excited all wrapped up in one," Drew told me.

That night, Ronnie David Jackson wore a black suit, a white undershirt, and a striped tie. His hair was wavy. His face was long and thin, clean shaven and handsome, his eyes piercing, not unlike those of Bundini.

While the conversation was friendly, a noticeable tension persisted.

"Ronnie [told Bundini] he was conceived in 1955. Momma was Daddy's wife in 1955. It was during those same months Daddy and Ruth had conceived a son. My father explained everything to Ronnie. He was obviously displeased. Unlike me, he hadn't spent his entire life dreaming of a long-lost brother. All of this brought Ronnie no joy. You could see it on his face. If anything, Ronnie looked disappointed or betrayed. The feelings weren't mutual," Drew told me.

"I think Ronnie was just grappling with the idea," Drew's first-wife, Laurie, said. "His famous mother, Ruth Brown, had lied to him his entire life about who his real father was. Ronnie was performing in a nightclub. What Bundini told him that night really knocked him for a loop. We did stay in touch with Ronnie for some time. It eventually fell apart. The relationship faded. It was a difficult situation for everyone. Ronnie told us that he just didn't know how to handle it."

As a young boy, Drew III had struggled with his father's physical absence in his day-to-day life. Today, research tells us that boys raised without their fathers are more likely to drop out of school, develop drug and alcohol problems, and even demonstrate higher levels of aggression as children. For Drew, the problem wasn't that his father had abandoned him. The exact opposite was true. The underlying problem was that his father made his living as the sidekick to perhaps the most famous athlete on planet Earth, their names synonymous with one another. As a boy, Drew often felt as if he were competing with Muhammad Ali for his father's love and attention. He had convinced himself that in having a brother, the emotional gap would somehow be closed.

Ronnie David Jackson maintained a far different viewpoint. In Ruth Brown's 1996 biography, *Miss Rhythm*, the R&B legend affirms the story. She did not tell Ronnie about his biological father until he was a grown man. When Bundini showed up to that California nightclub, looking to claim the identity of his father, Jackson was understandably shaken. As the years went by, the revelation caused Drew Brown III more hurt than joy. The relationship faded, but the underlying confusion remained.

"Years later, we were living in Virginia Beach," Laurie said to me. "Drew was a lieutenant in the Navy. I was working too but we didn't have much money. One day Bundini calls and starts talking to Drew about David and I could see the conversation was tearing my husband up. Bundini told us that he needed money and Drew said 'Daddy, I don't have any money.' So, Bundini gets mad and says, 'I'll ask my real son.' I remember the look on Drew's face and him saying, 'But, I'm your real son, Daddy." I'm listening to this and I said, 'Give me that damn phone. Don't you ever call my house with this kind of nonsense. You know how Drew feels about you. I can't believe you had the gall and audacity to say that," Laurie continued.

After giving Bundini a piece of her mind, Laurie handed the phone back to her husband. The first words out of Bundini's mouth were, "Well son, I see Angel has grown up. You have a good wife. When you are wrong, you don't have power. I was wrong," Bundini added.

The men in her life, brilliant and flawed, both found and lost themselves amid the organized chaos of nightclubs and dreams of success.

"Bundini apologized to me afterward. And, after a few minutes, we were all good again. That's how it was with Bundini. Listen, when Bundini was good, he was great. When he was bad, he could be obnoxious. Regardless, you always ended up back on his side. That was his power," Laurie laughed, reflecting on her life in Bundini's world.

7

Make Sure You Be There, Waitin'

Under the tutelage of his manager and trainer Angelo Dundee, Louisville native Jimmy Ellis emerged from Bob Arum's heavyweight tournament with one sliver of the fractured heavyweight title. Joe Frazier, the undefeated Philadelphia brawler most experts viewed as the best active fighter in the division, reigned as the New York State Athletic Commission champion, racking up four consecutive defenses, three by way of knockout. The Ellis–Frazier unification match, scheduled for February 16, 1970, at Madison Square Garden, thus served as something of a pacifier for boxing fans clamoring for a legitimate champion. The sport's king remained in exile. Overshadowed by the anticipation of the Ellis–Frazier unification bout was an undercard match showcasing the formidable power of a rising heavyweight prospect from Houston, a 1968 Olympic gold medalist named George Foreman. During a public workout hosted at the Garden, two days before the event, a chance meeting occurred that, in hindsight, foreshadowed the golden era to come.

Looking back on his first encounter with Drew Bundini Brown, Foreman confided in me, with impressive detail and clarity, the beginning of a friendship that would last almost twenty years: "My first encounter with Bundini was when Muhammad was in exile. Jimmy Ellis was training at Madison Square Garden for his bout with Joe Frazier. Right in the audience was Drew Bundini, right there. He came over, somebody introduced us. And he just fell for me. 'George Foreman!' he shouted in a big voice. And he just showered me with affection. To be honest, that was the beginning of a wonderful relationship."

At twenty-one years old and only fifteen fights into his career as a professional, Foreman was instantly drawn to Bundini's charisma. The young heavyweight listened with both ears open. Even in his wildest dreams, Foreman could never have imagined that he and Bundini, in just a few short years, would find themselves in opposing corners, linked by one of the most famous heavyweight championship bouts in the history of the sport.

Almost fifty years after his initial encounter with Bundini, Foreman described for me a lasting impression. The two-time heavyweight champion spoke of Bundini as if he were a guru, a fortune-teller or soothsayer of the squared circle: "I characterize Bundini as someone that was full of depth. He joked a lot to kind of conceal the depth of his wisdom. I don't think he really wanted everybody to know that he really was so smart. He pulled me off to the side that day and gave me so many tips on how to be the champion of the world. And, he was right there with me all the way [throughout Foreman's career]. He really loved me. And I loved him too. But in boxing sometimes we think that we can't share that love. That was a fault of his, I suppose. He loved me equally as he did Muhammad Ali. I was really just a young boy when I saw him in the Garden with Jimmy Ellis and Frazier. He embraced me and everything he said came true. Bundini was a legend in his own way. And he treated me like I was equal to anyone."

Two days after conversing with Bundini, Foreman would defeat a tough Argentinian fighter named Gregorio Peralta, and Frazier would dispatch of Ellis to unify the titles. Ali and Bundini would take in the action from ringside. Unbeknownst to those in attendance, the true heavyweight tournament, a legendary series of fights that would forever change the course of boxing history, loomed on the horizon.

■　■　■

The irony of Muhammad Ali's three-year hiatus from boxing is that it transformed the former heavyweight champion into a figure of much larger social and political stature than could have ever been the case had he continued to reign as champion, uninterrupted by the war in Vietnam. Exile transformed Ali into a civil rights martyr, a symbol of opposition to the Vietnam War, a voice for the oppressed. While Ali's global profile grew, however, his bank account dwindled. For three painstaking years, Ali's handlers worked tirelessly to find a way to return the Champ to the sport of boxing. Harold Conrad, who promoted and worked publicity for the Liston fights, ran through an exhaustive list of personal and political connections in an attempt to find a location audacious enough to host a Muhammad Ali comeback fight. Bob Arum, Bob Kassel, and Gene Kilroy (each man tied to Ali's career) worked their own set of connections in hopes of securing bouts in Tijuana and Toronto. These efforts would prove fruitless. Nothing could be accomplished because Ali was unable to secure a passport. Many legal experts predicted the Louisville Lip would not be able to return to boxing until after his Supreme Court appeal was resolved.

The state of Georgia, an unlikely candidate to say the least, would, in the end, prove to be an ideal location for the fight. First and foremost, there was no state athletic commission in Georgia, a major hurdle in other states. New York's boxing commission had stripped Ali of his right to box and other prominent boxing states, such as Nevada and California, quickly followed suit. Because there was no boxing commission in Georgia, an Ali comeback fight could be licensed in Georgia if Sam Massell, mayor of Atlanta, and the Board of Aldermen approved. "Politics was what kept him out of boxing, and in the end, it was what got him back in," Harold Conrad later reflected.[1]

In the 1996 documentary *Muhammad Ali: The Whole Story*, Bob Kassel credits the legal breakthrough to the visible presence of Black political and socioeconomic power in the Atlanta metropolitan area: "[Atlanta] struck me as a strange venue and I knew it was when I called. But, we hadn't made any progress in any other venues, which weren't so strange. I did know that the Black community, in Atlanta, wielded a lot of power. They had a lot to say about what went on in city government. And there was a Jewish mayor, so it was kind of a good mix."

In an attempt to gain some measure of political ground, Kassel sought out Leroy Johnson, the state's prominent Black senator, a man who held sway over Black voters. Johnson, who was offered money from ticket sales, was able to use his impressive business acumen to gain the support of other local entrepreneurs and politicians, including Mayor Massell. Johnson, ever the shrewd rhetorician, pitched the idea to the mayor as an opportunity to promote Atlanta as a progressive urban center for business. Despite his initial trepidation, Massell agreed to support the fight if Ali's team donated $50,000 to one of his anti-crime programs.

Once Arum and Kassel were able to gain favor with Georgia governor Lester Maddox—no easy task when considering the governor's conservative background—the team sprang into action, scheduling an exhibition event that would, in many respects, test the waters.

In September of 1970, Ali sparred with three opponents in an eight-round exhibition at Morehouse College in Atlanta.

"If you can't seize the title, then win the people," Bundini instructed Ali beforehand, dubbing the exhibition "The Champ's Resurrection."

Had it been any other boxer in the world, the event would have been viewed as little more than a sparring session. Ali was, of course, no ordinary boxer. While the Morehouse crowd of just over 5,000 fans were ecstatic to see Ali back in the ring, nobody in the arena was more pleased to see the Champ float like a butterfly than his loyal cornerman. With Bundini's World no longer in business and no legitimate job prospects on the horizon, Bundini, for a brief period of time, had earned a meager income working for a heavyweight journeyman named Jeff Merritt, a far cry from his once lofty position with the greatest of all time. Ali's return to the fight game was thus a prayer answered for Bundini. It should be noted that, at this point in his life, Bundini had only worked in three of Ali's twenty-nine professional training camps. He had yet to earn a sustainable income from Ali. Ironically, it was during those three years of exile that Ali and Bundini's friendship truly began to grow.

"When Ali was on Broadway, working on *Buck White*, Bundini was with him every day. If Ali was in New York, you could almost guarantee he was with Bundini," Khalilah Camacho-Ali said to me.

"My father was loyal to Ali during exile, when nobody thought he would ever fight again," Drew Brown III recalled. "Back then, it wasn't 'Is the Champ going to fight again?' He wasn't going to fight again. But Daddy was by Ali's side. His loyalty proved something to the Champ. There are a lot of other people who couldn't say they stayed loyal during those difficult times."

For both Ali and Bundini, but perhaps for different reasons, the exhibition at Morehouse College served as something of a spiritual rebirth. In Ali's 1975 autobiography *The Greatest*, Richard Durham portrays Bundini's elation via a locker-room conversation that allegedly took place between Bundini, Ali, and Ali's brother, Rahman, an exchange that reveals just how much the forty-one-year-old trainer had been hurting during Ali's exile.

"Angelo has the complexion and the connections but Bundini makes the fight," Ali proclaims to his brother, joyous that the event went off without a hitch.

Bundini's reaction to Ali's comments are telling.

"[That] was the first time he ever give me my mojo back," Bundini tells Rahman, beaming with pride.

Overcome with emotion, Bundini launches into one of his trademark philosophical musings, a commentary on boxing and life.

"I give it to him and he gives it back. I feel my body get younger. A man gets old quick when he don't get love. An unloved man is the endangered species. A man gets ulcers and brain damage when he ain't around love. But what he said smoothed out the wrinkles in my body. A man minus love is a wrinkled man, but a beloved man is smooth," Bundini tells Rahman.

Echoing Durham's characterization of his father, Drew III attempted to explain for me the importance of the Morehouse exhibition for his father: "Daddy had sacrificed himself during exile. Even when he was not Ali's employee, my daddy remained as a friend and an encourager to the Champ. Others, except for my father and Gene Kilroy, went their separate ways for income during those years. But when Ali needed them, Daddy and Gene were never more than a call away. The only difference is that Gene had other financial means and my father did not. Daddy's loyalty was unwavering and special."

The Morehouse College exhibition proved to be a success, bereft of any incidents of violence or demonstrations from the Ku Klux Klan. Shortly thereafter, Ali's official return to boxing was announced to the public. Seven weeks later, on October 26, 1970, Muhammad Ali would square off against "Irish" Jerry Quarry, "the Bellflower Bomber" of Bakersfield, California, a durable but undersized heavyweight known for his propensity to shed blood. Quarry's whiteness was unquestionably a factor in the promotional team's choice of opponents. When Ali was granted the opportunity to face Quarry at City Auditorium in Atlanta, Bundini was officially brought back into the fold. Angelo Dundee, despite his ties to Ali's hometown rival, Jimmy Ellis, also returned. Wali "Youngblood" Muhammad (formerly known as Walter Youngblood), served as the only new addition to the Ali corner. Born in Louisiana but raised in Harlem, "Blood" had previously worked as a member of security for Sugar Ray Robinson, and in doing so befriended Bundini.

"I loved Uncle Youngblood. He was like family to me," Drew III recalled. "Daddy was the one who helped get him into the entourage. Uncle Youngblood worked all of Ali's fights after exile, all the way to the end. He always looked after me when I came to camp, my Uncle Blood."

With his entourage reassembled for the first time in three years, Ali now faced the challenge of squaring off against the younger Quarry after an extended layoff. The bout would mark the first time Ali would face an opponent younger than himself.

Unlike many pundits who viewed Quarry as nothing more than "A Great White Hope," a punching bag with the ability to bleed, Ali's corner expected a challenge. Quarry was, aside from Frazier and Ellis, the highest-ranked contender in the division, according to *The Ring* magazine. By today's standards, such a risk would be almost unthinkable. Bundini, in particular, worried that Ali, anxious to prove he was still the true king of the heavyweight division, would overexert himself in preparing for the bout.

"Shorty wants you to rest. Rest's the most powerful medicine in the world for a fighter. Sugar Ray taught me that," Bundini instructed during the training camp.

Dundee, in a 1996 interview with Turner Home Entertainment, painted the Quarry training camp in a similar vein: "You gotta remember, Muhammad, for as beautiful an athlete as he looked, didn't do anything when he wasn't fighting. In fact, he tried to use that Archie Moore routine with the plastic [sweat suits]. But, don't ya know, he put the plastic on and he went into the gym and tried to rush his conditioning, which you can't do."

With only six weeks to prepare, nobody in the entourage could be certain which version of Ali was returning to the squared circle. Because of the controversial nature of the bout, threats of violence would abound. The 5th Street Gym in Miami, open and accessible, no longer appeared to be an appropriate venue to host Ali's training camp. In an attempt to secure a safe environment for all involved, Ali's team constructed a makeshift training camp in rural Georgia, just outside Atlanta. Ali's 1977 biopic, *The Greatest*, paints the experience in a less than positive light. In one of the more dramatic scenes in the film, Ali and Bundini, playing themselves, drive down a secluded rural backroad on their way to training camp. As the duo makes their way down the twisting country roads, a haunting soundtrack plays in the background.

"You see those evil eyes looking at us? When they saw us they eyes popped," Bundini says to Ali.

Later in the scene, underneath the moonlight, Ali shadowboxes outside his cabin. Bundini is, as always, by the Champ's side, providing verbal support. The moonlit shadowboxing session is interrupted by shotgun fire.

"Get out of Georgia, ya black son of a bitch!" a menacing voice calls from the shadowy wilderness.

"Nigger, you're gonna die!" another voice shouts as more gunfire erupts. Ali and Bundini duck for cover, scrambling to seek shelter.

This scene is, of course, heavily influenced by Durham's account of the events in his 1975 Ali autobiography. There, as is the case in the film, Bundini is portrayed as riddled with nerves. He answers threatening phone calls in multiple scenes, his trepidation exemplified by the two Colt .45 pistols in his suitcase. Regardless of whether these events actually took place—reliable sources suggest they did—one thing is for sure: The Jerry Quarry training camp served as a bonding experience for Ali and Bundini. One scene in Durham's book, for example, playfully depicts Ali waking early before roadwork to pour carrot juice in the mouth of Bundini while he sleeps. In another scene, Ali discovers Bundini up late into the night, unable to sleep, awaiting a phone call from his son.

"Can't sleep until I talk to his blood in the Holy Land," Bundini says.

This exchange is undoubtedly true. At the time, Bundini's son was on the other side of the globe, in the Upper Galilee section of Israel, experiencing his own spiritual awakening.

■ ■ ■

Shortly after she and her son relocated to Brighton Beach, Brooklyn, to live with her parents, Rhoda spotted a *New York Times* advertisement seeking high school exchange students to go to Israel. The program, sponsored by the Kfar Blum Regional School in Galilee, located on the site of a famous kibbutz, was designed to offer a spiritually enriching immersion experience for young Jewish children from the United States. Both Rhoda and her mother viewed the experience as a once-in-a-lifetime opportunity for young Buddy Drew. Upon moving to Brooklyn, the teenager had become impulsive and reckless.

"Bubba could see that I was troubled," Drew III recalled. "She always knew. Bubba believed that life on a kibbutz would steep me further in the Jewish faith and would discipline me in ways that no one in our family could. Bubba was excited and yet cautious. This was a pie-in-the-sky dream that was far from being a reality, especially since we didn't have the money to do this in the first place."

Driven by a combination of love and concern, the family pooled their collective resources. Rhoda helped her son with the entrance essay. Bundini secured recommendation letters from a few of his famous associates, theater and film director Otto Preminger and renowned literary daredevil George Plimpton. A few months later, the family was thrilled to learn that Drew had become the first Black Jewish student to receive a partial scholarship from the program. When it came time to pay for the cost of airfare, an expense the scholarship didn't cover, Bundini was unable to secure the funds. He had not received any money for the Morehouse College exhibition.

"Even though we had the partial scholarship, we were $2,000 short," Drew told me. "Momma had an idea. She took one of her Camel cigarette packages and cut out the camel and placed it on a sheet of construction paper with a mountain drawn on it, with $0 to $2,000. As everyone chipped in, and Momma continued to work, the camel climbed the mountain. I never had a doubt the camel would climb to the top."

Drew began his time in Israel living in dormitories with other exchange students. A few months into the experience, he was taken into the home of a kibbutz family, an Israeli couple named Zvi and Mazel Rauch. The experience of living in a kibbutz was profoundly illuminating for the fifteen-year-old boy. Drew's identity as a Black Jew no longer relegated him to a marginalized status. In Israel, the troubled teenager found his Jewish roots. He worked and studied Hebrew with other dark-skinned Jews, with hair just as kinky as his.

"As a younger person, I had wondered how meaningful it was for me to speak Hebrew and pray to God, when I don't even know what I'm saying. The emphasis in America had been on if I pronounced the words correctly rather than what the passages meant," Drew reflected.

For the first time in his young life, Drew began to think critically about his identity as a Jewish man. Much like his philosophical father, Drew began to view concepts such as racism and prejudice as a product of deep-seated insecurity and self-hatred. There is a certain wisdom that comes with traveling the world, Drew came to believe. Israel had welcomed him with open arms. The world was now his home.

Drew's time in Israel was not without its difficulty, however. The experience also introduced the young boy to the horrific nature of war. His kibbutz was located near the border of Lebanon and Syria. Israeli jet fighters, in retaliatory attacks against the Arab opposition, made frequent appearances in the sky. Despite the danger, Drew became instantly fascinated by the technological precision of the Israeli F-4 Phantom jets zipping across the sky.

"In Israel, fighter pilots signed autographs like celebrities. They were defenders of the people. Watching those jets fly overhead blew my mind. I never thought of actually doing that one day. I knew fighters; these bad asses were fighter pilots," Drew recalled.

At night, from the vantage point of his bedroom window, the teenager watched the pyrotechnic light show birthed by the four-to-one tracer bullets of Israeli machine guns and witnessed firsthand the aftermath of Soviet-made Katyusha rockets and mortar shells. War, the fifteen-year-old boy thought to himself, was the ultimate form of racism. Seeing war up close, recognizing its presence in the daily lives of a people, opened the young boy's mind to his own American privilege, despite growing up in the projects of Harlem.

As the months shuffled along, Drew grew tired of life on the farm. A true city boy, he longed for the fast pace of life in New York City. As his boredom mounted and his Hebrew improved, Drew began to wander outside of the kibbutz. Tired of cleaning cow dung out of barns, his daily Kibbutz duty, the teenager took to exploring the Galilee area, meeting strangers and looking for adventure. When the director of the school discovered his actions—clear violations of the exchange-student arrangement—he was subsequently expelled.

Two months before graduation, Drew was sent back to Brooklyn. Having to attend summer school to make up the work he had not completed in Israel was a humiliating experience. Drew was loved and accepted by the people of the kibbutz. He didn't get the certificate but he got the experience of a lifetime, one that would change him forever.

■ ■ ■

In October of 1970, Drew Brown III's melancholy was interrupted by a surprise phone call from his father.

"Buddy Drew, do you have school? Okay. You're coming to Atlanta. We are fighting Quarry. Told you I'd be back, boy. Told you I'd never leave you," Bundini said.

The exile was over for Buddy Drew as well.

"I was thrilled. Daddy's invitation proved that, even though he and I were apart, he had not forgotten his boy," Drew reflected.

At Atlanta's Hyatt Regency, the week before the fight, Bundini introduced his son to prominent Black figures such as Coretta Scott King, Harry Belafonte, and Sidney Poitier. At ringside, Drew was reunited with the man he had, as a child, affectionately referred to as "Uncle Ray," Sugar Ray Robinson. The trip to Atlanta served as a much-needed return to the excitement he once knew. Now a teenager, he could be a full member of the entourage. Witnessing Ali's resurrection, a three-round technical knockout of Jerry Quarry, was hardly the highlight of the trip. Drew was simply grateful to be back in his father's life as he returned to work.

Despite some apparent ring rust, Ali had proved there was plenty of gas in his metaphorical tank. It was a night of whipping right hands and stinging jabs, damage resulting in a severe laceration over Quarry's left eye in the third round. When referee Tony Perez called a halt to the contest before the start of the fourth round, Ali achieved more than simply earning the thirtieth victory of his professional career. The measure of his accomplishment extended far beyond the boxing ring.

"The ghost is in the house!" Bundini called, the first to greet Ali in a victory embrace, one arm wrapped around the champion's neck and the other extended to the heavens.

The ghost Bundini was referring to was that of Jack Johnson, the controversial heavyweight champion who, at the height of Jim Crow America, became the first Black man to win the title.

"The ghost of Jack Johnson is in the house!" Bundini repeated as he paraded around the ring with Ali, signaling the sociopolitical importance of the comeback victory.

For Bundini, and much of the Black American public, Ali's career now held a measure of importance that far surpassed his place in boxing history. After the Quarry victory, new opportunities emerged. In a surprise turn of events, the New York State Athletic Commission followed Atlanta's lead and reissued Ali's boxing license. Now that the ice had been broken, so to speak, New York boxing's movers and shakers were not going to sit back and simply allow Ali to make money fighting in other states. On December 7, 1970, just a few months after his victory over Quarry, Ali would continue his comeback against battled-tested Oscar Bonavena at Madison Square Garden. The news of Ali's return to the Big Apple held special importance for Drew Brown III. The location of the bout would assure that the teenager would once again be able to tag along with his father. For Bundini, Ali's continued good fortune would usher in, for the first time in his life, an era of temporary financial stability. Bundini would work the corner of Ali's final thirty-one contests. He would never again miss a Muhammad Ali fight.

While the success of the Quarry fight changed the fickle minds of boxing's business contingent, Ali's victory did little to silence his detractors. The continued animosity, and variety of public opinions, surrounding the controversial ex-champion was on full display in the buildup to the Bonavena bout. In the weeks before the fight, Bonavena would take a page out of the Ernie Terrell playbook, referring to Ali by his former name and mockingly calling him a "chicken" for not fighting in Vietnam. Ali, who proclaimed that he "had never wanted to whup a man so bad," beat up and then knocked out his opponent in the fifteenth and final round. After the fight, Ali took the microphone and called out the so-called heavyweight champion of the world, "Smokin'" Joe Frazier.

The stage was now set for perhaps the most anticipated event in the history of the sport. What Bundini couldn't have possibly predicted, however, was that the potential Ali–Frazier megafight was not the only good fortune waiting around the corner. Bundini was about to be linked with another mythic figure in Black culture, an outspoken and iconic personification of Black masculinity who, not unlike Ali, would have a profound impact on the American imagination.

■ ■ ■

In addition to his duties as Muhammad Ali's business manager, Gene Kilroy also worked as a marketing executive at Metro-Goldwyn-Mayer. In the early 1970s, Kilroy established a relationship with a talented young photographer-turned-filmmaker named Gordon Parks. Born in Fort Scott, Kansas, the youngest of fifteen children, Parks relocated to the South Side of Chicago shortly after the market crash of 1929. In Chicago, he earned a reputation as one of America's most talented young photographers, documenting Black poverty in the Windy City. Largely because of the success of his photograph "American Gothic, Washington D.C.," Parks secured a job with the Farm Security Administration, a New Deal agency that documented the nation's social conditions. By the 1950s, Parks regularly served as a consultant to Hollywood films. These opportunities inspired Parks to try his hand at documentary filmmaking. His first project would be a series of films on Black poverty commissioned by National Educational Television.

Parks's Hollywood debut would come in 1969, with the film adaptation of his semiautobiographical novel *The Learning Tree*. The success of the film subsequently opened the door for Parks's first project for MGM, a gritty crime drama called *Shaft*, which was set in the underbelly of Harlem and would soon position Parks as Hollywood's first major Black director.

Because of his background as an ethnographer, Parks was more than qualified for the task of capturing the essence of Harlem's mean streets—a world of pimps, pushers, hustlers, and gangsters. The territory Parks was looking to re-create for moviegoers was, of course, a world that Bundini had once called home. When Kilroy first read the script, he instantly thought of the Black Prince.

"I got Bundini in the *Shaft* movies, with Gordon Parks," Kilroy told me. "I was working for MGM at the time and they were doing this new movie called *Shaft*, about a Black police officer in Harlem. Bundini always wanted to be a big star. He liked the camera. He was good in front of the camera. So, I got him an audition."

Parks, an admirer of Ali, was aware of both Bundini's personal story and cultural persona. After considering Kilroy's suggestion, he asked Bundini to read for the part of Willy, sidekick to Harlem kingpin Bumpy Jones, a self-made overlord of prostitution, drugs, and racketeering. In the film, Bumpy's daughter has been kidnapped by rival gangsters. Private detective John Shaft, who serves as a go-between for the crime world and the NYPD, is thus hired by Bumpy to solve the case. Willy, who maintains both an antagonism and a partnership with Shaft because of his relationship with Bumpy, is charged with the role of maintaining his boss's reputation on the streets. While Bundini's part in the original film was small—Willy only appears in a handful of scenes—the opportunity and exposure was colossal.

The role of Willy, as Kilroy suggested to Parks, was tailor-made for Bundini. Willy's turf, the 125th Street neighborhood that surrounds the Apollo Theater, the Theresa Hotel, and the Amsterdam strip that once was home to Sugar Ray's, was essentially Bundini's old stomping grounds. Bundini was fluent in the ways of the Harlem streets, from the lingo to the body language.

"When I was a kid, I would hear my father talk to his friends on the phone," Drew III remembered. "Their street lingo sounded almost as if they were speaking another language. Even though I thought of myself as a cool kid, I couldn't understand none of it."

From a pragmatic vantage point, however, the problem was that Bundini, because of his inability to read at an adult level, could not fully comprehend the script. Thus, memorizing his lines proved to be difficult at first. The conundrum, a blessing in disguise for Bundini's teenage son, was one that would bring the two men back together.

"My father brought the script to me," Drew remembered. "I read it, memorized the lines myself, and helped him do the same. We had a wonderful time rehearsing and practicing together. We had so much fun with it."

Over fifty years later, Drew is still able to recite, without error or hesitation, his father's lines from the *Shaft* movies. Drew's impeccable memory serves as evidence of a powerful bonding experience that continues to hold importance for him today. As made evident by the 2019 Hollywood reboot, staring Samuel L. Jackson, Jessie Usher, Regina Hall, and the original lead actor, Richard Roundtree, the *Shaft* franchise continues to hold some measure of nostalgic importance for American moviegoers as well.

Partially because of the popularity of Isaac Hayes's Grammy-winning score, which opens the film as the camera descends on 1970s Times Square, *Shaft* proved to be a tremendous box-office success for the then-struggling

MGM studios. This was *James Bond* set in Harlem, an untapped pop-culture formula. Consisting of five feature films in total, ranging from 1971 to 2019, the staying power of the *Shaft* films is in part connected to the long-standing cultural void occupied by the series. Before the release of Gordon Parks's movie, Black actors were largely relegated to the cinematic margins, rarely given heroic roles or even opportunities to act in films centered on the Black experience. The original *Shaft* film, a 1971 Hollywood blockbuster, would fuel a new era in cinema, colloquially known in the industry as the blaxploitation genre. While some suggested Parks's films promoted negative stereotypes of Black men, particularly in regard to drug use, violence, and misogynistic views toward women, others applauded the groundbreaking nature of the films, the first generation of action films specifically crafted for Black audiences.

Muhammad Ali, like many film critics, maintained something of a love-hate relationship with the Shaft franchise.

"Ali's first reaction was, 'Why they always portraying Black people as nothing but pimps and players? Why can't we ever be men of education and respect? These movies are a tool they use to keep portraying our people in a negative fashion,'" Khalilah Camacho-Ali told me.

Her husband's disdain would, however, soften when Harlem gangster Bumpy Jones, accompanied by his sidekick Willy, dressed in tailored suits and fedora hats, entered the disheveled office of detective John Shaft for the first time, a scene that would be Bundini's cinematic debut.

"Look. If the man ever come here . . . again to see you, you make sure you be here, waitin'," Willy, in a slow and serious voice, warns Shaft, his long fingers pointing toward the movie's hero in a threatening fashion.

"When Bundini came on the screen, Ali got a kick out of it," Khalilah Camacho-Ali remembered. "He cracked up. I mean, he enjoyed the movie. He watched both movies. But he enjoyed watching them because of Bundini. I'd see Ali light up with a big smile when Bundini came on. He'd say, 'Look at Bundini go.'"

"My dad absolutely loved the movie. We went and watched both *Shaft* movies together," Jim Dundee told me. "I remember his grin when Bundini came on the screen dressed like a gangster. Dad loved seeing Drew succeed. Dad worried about him. We were thrilled when he got the part."

When Ali returned to training camp, his movie-star cornerman became the focal point of downtime between workouts.

"Drew kept us all laughing," Victor Solano, Muhammad Ali's longtime friend and training camp stablemate, told me. "Muhammad would always say, 'Say that part.' Drew would say it the same way he did at the beginning of the *Shaft* movie—the part when he came in with Bumpy and those guys. Sometimes Muhammad would say, 'Do it again' and Drew would recite the entire scene for us. Perfect. Every time. Whether it was just us or in front of twenty people, it always came off perfect. We would fall over laughing. He would do it perfect every time. It was classic. It could be after a hard day of work, working with Larry Holmes. It didn't matter if we were doing roadwork. Muhammad always asked him to say the part."

Despite Ali's objection to the messages found in the *Shaft* films, one could argue that he was indirectly responsible for their rise and popularity. It is next to impossible to quantify the lasting impact of Ali's braggadocio persona on American popular culture, particularly Black culture in the 1960s and 1970s. Ali's original mix of bravado, poetry, and vernacular changed the way American audiences viewed Black men and shaped how Black men thought about themselves. Ali was, after all, the first Black athlete to proclaim he was the greatest of all time. His talent, bravery, beauty, and brilliance served as a source of pride for a generation of disenfranchised Black youth. Ali's in-your-face persona and his willingness to bravely call out White America on their injustices served as a precursor to the rise of over-the-top pop culture figures made famous by the blaxploitation genre. Ironically enough, Drew Bundini Brown would play Sancho Panza[2] to both Ali and Shaft.

For a generation of young Black men raised on Ali fights and *Shaft* movies, Bundini came to be seen as a personification of street-smart poetic brilliance. Bundini's proximity to both enduring sources of Black pride bolstered his own credibility in the larger cultural circles. Ali's popularity, coupled with the success of the *Shaft* franchise, would, in many respects, lay the rhetorical groundwork for an identity performance that would one day become the dominant rhetorical formula of the hip-hop generation.

When MGM gave the green light for production of *Shaft's Big Score!*, studio executives had no choice but to ask Bundini to reprise his role as Willy. The sequel, released in June of 1972, elevated director Gordon Parks to new commercial heights. This time around, MGM's budget was twice that of the original film. Bundini's role in the film would also be expanded. The plot of the sequel, centered on an all-out turf war between the mob boss Gus Mascola and Bumpy Jones's gang, once again finds Shaft joining forces with the Harlem racketeer, who this time around lends Shaft his right-hand man.

In *Shaft's Big Score!* Parks makes no effort to hide Bundini's celebrity. For example, in one scene, Willy drinks a shot of vodka as Shaft does battle with one of Mascola's henchmen. As Shaft struggles to overcome his foe, Willy encourages him from the sidelines, a routine that audiences would have easily recognized.

"Rumble, young man!" Willy calls to Shaft.

The fact that Willy is featured much more prominently in the second *Shaft* film, despite Bundini's limited acting experience and inability to read, signals that both Parks and MGM recognized his value to the franchise, his raw talent, and his magnetic personality.

Bundini's initial foray into acting, coupled with Ali's return from exile, can be seen as the apex of Bundini's financial life. These were, without question, some of Bundini's happiest and most prosperous days. For the first time, Bundini had money to spare—the ability to shower his family and friends with gifts. Bundini's wave of good fortune would, of course, coincide with the long-awaited news that Muhammad Ali would be granted an opportunity to win back the title that was unjustly stolen from him upon his refusal to serve in the U.S. Armed Forces.

Dubbed "The Fight of the Century," the Muhammad Ali vs. Joe Frazier megafight provided both undefeated champions with an opportunity to put to rest years of trash talk, a bubbling animosity that dwarfed the rivalry Ali had experienced in facing Sonny Liston. Polar opposites, in both fighting style and public persona, Ali and Frazier embodied the essence of the term *nemesis*. Their initial bout, rife with political, racial, and sociological significance, divided the nation. On March 8, 1971, at Madison Square Garden, Drew Bundini Brown found himself in the best seat in the house, front and center at both the box office and the boxing ring.

■ ■ ■

Hours before the opening bell, Bundini gathered up the entourage's gear, a simple task but one of great importance. It was Bundini's job to set up the locker room. When the hotel lobby elevator opened, a swarm of reporters, pundits, and boxing fans rushed the doors. A palpable energy filled the lobby of the Statler Hotel, Ali's prefight headquarters. Drew Brown III, attending his third straight Ali bout, invited his high school friend Jeff Hofstein to Madison Square Garden. Hofstein, his mouth agape for much of the night, was overcome by the significance of the event he was about to witness. Pushing their way through the lobby, parting a sea of boxing fans and media, the teenage boys felt like nothing short of rock stars. As they made their way down the New York City streets with Bundini, the trio were met with cheers and words of encouragement.

At Madison Square Garden's side entrance, Bundini and his teenage entourage were ushered beyond the fencing and police barrels that restricted the general public from the arena. Some bystanders were hustling for last-minute tickets, others simply looking to catch a glimpse of the combatants as they entered the self-proclaimed "Mecca of Boxing." As the trio made their way to the door, a group of fans, perhaps fifty in total, screamed with excitement.

"Bundini! Bundini!" they cheered.

Pausing before entering, Bundini glanced back to acknowledge the crowd, tipping his cap like a baseball player who had just crushed a 400-foot home run. This move only served to intensify the calls.

"I've been waiting to see Ali my entire life!" one boy shouted, his face covered in desperation.

"Get us in! Get us in, Bundini!" another boy screamed.

"Bundini, you can get us in! Help us out, brother!" the crowd cheered.

For a brief moment, Drew Brown III experienced something akin to a psychic connection. He knew his father well enough to predict what was going to happen next.

"Let 'em in," Bundini instructed the police officer.

"Which one?" the officer reluctantly asked, after a moment's pause.

"All of them, sir," Bundini flatly responded.

"I can't let all those people in," the police officer laughed, perhaps wishfully reading Bundini's instruction as joke.

There was a momentary pause in the debate, one that felt much longer to the young Drew Brown III.

"If these people don't come in, I don't go in," Bundini threatened the officer.

As the officer looked to his partner for assistance, Bundini continued.

"I got the Champ's gloves and his jock. So if Bundini don't go in, the world's biggest fight don't happen. You understand?" he instructed.

When the officers did not acquiesce to his demands, Bundini called their bluff. He turned and motioned to his teenage entourage.

"C'mon, boys," Bundini called.

"Wait . . . wait!" the officers shouted in unison, motioning to the crowd of young people with a sharp gesture that roughly translated to "make it quick, kids."

Leaping over the barricade and scurrying into the Garden like children on Christmas morning, the boys showered Bundini with high fives, handshakes, and hugs.

"Ain't nothing like walking to the back of the line and getting invited to the front," Bundini instructed his son, who was smiling ear to ear, brimming with pride.

"My dad was the bomb that night. I was so proud Hofstein saw him do that," Drew reflected, unable to contain his smile.

Inside Ali's locker room, Drew motioned for Jeff to be silent. Drew, who had accompanied his father to the Quarry and Bonavena fights, understood the routine. Bundini was a man who went about even the most menial of tasks with a meticulous attention to detail. When Bundini entered the locker room, he was on the clock. The robe and cornermen jackets had to be hung a particular way. The trunks had to be laid out accordingly. From the placing of the hand wraps to the positioning of the boxing shoes, every detail of the setup held symbolic importance.

"He was like a priest handling sacraments at the altar," Drew recalled.

When the setup was complete, Bundini sat in silence, perhaps talking to Shorty, maybe resting his voice, the instrument by which he made his contribution. When Ali entered the locker room, a few hours later, Bundini came to life. There would be no talk of strategy. No mention of Ali's impending Supreme Court case. Instead, the topic of Bundini's sermon, perhaps inspired by his entrance to the arena, was the common people of the streets, the masses of disenfranchised Black youth who sought pride in the Champ's symbolism.

"You are fighting for all of them and Ole' Joe Frazier is fighting for himself. You're fighting a man who is like a wild animal, you made him mad. But a mad fighter can't think. You're fighting for all of those kids.

This is bigger than you, Champ. You've been fighting your whole life for this moment. Shorty gave you this moment. They took your belt and you are here to get it BACK. You are going to use the gifts Shorty gave you and you're going to float like a butterfly and sting like a bee. We are going to war, Champ. You can shock the world again. You've been chosen to be a symbol of freedom. With that responsibility comes power and when you are fighting for more than one, you have the power of more than one. You beat the United States government, now go beat Frazier," Drew recalled his father saying, describing him as a military admiral outlining the who, how, and why of combat.

"Bundini told Ali, 'When other fighters lose, nobody gives a shit. If you lose, there will be kids in Harlem crying tonight,'" Gene Kilroy, who was also present in the locker room, remembered.

The subject matter of Bundini's prefight oratory is key to understanding the larger cultural symbolism at play. When Ali won the heavyweight championship at twenty-two years old, he was far too young to understand the significance of his accomplishment. The process of having his title taken away, not to mention his livelihood, transformed Ali's sociopolitical ethos into something far bigger than himself. His greatness was no longer a testament to his speed or athletic skill. After exile, Ali's ring victories had a newfound cultural symbolism. Frazier, because of factors completely out of his control, served as the primary rooting interest for those who opposed Ali's religion, personality, politics, and color. Frazier, at least for one night, would personify the establishment, Ali the struggle. On March 8, 1971, audiences from around the world would bring their own morals, beliefs, attitudes, and ambitions to the event. Separating the hero from the villain had much more to do with the viewers than the fighters themselves. And, as Bundini attempted to point out in his prefight sermon, it was evident which contingent was on Ali's side.

Symbolism aside, Bundini likely saw some of his own story in that of Joe Frazier. The twelfth child born to poor Black sharecroppers, Joe had grown up amid the tough and unforgiving circumstances of Black life in rural Jim Crow South Carolina. The Frazier family worked their small farm with two mules, the land only suitable for cotton and watermelon. Smokin' Joe understood the struggle of Black people in the United States. By age fifteen, he, like Bundini, was on his own. The sport of boxing saved Frazier's life, took him around the world, first to the 1964 Olympic Games in Japan, where he would win gold, and later to Philadelphia, where he would serve as a key contributor to the city's long-standing boxing history.

"My father called himself a small piece of leather, well put together," former heavyweight contender Marvis Frazier, Joe Frazier's son, said to me.

"Pops would say, 'There is a wrong way to do right but no right way to do wrong. And, if you do wrong, I'm gonna make you smell this' (holding his fist underneath young Marvis's nose)," Frazier chuckled.

Joe Frazier had not chosen to be conservative White America's champion. He was not motivated by the hopes and dreams of the establishment. For Frazier, the fight was personal. The path to defeating Ali was, in many ways, a quest for personal legitimacy. Frazier had risen to the top of the heavyweight division despite the long list of sociocultural obstacles that stood in his way, and had successfully reigned as heavyweight champion for three years, only to be continuously reminded that he was not, in fact, the true champion. Listening to Marvis conjure memories of the fight that forever cemented his father's legacy, it was impossible to see him in any other way than a son who admired his father.

"I was eleven years old. Me and my sisters listened to it on the radio. I was like, 'Be careful, Daddy.' I was scared. But Pop wasn't afraid of him at all. Maybe more than anybody in the world, Pop wasn't afraid of him. My Pop didn't care about the trash talk. Pop gave him a few dollars while he was in exile. He wanted Mr. Ali to be able to fight so that he could prove that he could beat him. He said, 'I got the trash talk when we get in the ring.' He knew what was going on," Marvis Frazier said to me.

As Marvis and his sister huddled around their radio, hundreds of millions of boxing fans around the world were watching the fight on closed-circuit television. Madison Square Garden had broken all of its records by selling $1.35 million worth of tickets.

From his vantage point at ringside, Drew Brown III watched with great trepidation as his father led Ali into the ring. "My father often described this prefight moment as being pregnant in public—pacing, praying, and anticipating, waiting for the baby to be born," Drew remembered.

By night's end, the names Ali and Frazier would forever be linked.

■ ■ ■

The first stanza of the Ali–Frazier trilogy would go to Joe Frazier via a unanimous decision, a victory most eloquently symbolized by the leaping left hook that connected on Muhammad Ali's chin midway through the fifteenth and final round, momentarily planting the former champion on the seat of his pants. Seated at ringside was the man who would eventually usurp the title from Smokin' Joe, Bundini's old friend, George Foreman. For Big George, one of the more memorable moments of the night had nothing to do with the two men in the ring.

"I remember the night Joe Frazier knocked him down at [Madison Square Garden]. I was there. Ringside. Bundini picked up some water and I've never seen someone throw some water with such accuracy. It hit Muhammad right in the face. It gave him chills. Woke him up. Bundini got a fine [from the New York State Boxing Commission] and all that. But he said 'what the heck.' Never seen no one do that. He was willing to make the ultimate sacrifice for his fighter, that no one else would have touched. It just came with his heart. It was a move from the heart. Bundini was one of a kind. You gotta understand, Muhammad didn't have a big punch. Muhammad Ali, the second time around, didn't have the constant dynamics that he did originally. He came back with half of what he had," Foreman said.

After earning the distinction of becoming the first man to defeat Muhammad Ali as a professional, Joe Frazier was rushed to the hospital. Only Ali's detractors were given a chance to bask in the glory of Frazier's accomplishment. Frazier's face was grotesquely misshapen.

While Ali was also taken to Flower-Fifth Avenue Hospital as a precautionary visit, because of his swollen cheek, it was Frazier who suffered the far greater physical damage. With hypertension and a kidney infection, Frazier would remain in the hospital for weeks. Ali, who had far too much pride to be hospitalized by his rival, recovered from his injures from inside his suite at the New Yorker Hotel.

Because of the numerous injuries Frazier suffered, he did not fight again in 1971 and would defend his newly legitimized heavyweight title only twice in 1972, a pair of technical knockouts against journeymen Terry Daniels and Ron Stander. Frazier's handlers were undoubtedly concerned by what the fifteen-round war had done to their fighter. Ali, on the other hand, was quick to get back on the saddle.

After the fight, Bundini would serve as Ali's stand-in during the postfight press conference, proclaiming Frazier a true heavyweight champion but also vowing that Ali would return to reclaim the crown. There was plenty of reason to believe Ali's loss was connected to ring rust rather than his inability to match Frazier's dogged style. In fact, many in attendance felt Ali had won enough of the early rounds to pull it out despite the knockdown. Still, two judges scored the fight 9-6 in favor of Frazier while the third judge scored it 11-4 in favor of Frazier.

Despite Ali's crushing defeat, the Ali–Frazier bout would prove to be a lucrative occasion for Bundini.

"My father earned over $70,000 from the $5 million purse Ali and Frazier divided. It was the largest amount of money he would ever make, period. Back then, that was a lot of money," Drew recalled.

Upon receiving his share of the purse, Bundini showered his ex-wife Rhoda and his son with gifts. First, Bundini sent Drew and a few of his high school friends on a spring-break trip to Miami and the Bahamas. Next, Bundini hired contractors to transform Rhoda's Brighton Beach home. Bundini purchased new carpet and black-and-white ornamental title, and had the kitchen redone to include a bar, complete with western-style saloon doors. Bundini also purchased a new couch, chairs, a color television, and a giant waterbed, and had every room in the house repainted.

"In a platform behind the bar, he had an artist come in and paint *float like a butterfly and sting like a bee*, with an awesome bee and a beautiful butterfly," Drew remembered.

Securing income from both the Ali–Frazier fight and the *Shaft* film, Bundini, unbeknownst to his son, made one last attempt to woo back Rhoda. Less than a month after Ali's loss to Frazier, Bundini moved back in with his ex-wife and son. Buddy Drew's prayers were answered.

"April through June were remarkable months in our family. They seemed almost too good to be true," Drew told me, looking back on his mother and father's brief reconciliation. "It was wonderful to wake up each morning and know that my parents were in their bedroom and I was in mine. I took great pride in bringing my friends to the fancy place my father created."

Shortly after moving to Brighton Beach, Bundini proposed to Rhoda. His proposal was met with awkwardness and trepidation.

"I said no," Rhoda wrote to her son, years later. "I didn't want to put myself back in the same position. I simply wanted to let things be the way they were, and see if they worked out. I knew that he wanted things right—a home and the three of us together again—at least for your sake," Rhoda reflected.

When Bundini's proposal was rejected, he began seeing a younger woman named Sherrie. When Rhoda decided to move out, Sherrie moved in. When Rhoda returned to collect her belongings from what was her own house, a violent altercation ensued.

"Here it goes again, I thought. But this time I'm not going to get them back together," remembered Drew. "The memories of the past were rushing through my head as the argument increased in volatility. My father put his hands on my mom for the last time. I leaped from where I was, and I picked him up and put him on the ground as forcefully as possible. I looked him in the eyes and grabbed him by the collar and I said, 'If you ever touch my mother again, I will fucking kill you.' Suddenly, his body went limp. He looked me in the eyes and said, 'I'm proud of you son, you take care of your momma . . . you're a good boy.'"

The altercation would in effect end Bundini and Rhoda's twenty-year relationship.

At first, Rhoda moved back in with her parents. Drew, stubbornly clinging to the material possessions of his newly refurbished home, chose to stay with Bundini and Sherrie, making life hard on the new couple. The arrangement, like many of the fleeting *Brady Bunch* moments in the young boy's life, would not last.

Despite the many renovations, the home was still in Rhoda's name. In the end, Bundini and Sherrie left Brighton Beach, taking the waterbed and new furniture and leaving Drew III behind. The incident resulted in a bitter divide between Bundini and Rhoda.

When Rhoda returned home, she took a paintbrush to the butterfly and the bee.

■ ■ ■

Just a few months after being handed the first loss of his boxing career, Muhammad Ali would rebound by pulling off the biggest upset of his life, a unanimous decision victory in his U.S. Supreme Court case. Cleared of all charges, Ali was now a free man. The game plan was to fight early and often. Many boxing insiders felt that Ali had rushed back into the upper crust of the boxing world far too soon. Maintaining a busy fight schedule would allow Ali to sharpen his skills as he awaited the high-stakes rematch with Frazier.

On September 27, 1971, Ali officially began his comeback, facing off against fellow Kentuckian, and former boyhood sparring partner, Jimmy Ellis at the Houston Astrodome. Ali would, for the first and only time in his career, find himself on the opposite side of the ring from his longtime trainer Angelo Dundee, who because of his managerial ties to Ellis chose to side with the fighter who would earn him the higher percentage of the purse.

With Dundee in the opposite corner, the task of preparing Ali fell to Bundini, Wali "Youngblood" Muhammad, and Harry Wiley, the former chief second for Sugar Ray Robinson. Ali would easily win the fight via a twelfth-round technical knockout.

"If I remember correctly, the bout was just a way for Ali to help Jimmy [Ellis] get a payday," Jim Dundee suggested to me. "Ali loved Jimmy. He'd known him his entire life. Jimmy was a great fighter but he was really a blown-up light heavyweight. He didn't stand a chance against Ali. After the fight, Ali and Bundini came to Jimmy's locker room. Everyone was friendly. The fight didn't hurt Ali's relationship with my father or his friendship with Jimmy."

"When the Champ fought Jimmy, it was one of the hardest fights I have ever watched for the mere fact that it felt like family fighting family and I was rooting for my friend Jimmy because he was the lesser of the two," Drew remembered.

After the Ellis bout, Angelo Dundee returned to the Ali entourage. With the conflict of interest behind them, the team set a frenetic pace geared toward a Frazier rematch.

Before Smokin' Joe Frazier returned to the ring to defend his newly legitimized heavyweight championship, Muhammad Ali racked up four consecutive comeback wins. After Frazier's meaningless tune-up bout, Ali would continue his blistering pace with rematch wins over George Chuvalo (May 1, 1972) and Jerry Quarry (June 27, 1972), followed up by effortless wins over Alvin "Blue" Lewis (July 19, 1972), Floyd Patterson (September 20, 1972), also a rematch, and Bob Foster (November 21, 1972). To Frazier's two non-eventful post-Ali tune-up fights, little more than boxing exhibitions, Ali compiled nine straight victories over ranked opponents. Ali's busy schedule would, for Bundini, usher in a time of financial prosperity. Bundini was making more money than he ever imagined.

In early 1973, all that separated Joe Frazier from his rematch with Muhammad Ali was an undefeated mandatory challenger by the name of George Foreman, who despite being five years younger and heavier, was seen by boxing experts as a clear underdog. Foreman's biggest professional achievement, at this point in his career, was a technical knockout over tough Canadian George Chuvalo. In attendance for Foreman's first title shot was Drew Bundini Brown, who had made the journey to National Stadium in Kingston, Jamaica, to both scout Frazier and support his friend. By all accounts, Bundini was swept up in the emotion of Foreman's two-round, six-knockdown dismantling of Frazier, immortalized by Howard Cosell's iconic call: "Down goes Frazier." The possibility of Ali–Frazier II, with each thudding Foreman uppercut to Frazier's chin, began to dissipate. When the referee mercifully stopped the contest, the heavyweight division instantly became a three-man show.

Looking back on Bundini's postfight exuberance, Foreman said the following to me: "Bundini got in big trouble because I fought Joe Frazier and there Drew Bundini was, screaming and cheering, proud of me. Ali found out about it and suspended him because of that. Ali thought he shouldn't have been there, crying and everything. When I dethroned Frazier, Bundini looked at me and said, 'the real champ is back.'"

Bundini's support of Foreman would, for a brief period of time, cause discord between him and Ali. Bundini was told that his services were no longer needed. The path ahead, for both men, would be winding.

Ali's road to redemption would take an unexpected detour, thanks to a broken jaw and a new rival.

Ali and Bundini Brown go into their war cry, "float like a butterfly, sting like a bee," during a press conference at Ali's training camp in Chicopee, Massachusetts, on May 4, 1965. Ali trained there for his rematch against Sonny Liston, which was scheduled for May 25 at Boston Garden. *AP Photo*

Argentina's Oscar Bonavena, left, fakes a left to Bundini's head, as Ali looks on during the press conference after their fight at Madison Square Garden, December 7, 1970. Ali won the fight in the fifteenth round. *AP Photo*

Ali and Bundini training in Miami Beach for "The Fight of the Century" versus Joe Frazier at Madison Square Garden on March 8, 1971. *AP Photo*

Saturday, February 17, 1968: Drew Bundini Brown, Drew
Brown III, and Rhoda Palestine, at Drew's Bar Mitzvah at
Oceanview Jewish Center in Brighton Beach, New York.
Courtesy of Drew Brown III

Jack Palestine, Drew Brown
III, and Drew Bundini Brown
pose for traditional Bar
Mitzvah photos. *Courtesy of
Drew Brown III*

Drew Brown Sr., Drew Brown
III, and Jack Palestine.
Courtesy of Drew Brown III

Drew Brown III and his father celebrate his Bar Mitzvah.
Courtesy of Drew Brown III

Muhammad Ali victorious with Drew Bundini Brown after defeating Jerry Quarry by a third-round TKO at City Auditorium in Atlanta on October 26, 1970. *Sports Illustrated via Getty Images*

Drew Brown III celebrates with his father after
Muhammad Ali knocked out Quarry.
Courtesy of Drew Brown III

Muhammad Ali and Drew Bundin Brown during the postfight interview
following his victory over Quarry. *Paris Match via Getty Images*

Don King speaks at a press conference on October 22, 1974, in Kinshasa, Zaire, before "The Rumble in the Jungle." Muhammad Ali holds the head of his cornerman Drew Bundini Brown. The legendary fight between Ali and George Foreman took place on October 30, 1974. *AP Photo*

Actors Richard Roundtree and Drew Bundini Brown on the set of the movie *Shaft's Big Score!* in 1972. *Getty Images*

Muhammad Ali and Drew Bundini Brown at Ali's training camp in Deer Lake, Pennsylvania. *Courtesy of Drew Brown III*

8

The Road to Heaven

Sunrays peeking through thickets of trees, illuminating pollen suspended in the air, gave way to dancing shadows along the snaking contours of Sculps Hill Road. The unassuming pathway held no visible measure of significance. There were no billboards welcoming tourists, no indication that just around the bend of a curve was the historical site of "Fighter's Heaven," the legendary training compound where boxing's most celebrated gladiator readied himself for the final thirty-one fights of his storied career. If not for a few modest homes sprinkled along the way, one might mistakenly assume Sculps Hill Road leads to nowhere. Or maybe it does. Maybe that's the point.

On a warm June morning, I made the pilgrimage to Orwigsburg, Pennsylvania, located just outside the nearby town of Deer Lake, together with my father. Thirty-eight years had passed since Muhammad Ali's final morning jog down the curvy dirt road that led to town. Truth be told, I was unsure of what I hoped to gain from the visit—something metaphysical perhaps. I'd convinced myself that Bundini's spirit would be waiting for me at Cabin No. 7, lurking in the shadows of the Schuylkill County wilderness. The more romantic side of me anticipated the specter of Ali. No such incidents would occur during my visit. In the end, the journey itself proved to be the lesson. What I found was tranquility, the beautiful stillness of nature described in the stanzas of poet William Wordsworth. And, in the beauty of perfect silence, I found "Fighter's Heaven" just as did Ali and Bundini.

Shortly after Muhammad Ali's passing on June 3, 2016, Mike Madden, son of Hall of Fame NFL coach John Madden, bought the Pennsylvania property in hopes of restoring and preserving the site as a historical marker for future generations. Ali owned the secluded training camp from 1970 to 1997 and trained at the facilities from 1970 to 1981. As a young boy, Madden accompanied his father to several of Ali's training camps, experiences that made an indelible mark on his life.

"The right guy bought the property. Mike is doing this for all the right reasons," boxing photographer Jeff Julian assured me upon my arrival. "He isn't out to make a profit. Fans can tour the facilities free of charge. This is an attempt to preserve history."

Under Madden's supervision, Amish workers, using many of Julian's photographs as blueprints to guide their way, have meticulously reconstructed the compound. Julian frequently travels to local auctions with the aim of securing antique furnishings to help restore the insides of the log cabins to their original form. Thanks to the tireless efforts of Madden's team, particularly camp managers Mick Stefanek, Sam Matta, and the original Deer Lake headmaster Gene Kilroy, even the most hardened pragmatist cannot walk the grounds without feeling transported back in time. This is boxing Holy Land, even if the log cabins themselves have been rebuilt, restored, and refurnished.

At the height of his career in boxing, Jeff Julian worked as the personal photographer for welterweight champion Kermit Cintron. In Atlantic City, Julian shot a host of Arturo Gatti fights, most notably Gatti's pay-per-view showdown with Floyd Mayweather. I found Julian to be a kind and thoughtful tour guide, careful with his words and respectful of the historic ground on which we were walking. As Julian showed me and my father around the cabins, pointing out Bundini's living quarters and other landmark spots, it occurred to me that "Fighter's Heaven" held a special place in his heart. As the day progressed, I found myself more interested in Julian's story than in the newly restored relics.

In Ali's mess hall, sitting at the same table where the legendary champion frequently entertained local children with magic tricks, Julian recalled his first visit to Deer Lake.

"I was in my early twenties. I had just bought a second-hand camera, an old 35-mm camera. I'd bought it from an ad in the newspaper. I was living in Reading, Pennsylvania, at the time, about thirty miles away. I thought this might be an interesting place to shoot so I drove up here on a whim," Julian said.

When the young photographer arrived at "Fighter's Heaven," he found the compound packed with Ali fans, a carnival atmosphere of sorts.

"The gym was intensely hot. There were all different kinds of people here. Black. White. Construction workers. Hippies. Everything. I don't remember seeing any security. I just walked right into the gym, found a good spot, and began to shoot," Julian remembered.

Overcome by the thrill of photographing the iconic boxer, Julian rushed back to his home to develop the pictures in his makeshift darkroom.

Julian returned to "Fighter's Heaven" the following day with his girlfriend, now his wife, in hopes of hand-delivering copies of the photographs to Ali. When Julian approached Ali with the photos, catching him alone just outside the mess hall, the Champ invited the young couple into his cabin. There, Ali took his time looking through the photos, pausing briefly to say, "Hey, man, I look pretty in that one."

Julian admitted to me that, before venturing to Deer Lake, he had rooted for Joe Frazier in the first fight of the Ali–Frazier trilogy, largely because of Frazier's Pennsylvania connection.

"But, when I saw how he [Ali] treated people, it completely changed my perception. He was so soft spoken and kind. When I saw what he was really about, I became a fan. At the time, he was the most famous man in the world. He didn't have to be so kind and patient with us. He didn't have do that," Julian reflected.

The photos Julian shot during his first visit to Deer Lake were the ones now being used to reconstruct Ali's secluded boxing compound.

As the years passed, and the visits to "Fighter's Heaven" became more frequent, Julian befriended many of the key members of the entourage. Capturing images of Ali's daily training routine without also including Bundini in the photo proved next to impossible.

"It was clear to me that Bundini was the motivator," Julian said as he watched me study his photographs. The expression on my face must have been easy to read. I was struck by how frequently Bundini appeared somewhere in Julian's shots.

"Bundini was always there. Every single day. Calling out those famous lines. Shadowing Ali," Julian told me as I thumbed through his photos. "And Bundini was just as approachable as Ali," he added.

Reviewing Julian's portfolio, seated at Ali's mess-hall table, I began to feel as if I had taken in a day's training. Some photos featured Bundini in the background, his mouth agape as he shouted instructions to Ali. Others were far more intimate, images of Bundini securing Ali's mouthpiece, providing water as the Champ leaned over the top rope, beads of sweat coating his arms and shoulders. The image that struck me as the most compelling featured the two Deer Lake comrades standing chest to chest, both looking downward, as Bundini removed Ali's left hand wrap following a workout. The expression on Bundini's face, that of concern and concentration, was just as obvious as the six-inch scar he had received in the 1968 Bundini's World robbery.

"That picture reminds me of a father tying his son's shoes. It's a touching image. You can definitely see the love and friendship they share," Julian remarked.

This unique friendship was also apparent to sparring partners that frequented the Deer Lake training compound.

"I met Bundini during the Ali–Holmes training camp. Bundini wasn't scared to say nothing. You always knew he was there. At first, I thought he was grouchy. He would encourage us young boxers. You need to get your butt up there and be chopping wood! You need to get up and run with the Champ. Stuff like that. I was just a teenager, a young baby coming into a new world. I was thrilled to watch Bundini and Ali work their magic together," former WBC and WBA heavyweight champion Tim Witherspoon said to me.

While Ali's Deer Lake compound is clearly off the beaten path, labeling the training camp "secluded" feels like a misnomer. Andy Warhol, Michael Jackson, Kris Kristofferson, Cheryl Tiegs, and John Madden are just a few of the celebrities who visited Deer Lake to see Ali train. Aside from nighttime hours—visitors were sometimes greeted by a pair of German Shepherds, who doubled as a security detail—the doors of the facilities were never locked, except Ali's cabin. One did not need to be famous to be granted access to the most famous athlete on the planet. Boxing fans could come and go as they pleased. There were no gates or ropes or security guards. If you could find Deer Lake, you could find Muhammad Ali. In maintaining this unique training arrangement, Ali made himself accessible to boxing fans in a way that is unfathomable in today's smartphone-driven society. Every fan who made the pilgrimage to Deer Lake seemingly came away with a memorable Ali story.

One such example is that of Rick Kaletsky, author of *Ali and Me: Through the Ropes*. Kaletsky's book, folksy in its approach, captures Ali's career via the gaze of a lifelong fan. In talking with Kaletsky, it became apparent that visiting Deer Lake, if only once, could be a life-changing experience.

Similar to photographer Jeff Julian's story, Kaletsky's first visit to "Fighter's Heaven" was something of a spontaneous gesture. He'd driven all night from Connecticut hoping to capture a glimpse of Ali as he trained for his upcoming bout with George Foreman. Unsure if he would even be permitted access to the compound, Kaletsky made his pilgrimage on good faith. As fate would have it, the self-proclaimed "Ali-ologist" came away from the experience with more than a souvenir.

In my conversation with Kaletsky, his narrative enthusiasm, forty-five years later, remained intact.

"I approached Bundini first," Kaletsky told me. "Ali had just finished up a training session and he was being swarmed by people. Bundini was wearing this white T-shirt that said 'Float Like a Butterfly, Sting Like a Bee.' I walked over to him and asked where I could get one of those. He looked at me and said, 'Stay here.' Two words. He walked up the hill to his cabin and returned wearing a clean shirt. I believe it was red. He then tossed me the one he had been wearing. Drew Bundini Brown literally gave me the shirt off his back, with his DNA still on it."

Kaletsky's visit would mark the beginning of his impressive side career as a Muhammad Ali memorabilia collector. Over the years, he and Ali would eventually become friends, both inside and outside the confines of "Fighter's Heaven." Today, the basement of Kaletsky's Connecticut home doubles as perhaps the single most impressive noncommercial Muhammad Ali museum in the United States. One random visit and Kaletsky's life was forever transformed.

In the early 1970s, Drew Brown III found himself on the seller's side of Kaletsky's memorabilia narrative. During his high school years, when Ali was in training, Drew spent much of his summer months with his father in Pennsylvania, selling merchandise. Because Bundini was busy attending to the Champ's every beck and call, the fiduciary responsibility fell to the teenager.

"Daddy had T-shirts, buttons, and hats made up that said 'Float Like a Butterfly, Sting Like a Bee.' Ali allowed him to sell the merchandise to the fans who came up to camp to watch him train. It was the least he could do. Ali wasn't in control of his money. He felt bad, actually. I guess he was okay with my daddy being severely underpaid. When I wasn't in school, I was selling hats and T-shirts at Deer Lake. They had this little table outside of the gym and I would set up shop and sell merchandise to fans. I was a teenager—I didn't want to be doing that. I wanted to be out having fun," Drew laughed, outlining the obligations of his unique summer job.

For the born and bred New Yorker, life at Deer Lake could be described, at times, as "boring." When new sparring partners were brought in, however, there were always opportunities to make new acquaintances. Some of Drew's closest Deer Lake friendships were formed with the men brought in to take punches from Ali.

"You got to remember, Larry Holmes wasn't Larry Holmes back then. Larry was a sparring partner. Nobody was after his autograph. We were a little closer in age. We would hang out. We played basketball together. Larry and I became like friends at summer camp," Drew reflected.

In my conversations with Holmes, the former heavyweight champion framed his five years at "Fighter's Heaven" as analogous of going off to college. When Holmes first arrived, he was in awe of Ali and his team.

"It was just an honor to be around those guys. Ali. Bundini. Gene Kilroy. I was just honored to be there. It was a great pleasure," Holmes said.

Early into Holmes's time at Deer Lake, Bundini christened the young sparring partner with a nickname, a moniker used only by members of the entourage.

"Bundini gave me the name 'Big Jack,' because of Jack Johnson. He said I had small legs and big arms like Jack Johnson. He'd rhyme—'Holmes hit 'em and they don't hit back, that's why I call him *Big Jack*,'" Holmes reflected, doing his best Bundini impersonation, placing a noticeable emphasis on the end of the rhyme.

Holmes described Bundini's daily routine in the gym in a similar fashion as photographer Jeff Julian had. "Bundini was always in the corner, motivating Ali. He and Youngblood were right there all the time. They'd wipe Ali down. Give him a drink of water. Whatever he needed. And, if you needed anything, they would get it. But Bundini was Ali's right-hand man. He was always there for Ali," Holmes recalled.

Despite Bundini's amiable personality and overall generosity, there was no mistaking the fact that his job was to serve the Champ. During sparring sessions, when Ali would score a telling blow against Holmes, he would shout "Cook! Cook, Champ! Cook!" Holmes recalled. When the bell rang, the metaphorical switch flipped. Motivational slogans poured out of Bundini like a verbal geyser.

While the isolation of Ali's training compound fostered a sense of family and comradery, cabin fever occasionally set in.

"At first, my father hated it," Jim Dundee confided to me. "It was rustic. My father wasn't a rustic type of guy. He was shocked that Muhammad stuck with it. He couldn't believe how much Muhammad liked it up there."

Larry Holmes, like Angelo Dundee, was not a fan of the bucolic isolation. Holmes did not stay in the cabin designated for sparring partners, instead opting to spend his nights in a nearby Deer Lake hotel. When the day's training was over, Holmes would, on occasion, venture off into town with Bundini.

"I had dinner with Bundini numerous times. We would go down to this little club they had. It was just Bundini Brown, checking out the girls. Making everybody laugh. He was a great guy. He was a lot of fun to be around," Holmes told me.

"Outside of boxing, there was nothing to do. After a week or so, some of us got stir crazy. It was in the middle of freaking nowhere," Drew Brown III recalled, echoing Holmes's assessment.

It goes without saying, the rugged conditions were not for everyone. In touring the newly restored facilities, reflecting on how difficult the compound must have been to find before the days of GPS, I tried to imagine the silent campgrounds alive with excitement, a mix of celebrities, fight fans, and boxing royalty.

"How did Ali find this property in the first place?" I asked photographer Jeff Julian, disappointed in myself for not having thought of the question sooner.

Like so much of Ali's career, "Fighter's Heaven," in its original incarnation, was orchestrated by Gene Kilroy, who was a native of Mahanoy City in Schuylkill County and first brought the secluded Pennsylvanian property to Ali's attention. When the Champ returned from exile, for better or for worse, he had outgrown the 5th Street Gym in Miami Beach. The goal was to seek refuge from the distractions of Ali's roller-coaster life. Vowing to take his preparations more seriously than ever before, seclusion, a term that holds a different meaning for a man of Ali's stature, was key to the plan for redemption.

After Ali purchased the Pennsylvanian land in 1972, an eighteen-building training compound was erected, mostly composed of log cabins. The original blueprint included cabins for visitors and sparring partners, a boxing gym, a small mess hall, a mosque, an office space for Kilroy, and a family house. The compound also included a five-stall barn for horses. Both Matthew Saad Muhammad and James "Quick" Tillis tell stories of riding horses with Ali at "Fighter's Heaven." For fighters of a certain disposition, the bucolic setting was the perfect place to ready one's mind for battle. Heavyweight sluggers Tim Witherspoon and Earnie Shavers, for example, speak of their time training at the compound with great affection.

"It was so beautiful up there," former heavyweight contender Earnie Shavers said to me. "Peaceful. You could take long walks and get your mind set on what you were doing."

"Ali would open the camp up to me, when I had a fight, free of charge," Shavers added. Ali would also open the facilities to Bundini, who on a few occasions hosted the Brown family reunion at the Deer Lake campground.

"Daddy loved it," Drew recalled. "He was excited to show it off to all of his family back in Sanford. My family had some wonderful times there. Daddy's spirit was at peace there. Those were some of the happiest times of his life, being by Ali's side, working with Angelo and Uncle Youngblood and the rest of the team."

Life at Deer Lake was anything but fancy. A large bell rang every day at four-thirty in the morning. Fighters were expected to be dressed and down at the main facilities by five o'clock for the daily morning run. Ali would jog in dirty work boots. The bell would ring again at eight o'clock for breakfast and again at five for dinner. Ali's one-room cabin was, in and of itself, an artifact. The wood used to construct the cabin came from a ninety-five-year-old Schuylkill County railroad bridge.

The inside of the cabin was furnished with a 200-year-old rope bed and a large table and bench constructed from an 850-pound oak tree. Under the light of an antique coal lamp, Ali would sit at the table each night reading the Quran. The cabin was heated by an old coal-fired stove, and water came from a well pump. The cabin's only other furnishings were a pair of wooden rocking chairs.

"Just like the days of Jack Johnson," Ali bragged to talk show host Dick Cavett when he came to tour the facilities in 1974.

The rugged conditions in Deer Lake clearly brought out something special in Ali, just as did the steady influx of fans from whom Ali drew inspiration and energy.

"Make no mistake about it, Ali did not like being alone," Jim Dundee said to me, speaking to Ali's willingness to allow fans to enter his secluded getaway.

"Deer Lake provided Ali with the perfect balance of seclusion and chaos," Dundee added.

In examining the stories of the fans, photographers, and celebrities who made their way to Deer Lake during the eleven years "Fighter's Heaven" was operational, we move closer to better understanding the atmosphere in which Ali and Bundini readied themselves for the second act of his legendary career. In telling their stories, we can also learn a thing or two about the Champ, the various ways in which a change in scenery accommodated the needs of a changing fighter. The Deer Lake years thus hold immense importance in telling the life story of Drew Bundini Brown. If Bundini was indeed the spark to Ali's inner motivational flame, "Fighter's Heaven" can be seen as the site where the fire burned. When Ali arrived in Deer Lake, he no longer possessed the blinding speed and fast-twitch reflexes he once used to whitewash his opponents. If Ali was going to become the second man in heavyweight boxing history to reclaim the world championship, he would need to harness untapped mental strength and inner toughness. "Fighter's Heaven," tough by design, is the location where Muhammad Ali cultivated those skills. Sculps Hill Road, it occurred to me during my brief visit, is a fitting representation of the Odysseus journey that was Muhammad Ali's winding and bumpy path to reclaiming the title.

■   ■   ■

George Foreman's two-round destruction of Joe Frazier reconfigured the landscape of the heavyweight division. With Frazier out of the picture, an Ali–Foreman showdown now appeared to be a foregone conclusion. All that stood in the way of Ali's third crack at the heavyweight championship was a hard-punching contender with a bodybuilder's physique and awkward style, a twenty-eight-year-old fighter from Jacksonville, Illinois, by the name of Ken Norton.

With a record of twenty-nine wins and one loss—that loss coming via a technical knockout to a little-known heavyweight journeyman named Jose Roman—Ken Norton was seen by boxing experts as a sizable underdog. For most pundits, Norton was nothing more than a tune-up fight for what appeared to be an inevitable showdown with George Foreman. The California-based heavyweight had fought mostly in the confines of his adopted home of San Diego, to little fanfare or national acclaim. Compared to Ali's style, which at times resembled ballet more than boxing, Norton's herky-jerky technique and crab-like defense was less than aesthetically pleasing. Ali glided around the ring like an ice-skater preparing for a double axel, whereas Norton dragged his right leg as if he were an injured dog returning to an alley fight. The danger of the Norton fight, according to most experts, lay not so much in Norton's talent but in Ali's ability to motivate himself for the fight. Ali, even at this point in his career, had a reputation for fighting down to the competition, as was the case in his bouts with Jimmy Young and Henry Cooper.

During preparations for the Ken Norton fight, Ali's Deer Lake training camp would be minus one key member, a move that would temporarily disrupt the hierarchy of the entourage. Still upset by Bundini's public display of affection for the newly crowned heavyweight champion, Herbert Muhammad stepped in.

"Using the so-called Foreman betrayal to his advantage, Herbert Muhammad, once again, manipulated Ali. Daddy wasn't invited to camp," Drew Brown III told me.

"It killed my father inside. I watched my daddy sit by the phone, staring at it as if staring would make it ring. It hurt me to see them do him like that. Then, a few days before the fight, they called and said, 'Okay, you can come back to work now,'" Drew remembered, the emotion in his voice signaling his father's pain.

For the first Norton fight, scheduled for March 31, 1973, at the Sports Arena in San Diego, Bundini was flown from New York to California only three days before the bout. While Ali likely viewed the suspension as nothing more than a time out, Bundini, guided by his own spiritual sensibilities, unquestionably viewed the punishment as a bad omen.

In George Plimpton's *Shadow Box*, Bundini reflects on the Norton fight, his assessment of what took place framed somewhat superstitiously: "[Ali] wasn't wearing my robe for the fight when Ken Norton opened up and busted his jaw," Bundini told Plimpton.

The robe tradition Bundini is referring to comes from a long-standing prefight ritual that paired Bundini up with members of the Everlast company to create custom designs for Ali's trunks, shoes, and ring robes. Unbeknownst to many boxing fans, Bundini was the fashion designer behind many of Ali's famous ring ensembles.

"My father didn't get paid for any of that. He didn't ask Everlast for money. He didn't do it for the money—he did it for the show," Drew told me.

When Ali entered the ring to face Norton, wearing garments Bundini had no hand in crafting, Bundini feared the worst. The robe that Ali did wear to the ring, a sparkling white garment with black trim, read "The People's Choice" on the back. The trunks and robe had been given to Ali by none other than Elvis Presley. In revisiting footage of the Ali–Norton fight, I was struck by Ali's ring walk. Angelo Dundee, Youngblood, and other members of the Ali team can be seen wearing matching jackets, in line with the Elvis motif. Bundini, because he was brought in at the last minute, wears a purple cornerman jacket, a garment reused from a previous fight.

"My father was hurt and wanted to show that he wasn't in line with what they did to him. He wore his own bow tie, his own jacket. He didn't want them to believe that he felt like part of the team," Drew argued.

Regardless of lucky robes, unfair suspensions, or bad karma, the impact of Bundini's absence from Ali's Deer Lake training camp is impossible to quantify. What we do know, in hindsight, is that Ali–Norton would, in the end, prove to be a painful endeavor for the former champion.

In Ali's 1975 biography, Richard Durham elects to open the book with a scene that harkens readers back to the end of the second round of Ali's first fight with Norton, a key moment in the careers of both fighters. Hit by a crushing left hook, followed by a powerful overhand right to the jaw, a shot that would change Norton's place in boxing history, Ali returns to his corner in immense pain.

In Durham's account of the events, Ali, with a mouthful of blood, asks Bundini "how you can tell when your jaw is broke." Bundini demonstrates the "click" that signifies when an injured jaw is opened and shut. Ali mimics Bundini's demonstration and hears the ominous clicking sound, instantly wincing from a sharp pain radiating down his face. Blood trickles down the back of Ali's throat and out of the corners of his lips as he struggles to breathe.

"What should I do?" Ali asks.

Before action resumes in the third round, Bundini whispers into Ali's ear, uttering the famous phrase that serves as the title of Durham's opening chapter—"Shorty is watching you."

Bundini's instructions to Ali, amid the chaos of discovering the severity of the injury, provide a window into Bundini's ability to tap into Ali's inner sensibilities.

"Shorty is in the living room, watching. Shorty is sitting down, crossing His legs and watching you. Just remember that. Shorty is watching you," Bundini instructs.

When the fight continues, Ali circles the ring, desperately attempting to evade another devastating hook to his broken jaw.

Bundini can be heard screaming from ringside, "Shorty's watching! In the living room! On TV in the living room! He's watching!"

Ali's heroic performance, even in a losing effort, would only serve to enhance the Champ's legacy. Battling through the pain, Ali desperately attempted to rally against the heavy-handed Norton.

According to fight doctor Ferdie Pacheco, who spoke often about the fight, each member of the Ali team took turns trying to convince the former champion to throw in the towel.

"I can get him this round," Ali consistently responded.

In a handful of the middle rounds, Ali was able to land effective lead right hands, sometimes stealing the show in the closing moments. By the championship rounds, however, Norton clearly understood that he was in the ring with an injured man.

Because Ali offered very little offense in the final two rounds, some have even speculated that Ali's injury did not happen until late in the fight. In the corner between rounds eleven and twelve, Ali can be seen awkwardly holding his mouth open, gasping for air, his face a contorted mask of discomfort. With Ali's long arms stretched along the ring ropes, Youngblood and Bundini massaged his chest and arms as if they were paramedics with defibrillators, attempting to shock the former champion back to life.

In the closing minutes of the bout, Norton charged ahead, swinging wildly, showing little concern for any return fire that Ali was planning to offer. Norton was gunning for the knockout and Ali was battling for survival. In battling ten rounds with a broken jaw, enduring unspeakable punishment at the hands of the powerful-punching Norton, Ali would capture nothing more than a moral victory. The little-known Ken Norton would win a split decision on the scorecards. At the time, the loss was viewed as a monumental setback to Ali's comeback journey.

According to Drew, Bundini knew something was wrong with Ali when he arrived in California three days before the bout.

"Daddy told me that he knew the Champ was in trouble before that fight. For the first time in their years together, my father could not find the right buttons to press in order to motivate the Champ. He knew something wasn't right," Drew insisted.

Taking nothing away from Norton, who would later prove to be a Hall of Fame boxer in his own right, one could argue Ali was in no physical condition to compete at an elite level. He had clearly overlooked the unheralded slugger. Before the fight, the bookmakers had made Norton a five-to-one underdog; the promoters struggled to frame the fight as a tussle between a draft dodger and an ex-marine. Norton, unwilling to criticize Ali's antiwar stance, did little to fuel the promotion. Perhaps the most telling evidence of Ali's lackluster preparation came at the scales. Ali weighed in at a flabby 221 pounds, one of the heaviest weights of his career.

After the upset loss, Ali was transported to Clairemont General Hospital for surgery on his broken jaw. Following surgery, Ali's jaw would be wired shut for three months. The first to arrive at the hospital each morning, Bundini relayed the mass media's reaction to the stunning upset to Ali.

"Howard Cosell is predicting you're finished. He's saying that three-and-a-half-years' exile took too much out of you. The sucker is taking you cheap. Only yesterday, he was saying how great you were," Bundini told Ali.

It is Bundini who worked to lift Ali's spirits, proclaiming that the loss to Norton would only make his comeback that much greater.

"I'll train harder than ever now," Ali said to Bundini, his jaw wired shut.

By all estimations, Muhammad Ali followed up on his postfight promise. When he returned to Deer Lake, Pennsylvania, the compound still under construction, he found new levels of determination. Ali was relentless in his preparations for the second Norton fight.

At the prefight weigh-in for Ali–Norton II, Angelo Dundee would declare his fighter to be in the best shape of his life. Ali would step on the scales at a trim 212 pounds, clearly a different physical specimen. When the opening bell sounded, less than six months after the original bout, an electric atmosphere filled the Forum in Inglewood, California.

"You the boss with the hot sauce! Be a pitcher, not a catcher!" Bundini, wearing his lucky bow tie, screamed from ringside.

Minutes into the fight, it would be clear that both Ali and Bundini were back in full form.

In the opening round, Ali fought brilliantly, dancing around the ring, moving in and out of danger, stinging Norton with sharp jabs and whipping uppercuts. After the first round was complete, referee Dick Young made his way to Ali's corner, warning Bundini that he would be removed from ringside if he did not pipe down, an action noted by the color commentators during the broadcast. Ali, clearly attempting to send a message to Norton, refused to sit on the stool between rounds, instead opting to bounce on his toes, breaking into his famous Ali shuffle to the delight of his fans. Ali would repeat the performance after the second and third rounds. "This is the old Muhammad Ali!" the play-by-play analysts shouted with excitement.

"An action took place after the first round that has never happened before in boxing history," Drew Brown III told me. "The referee came to my father and told him to keep the volume down or he would be removed from the corner. They were in the Los Angeles Forum, where the Lakers played, with a full-capacity crowd and you could only hear my daddy. Imagine how I felt in the kitchen when I was seven years old!'"

Bundini was back on his A game as well. In some respects, Bundini's ringside antics stole the show. As the fight progressed, the ABC television production crew chose to include a small window in the bottom left corner of the screen, providing fans the opportunity to watch Bundini watch the fight. Shadowboxing, agonizing, feinting, and dodging, Bundini behaved as if he were a man spiritually connected to his pupil.

In an interview with *Sports Illustrated*, Bundini later reflected on the experience: "I give the champ all my strength. He throw a punch, I throw a punch. He get hit, it hurt me. I can't explain it, but sometimes I know what he's gonna do before he even knows it. Some of my duties with the champ, anybody could do—use the watch, carry stuff, all like that. Other things couldn't nobody else do because I don't even know how I do them myself," Bundini stated.

In the fourth round, Norton finally entered the fight, landing several crushing blows to Ali's jaw, resulting in a collective gasp from Ali's team.

The expression on Bundini's face, there for all the world to see, told the story. Nobody in the entourage could be sure how his jaw would hold up to Norton's onslaught. Because of his injury, Ali had gone four months without sparring. As Ali staggered against the ropes, attempting to escape Norton's attack, the stakes couldn't have been higher.

As the fight progressed, Ali stayed true to his promise to dance. At times, Ali used his superior footwork to keep Norton off balance. By the sixth round, Norton's sweeping hooks to the body and head began to consistently find their targets. Because of Ali's much improved jab, Norton's right eye began to swell shut. Norton's style continued to give Ali problems. Just when it appeared that Ali was about to pull away with the fight, Norton would land a thudding shot that would stagger the former champion. George Foreman, who was ringside to scout his two most worthy challengers, left the arena midway through the fight, perhaps signaling to the television audience that neither man was a true threat to his crown. Norton's aggression neutralized many of Ali's physical gifts. The fight, going into the twelfth and final round, was clearly up for grabs.

For a second straight fight, Muhammad Ali and Ken Norton battled to a split decision. This time around, Ali would find himself on the right side of the verdict. One judge would score the fight 6-5 in favor of Ali, the other would give the same score to Norton. Referee Dick Young, the deciding vote, scored the fight 7-5 in favor of Ali. After the decision was announced, there would be no gloating. Ali would not even crack a smile in the postfight interview.

"I'm more tired than usual because of my age," Ali commented.[1]

"I'm in shape because I'm building a training camp," Ali added, thanking Louie, the man who transported the boulders to his compound via crane.

The boulders that Ali was referring to are perhaps the most iconic images from "Fighter's Heaven," a collection of large rocks famously inscribed with the names of team members, legendary champions, and vanquished Ali opponents, an idea inspired by Ali's lone training camp at Archie Moore's "Salt Mine" compound in California. Cassius Clay Sr., a painter by trade, served as the original boulder artist. Legendary heavyweights Jack Johnson, Jack Dempsey, and Rocky Marciano each have their own boulders, as do Ali rivals Sonny Liston, Floyd Patterson, Jerry Quarry, and Joe Frazier. Today, the boulders remain just as they were in the early 1970s, monuments to Ali's many triumphs and inspirations.

Four months shy of his thirty-second birthday, Muhammad Ali's victory over Norton did little to detract critics. The razor-thin victory merely kept Ali alive as a viable contender. Despite the loss, it would be Ken Norton who would be offered the title shot against George Foreman. The result of Foreman–Norton would aid the argument that Ali was no longer the man he used to be. Ringside for the fight, March 26, 1974, in Caracas, Venezuela, Ali would call the action with Hall of Fame boxing analyst "Colonel" Bob Sheridan.

After the first round, Sheridan turned to Ali in an attempt to get his assessment of the action. Ali was confident that his man, Ken Norton, was in control of the fight.

"Just like I thought it would be. Kenny Norton boxing. George Foreman not throwing all of those hard punches and not punching him out like he did Joe Frazier. Because Kenny Norton is a great fighter, any man that goes twenty-four rounds with me is gotta be great and ain't no George Foreman, who is still a good amateur, gonna destroy Ken Norton because I couldn't do it. I'm proud of what Norton did because it shows the world Norton is a great fighter," Ali commented. In the following round, George Foreman would plant Norton onto the canvas on three separate occasions, decimating the man who had just battled twenty-four life-or-death rounds with The Greatest of All Time.

■　■　■

While Bundini was away in the secluded confines of Muhammad Ali's Deer Lake training camp, preparing the former champion for what seemed to be an impossible task of regaining the heavyweight championship of the world, his son was, at the same time, embarking on his own unlikely journey, plotting his path to becoming the first member of the Brown family to attend college.

Basketball, in Buddy Drew's young mind, was his only ticket to turning his father's collegiate dreams into a reality. Facing the prospect of entering the so-called real world, the teenager began dedicating all of his free time to sharpening his skills on the court.

"It happened almost overnight. It was like Drew grew six inches over the summer," Rick "Cubby" Katz, Drew's high school best friend, recalled. "And, all of a sudden, he was the best player on our team."

During his senior year at Abraham Lincoln High School in Brooklyn, Drew Brown III, now standing six feet five, emerged from off-season workouts bigger, stronger, and more athletic than his peers. While Drew had spent much of his early high school days languishing on the bench, his final year of high school was filled with breakout performances. The teenager's size and athleticism, along with his ability to jump, rebound, and block shots, began to draw the attention of college scouts.

During the winter months of 1971 and 1972, Drew, with assistance from his mother Rhoda, wrote to numerous college coaches, relaying his abilities and accomplishments. Looking back on his desperate attempt to make up for lost time, Drew said the following: "I promoted myself the way my daddy promoted Ali, and I got some offers. Several schools extended partial scholarships or grants, and in New York, both Yeshiva University and Hunter College wanted me for a full ride. But my number-one criterion was to go as far from the Big Apple as possible. No matter what our family faced over the years, I was always expected to go to college. I didn't really have a choice. My father repeatedly said, 'I'm giving you two choices in life, son: college or death . . . I picked college.'"

Drew's prayers would be answered in the form of a return letter from head coach Lue Henson, offering the Brighton Beach youngster an opportunity to walk on at New Mexico State University in Las Cruces, New Mexico. Soon thereafter, Drew applied to NMSU and was accepted to the university.

While the family was initially elated over the news, the economic reality quickly set in. Neither Rhoda nor her parents had the money to pay for college. With nowhere else to turn, Drew asked his father for assistance. Bundini, equally joyful, promised to secure the funds. His boy was going to be an Aggie, a college basketball star, a real-life college graduate.

With only $200 in his pocket, Drew Brown III arrived in New Mexico, amid an unfamiliar backdrop of cacti and sandstorms, instantly feeling the doubt and indecision that comes with being a first-generation college student. Continually receiving letters and phone calls from the university business office, Drew had good reason to feel like an academic imposter. Even after moving into his dorm in August of 1972, the financial side of Drew's college dreams had yet to be settled. Drew, for reasons still unbeknownst to him, was allowed to register, move into his dormitory, and even attend classes without making any tuition payment whatsoever. Two weeks into the semester, however, Drew was given a stern ultimatum by the university: Pay up or leave campus.

"Bundini came to me and said he needed more money for his son's college tuition," Gene Kilroy recalled to me. "I told Ali about it but I was leery because I had heard his son had a basketball scholarship. We'd already given him money. But Ali said 'give Bundini the money.'"

In our conversations, Drew supported Kilroy's version of the events.

"Daddy had to go to Ali a second time, admit that he had squandered the first funds. Gene Kilroy intervened once again and told the Champ that a son shouldn't suffer because of what his father does. To Ali's credit, he paid twice for my first freshman semester," Drew insisted.

Even after the financial obligations of Drew's 1972/1973 academic year at New Mexico State University had been worked out, the social and academic pressures continued to loom large. The eighteen-year-old New Yorker had never been to a major university before arriving on campus. At the time, NMSU was composed of mostly white students. These students, more often than not, came from agricultural backgrounds.

As is the case for many first-generation college students, Drew's first year can be described as a continual search for a sense of community. Before classes began, Drew tried out for New Mexico State's struggling football team, despite having never played organized football. Much to his surprise, he made the spring team and eventually found his way onto the field for actual game action. At six feet five and 205 pounds, Drew had size and athleticism, so the coaching staff took him on with cautious optimism, trying him out first at linebacker and then tight end. While joining the football team might have been good for Drew's social life—it was the lone space where he found comradery with other Black students—the endeavor did little for his academic performance.

"Good athletes got away with not going to class. I hung out with the jocks. I did as they did. I skipped class. At the time, Blacks were a small minority within the NMSU student body and since most of us were athletes, we all hung together," Drew recalled.

After grades were released for the fall semester, the free-spirited freshman found himself on academic probation.

On the basketball court, just as was the case in the classroom, Drew Brown III felt like a fish out of water. He was overwhelmed by the talent and size of the NMSU basketball players. From 1950 to 1970, the Aggies had made nine appearances in the NCAA tournament. At NMSU, Drew was no longer one of the *big guys* on the team. He was average, in both height and talent.

"After two semesters of skipping classes and hanging out with the jocks, my grade point average was a 1.6. 'You won't be able to come back next year, that's the rule,' they told me," Drew remembered.

Drew spent much of the following summer back in Deer Lake selling hats and T-shirts to Ali fans, searching for his own source of strength.

"I was too proud to tell my family or friends that I had flunked out. Only Momma and I knew, and as usual, she was sympathetic but determined that I go back to school," Drew told me.

In the fall of 1973, Drew Brown III enrolled in Kingsborough Community College in Brooklyn, New York, neglecting to mention his first-year performance at New Mexico State University to KCC admissions officers. Within the familiar confines of his Brighton Beach home, Drew commuted to school each day by bus. The small-school atmosphere better suited the teenager in every way. Vowing to correct his lackluster efforts at NMSU, Drew made it a point to sit in the front row of every class; he never again skipped a single class session. The small class sizes and amiable professors, as research often shows for first-generation college students, also better suited his academic needs. As Drew began to succeed on tests and quizzes, his dream began to feel more like a reality. KCC could be a bridge to something substantial, Drew believed.

As Drew adjusted to his newly refocused approach to college life, he and his father began to mend the hurt caused by Bundini's mishandling of his son's NMSU tuition funds. When Bundini wasn't at Deer Lake working with Ali, he continued to offer his services to heavyweight Jeff "Candy Slim" Merritt, a New York–based slugger who Bundini worked with during Ali's exile.

"When my father was in New York, the best way for me to spend time with him was to show up for Merritt's workouts," Drew said. "Working alongside my father helped both of us heal some wounds from the previous year."

Early into Drew's first semester at KCC, the second-year freshman was faced with a unique opportunity. On Monday, September 10, 1973, the exact same night Ali was set to face Norton in their rematch, Jeff Merritt, with a professional record of 19-1, was scheduled to fight former heavyweight champion Ernie Terrell at Madison Square Garden. The undercard to Terrell–Merritt featured Drew's summer camp buddy, Larry Holmes, who was set to compete in his fifth professional fight. Merritt, boxing historians will likely remember, was the first fighter signed to Don King Promotions.

"Daddy had to be in California . . . because Ali had his rematch with Norton at the Forum in Inglewood so it was agreed that Daddy would train [Merritt] for the fight and I would take his place in Jeff's corner at MSG," Drew told me.

While Bundini was on the other side of the country, tending to Ali as he prepared to test his jaw against Norton a second time, his son, entering his second week of classes at KCC, was in the dressing room at Madison Square Garden, holding the mitts for Candy Slim.

"During our time in the gym, Jeff and I became true friends. I liked him, appreciated his kindness. It was just an added bonus that I would get to see my friend Larry fight as well," Drew said, reflecting on his one and only night serving as a chief second.

The first-time cornerman would not even need to bother with the stool. Merritt would knock out the aging Terrell in the first round of the fight, scoring one of the biggest victories of his young career. After Merritt's headlining victory, he and his team took to Harlem in search of celebration.

"Late in the evening, we ended up at a private affair, and within minutes Jeff was nowhere to be found," Drew recalled. "I started checking the apartment, room by room, until I located Jeff in the bathroom. There, sitting on the floor, his arm outstretched over the toilet, Jeff was shooting up heroin."

Shocked by what he had seen, conflicted as to whether he should report Merritt's behavior to his father, Drew waited a few days before making his decision.

"He was hooked on drugs but he was my friend. But I had a responsibility to tell my father. So, when Daddy made it back to New York after Ali defeated Norton, I told him what happened and he resigned from Jeff's staff," Drew told me.

The end of Jeff Merritt's boxing career, as told in the opening to Jack Newfield's Don King exposé, *The Life and Times of Don King: The Shame of Boxing*, would not be a pretty picture. In the coming years, Merritt would become homeless, largely because of his drug addiction. Something about the postfight incident, despite being no real fault of his own, snapped Drew Brown III back to reality. Attempting to walk in his father's shoes would only hurt his feet. It was time to become his own man, Drew believed.

At KCC, Drew's second attempt at becoming a walk-on basketball player proved much more fruitful than his first attempt. While the setting was far less glamorous than was the case in Las Cruces, New Mexico—KCC played in a small air dome called "The Bubble"—Drew would thrive on the basketball court, earning him the title of Captain.

By the end of Drew Brown III's lone year at KCC, he had proved to himself that he had what it took to succeed at the college level. He ended the year with a 3.2 grade point average. In the school newspaper, Coach Lopez wrote the following: "For Drew Brown this is just the beginning of something big. This 19-year-old sophomore out of New Mexico State is out to make a name for himself. When January came around, Drew became eligible. With his 6'5" muscular body, he paced the Kingsborough Basketball Lions to a convincing 12-11 season after a horrendous first half of basketball. Among Drew's best games was a 35-point performance against a Queens team, which also included 13 rebounds and five blocked shots. Between his basketball skills and his knowledge, Drew is destined to become a great man."[2]

With Coach Lopez's support, Drew was able to field offers from larger schools. The most attractive opportunity came from Southern University in New Orleans, a full athletic scholarship from head coach Joe N. Hornbeak. This would prove to be the most important opportunity of Drew's life, one that would, in many ways, change the trajectory of his family history.

"At the time, I could imagine nothing better than going to a university in the Big Easy," Drew told me. "What's more, the SUNO scholarship meant that my education would survive whatever happened in my father's boxing career."

The road to securing a college degree was, for Drew Brown III, anything but straight. It was a winding path, rife with setbacks and moments of humility.

"You can't have the smiles without the miles," Bundini would often tell Ali, as he woke the Champ for roadwork each morning. "Nothing good comes easy."

9

God's
Act

As I sat in Drew Brown III's kitchen outside Atlanta, looking through a box of memorabilia, the first item that caught my attention was a leather-bound Bible, inscribed with gold lettering at the bottom left-hand corner. I lifted the Bible out of the cardboard box and read the inscription: *To Drew Timothy Brown III.* Surprised to find a Christian Bible among Drew's father's keepsakes, I eagerly thumbed through the pages. The inside cover contained a personalized message from none other than Granville Oral Roberts, the charismatic and controversial American televangelist.

"You've got to be kidding me," I chuckled.

The thought of Drew Bundini Brown hanging out with Oral Roberts, a traveling faith healer who founded his own university in Tulsa, Oklahoma, was more than enough to make me smile.

Realizing what I had found, Drew Brown III returned to the kitchen table with our morning coffees. The smirk on his face quickly disappeared.

"I want you to know, my father didn't believe in religions. He didn't do Bibles. That was just a nice gift from Mr. Roberts. But my father used to pray. We used to pray every night to Shorty," Drew said to me, the tone of his voice sharply turning.

Like his famous father, Drew Brown III is a natural storyteller. His vocal prowess is marked by sudden changes in pitch, tone, and rate, and carefully measured pacing. Just when you think the story is complete, Drew continues.

"Daddy had one prayer. One prayer that he knew," Drew added, just before taking his first sip of coffee.

It was six o'clock in the morning, our final day of scavenging before I returned to New York. Forty-eight hours into my time in Atlanta and I'd already learned to be patient with the narrative arc of Drew's stories. They would wander, circle back, stray for brief interludes, and somehow find their way home for a powerful crescendo. Analyzing the narrative structure of Drew's stories quickly became something of a game for me. I would guess how his stories would end and be wrong every single time.

"When I was a little boy I called it the 'King Kong' prayer," Drew continued. My face no doubt showed my confusion.

"Our father who art in Heaven, hallowed be thy name. Thy kingdom come. Thy will be done," Drew recited, his eyes partially closed, sunlight spilling through the morning curtains. "When I was little, I thought Daddy said 'King Kong,'" Drew added, his warm smile returning.

When Drew Brown III was a young boy, his father would, on occasion, place a chair at his bedside, keeping him up into the early morning hours, espousing his views on God, spinning his philosophies on life. Shorty, for Bundini, was a God of his own understanding. It was important to Bundini, as a father, to pass this knowledge on to his son, holding nothing back. While the young boy was clearly in awe of his father's spiritual discourse, there were, of course, nights when he would much rather sleep than philosophize.

"My father loved going to churches," Drew told me. "Daddy took me to churches, mosques, synagogues, and little chapels. We would slip in, just the two of us, find a pew or whatever near the back, and pray, no matter what type of service was actually being held."

Drew's favorite church story, one that instantly sprang up when he laid eyes on the gift from Oral Roberts, begins on a brisk Sunday in Uptown Manhattan.

Bundini taps his son on the shoulder and directs him into a church service that is already in progress. Drew is ten or eleven years old at the time. Bundini, according to his son, enjoyed attending houses of worship but would only do so when the feeling struck him. These visits were always spontaneous. On this particular Sunday, Bundini sat quietly, taking in the music, the people, and the message. When the service was complete, the pastor made his way to the back of the church to greet the father and son.

"Thank you for coming," the pastor warmly said to Bundini, his hand extended.

"Thank you, sir," Bundini quickly responded.

"We would love for you to join us," the pastor continued, his eyes now glancing down at young Drew.

"We did join you," Bundini puzzled.

"Oh, I'm sorry. I mean join our church. Become a member," the pastor continued.

"That's okay. We already belong," Bundini answered, his eyes sharp and steady.

The story ends with the boy and his father exiting the church without saying another word. As Drew relived the story, I studied the curves of his face, the energy in his eyes. I could sense how much he had admired his father for having delivered that closing line.

Listening to Drew outline his father's concept of Shorty, I was suddenly struck by something Thomas Hauser, Muhammad Ali's second biographer, had said to me over the phone one week prior.

"One of the appeals of Bundini, for Ali, was that he wasn't grounded in the same reality the rest of us know and experience. Ali and Bundini had an aura of fantasy about them. These wonderful flights of imagination," Hauser said.

For casual boxing fans, this side of Bundini's personality is best exemplified in Leon Gast's 1996 Oscar-winning documentary *When We Were Kings*. In setting the table for the upcoming George Foreman–Muhammad Ali heavyweight championship bout, Bundini delivers some of his most famous and oft-quoted lines.

"The king is going home to get his throne. From the root to the fruit," Bundini spouts into the camera, standing among the backdrop of Zaire, Africa, his bucket hat tilted to the side, shading one eye.

"This is God's act and you are a part of it," Bundini adds, directing his gaze toward the interviewer.

Bundini's understanding of the significance of the Foreman–Ali bout, highlighted by his belief in a just and redemptive fate driven by an omnipresent and omnipotent God, speaks to Hauser's characterization of both Ali and his cornerman. Just ten years earlier, after upsetting the seemingly unbeatable Sonny Liston, it was a twenty-two-year-old Muhammad Ali who emphatically shouted, "If God is with me, can't nobody be against me" in his postfight interview. "I talk to God every day," the exuberant young champion said, interrupting the questions of the ringside analysts.

Drew Bundini Brown did not view the bout with George Foreman as merely an opportunity to cement Muhammad Ali's place in sports history. In *When We Were Kings,* Bundini talks of Ali's impending victory as if it were an act of God, an act of redemption.

"This is no Hollywood set. This is real. Hollywood come here and take these kind of things and set them up, have somebody in the movies playing his life. This is real. We don't pick up a script," Bundini philosophizes.

This concept of an omnipotent God is a connecting thread in all of Bundini's philosophical asides. When asked about his fighter's chances, Bundini continually responds in spiritual terms, referring to his boss as a prophet rather than a boxer. When pressed to defend his characterization of Ali, Bundini launches into the following soliloquy, perhaps one of the more dramatic verbal exchanges in the film:

Muhammad Ali was born to do it. He's a prophet. He's going to be a fisherman for Elijah Muhammad. We've been fighting ever since we met. We beat Uncle Sam. First man that ever did it. The rest of them they put out the country. This is God's act and we are just actors in it. I think Muhammad is a prophet. How you gonna beat God's side? Anybody that love poor people and little people got to be a prophet. He was champion of the world, had a long table full of food. Had a house for his mother. Had one for him. And he told them to take it and shove it if he couldn't love his God. What you think he is, Mister?

For Bundini, Ali's monumental upset victory would mark the culmination of a spiritual quest, a test of his faith and devotion. Like the Biblical story of Job, who was stripped of all earthly pleasures yet remained steadfast to his devotion to God, Ali had remained on the right side of Shorty's favor, according to Bundini.

The three years of political exile, even the losses to Frazier and Norton, would, in the end, only serve to make his resurrection that much greater.

In retrospect, it is hard to think of Ali–Foreman in any other way.

■ ■ ■

After avenging his loss to Ken Norton, Muhammad Ali stayed busy with an easy victory over Rudi Lubbers at Bung Karno Stadium in Jakarta, Indonesia. Despite Ali's unquestionable marquee draw, most boxing experts viewed a potential Ali–Foreman matchup as nothing more than a cash grab. Aside from his size and age advantages, "Big George" had scored quick and emphatic knockouts over both of the men who defeated Ali.

In an attempt to shift public perception, Ali's team first sought a rematch with Joe Frazier, who had rebounded from his loss to Foreman with his own easy victory over Joe Bugner. The idea, from a promotional standpoint, was that avenging the loss to Frazier would provide Ali with the added credibility boost of having defeated every man that he had faced as a professional. The winner of the Ali–Frazier grudge match would thus produce a worthy, if not more bankable, challenger to Foreman's crown.

When Ali–Frazier II was announced, scheduled for January 28, 1974, at Madison Square Garden, the matchup held half the luster as the original. Both men were coming off setbacks in the ring, and neither was viewed as a fighter in his athletic prime. To help stir the promotional pot, Ali launched into a familiar routine. Frazier was too ugly to be the champion. Frazier was too stupid to be the champion. Black America was on his side. The drama of the first fight, as well as the events that followed, provided Ali with renewed rhetorical venom.

In the buildup to the rematch, Ali's verbal attacks were more personal than ever before. His argumentative strategy, revisionist in focus, was to reshape the original bout in the minds of the American public. First, Ali set out to convince viewers that he had not lost the first fight. Citing the ridiculous scorecard that had Ali losing the bout eleven rounds to four, an unjust total even for hardcore Frazier fans, Ali argued that "white bigots" and "racists" had swayed the judges to err on the side of Frazier. In doing so, Ali was able to once again position Frazier as a racist America's symbolic champion. Ali represented the struggle, Frazier the establishment.

Second, Ali reminded audiences that Frazier had spent nearly a month in the hospital after the fight. Ali's logic would suggest that it was he, not Foreman, who had truly broken down Smokin' Joe. According to Ali's refashioning of the events, Big George had simply finished off a damaged fighter, an inferior version of the once-great champion.

Third, Ali continually cited his three-and-a-half-year layoff as the true challenge of the first Frazier fight. Ali had won many of the early rounds but was unable to close the show, particularly the fifteenth and final round. Had Ali been given more time to prepare, Frazier would have been no match, Ali argued.

Fourth, Ali chalked up the rounds he did lose emphatically to "clowning" and "talking." Vowing to be serious this time around, Ali continually cited the lost rounds as a tactical misstep, stripping Frazier of any agency.

"I learned a great lesson. And, it's good. Just what I needed. Same with the first Norton fight. I went and got in shape and I whupped him [in the rematch]," Ali argued.

This prolonged argumentative campaign, one that aimed to tarnish Frazier's victory, clearly wore on the Philadelphia fighter, as evidenced on January 24, 1974, four days before the rematch, when Ali and Frazier nearly came to blows on Howard Cosell's ABC special.

In the locker room before the fight, Drew Brown III noticed a different demeanor in the now thirty-two-year-old Ali. While the rematch was taking place in the same arena, Ali facing the same opponent, the environment, as Drew recalls it, felt noticeably different. Much was at stake for both boxers. Gone was the bragging and quick wit that Ali had displayed leading up to the fight. Ali was prepared, determined, but visibly shaken.

"He wasn't afraid of Frazier. No, Ali was scared because he had so much to prove. He was nervous. My father was the only person that Ali would let near him. There was something about Ali—this was different, he didn't want people around him," Drew recalled.

As was often the custom, Ali and Bundini went into the bathroom for privacy, sharing a prefight prayer that had very little to do with the tenets of organized religion.

"Allah is just a different word. Me and the Champ pray to the same God," Bundini once told his son.

This time Ali and Bundini stayed in the bathroom longer than usual.

"A lot of people don't know this but Ali was always nervous about the judges robbing him. He was particularly worried about that happening in the Frazier rematch. Because he wasn't a one-punch knockout guy, he had to count on the judges getting it right. This wasn't just paranoia, he felt they cheated him last time," Drew said, recalling the atmosphere in the locker room.

When Ali and Bundini returned from their prayer, both appeared to be physically restored.

"Champ, you don't have to worry about the judges this time! You just got to worry that they found a referee that can count to ten!" Bundini shouted, an attempt to restore the collective spirits of the team.

While the buildup to Ali–Frazier II packed more venom than its predecessor, the fight itself would not produce the same level of fireworks. In the early rounds, Ali stuck to his prefight promise, implementing a far more disciplined game plan. He used his superior footwork, moved laterally, and stayed off the ropes. When Frazier dove in, Ali clinched his shorter opponent, wrapping up Frazier's left arm, thus neutralizing his opponent's dominant weapon. More so than in the first bout, Ali mixed up his attack, feeding Frazier a variety of stinging jabs and whipping hooks. Using his superior ring generalship, Ali would successfully dictate the real estate of the action, avoiding the wild exchanges that had made their first fight classic.

While Frazier had his moments, occasionally landing hooks to Ali's head and body, Ali generally controlled the pace. Despite a few brief moments where Frazier was able to successfully cut off the ring and pin Ali to the ropes, he did not appear to possess the same speed and athleticism that he had in 1971.

Although the rematch lacked the same theatrics of the original, the bout was not without its violent exchanges. The true fireworks would not arrive until the final three rounds of the fight. Ali–Frazier II would come to a fitting close, both men exchanging toe-to-toe, each landing heavy punches. Some critics argued that Ali's choice to abandon the game plan in the final rounds was because of aging legs. Others viewed Ali's willingness to trade punches as a sign of ego, an attempt to show Frazier that he could also *fight*. Because the bout was not a title fight, it had been scheduled for twelve rounds as opposed to fifteen. The momentum Frazier gained in the final rounds would be halted by the sound of the final bell. Frazier, without question, could have used the extra nine minutes.

Awaiting the announcement of the decision, Frazier smiled for the television cameras, bounced up and down on his toes, as if to embody confidence. Ali's team, on the other hand, appeared to be the more nervous of the two entourages. Bundini's gaze was stoic; no tears were shed. Gene Kilroy and Angelo Dundee wore worried expressions on their faces as they paced around the crowded ring.

This time around, Ali won a clear-cut, unanimous decision.

After the fight, Howard Cosell rushed to Frazier, who had been handed the second loss of his career, asking him whether he believed he had won the fight.

"I thought I had the more effective punches but I have no argument over nothing," Frazier sternly replied, a noticeable mouse above his right eye, his left cheekbone severely swollen.

Unable to immediately secure an interview with Ali, Cosell turned his attention to Angelo Dundee.

"My man fought a more strategic fight, he was in great shape. I thought he offset him, I thought he won the fight. I don't know how you can make no baloney over this one—I thought he won the first one," Angelo injected.

To this Cosell sheepishly responded, "Do you really want Foreman?"

The expression on Dundee's face instantly shifted, his eyebrows narrowing behind his thick glasses. "The question is, does Foreman want us?" Dundee asked.

With an improved record of forty-two wins to only two losses, Ali validated his worthiness for another shot at the title. Edging out a close but unanimous victory over an opponent that George Foreman easily dismantled, Ali had not done enough to convince pundits that he was a true threat to the reigning champion.

In surveying the public perception of the rematch, *Sports Illustrated* journalist Mark Kram positioned Ali's victory as one that exceeded expectations, be it only slightly. Before the rematch, the bout "promised to be a match that would provide nothing more than a wistful reminder of the past, a bout between two men with bankrupt talents," Kram wrote.

With the Norton and Frazier losses avenged, there was little doubt that an Ali–Foreman bout would be made. Ali–Foreman, at this point, made more economic sense than competitive sense. The first upset victory scored in the unlikely and unpredictable series of events that would eventually come to be known as "The Rumble in the Jungle" would belong to a relative newcomer to the sport, a little-known ex-convict turned boxing promoter from the streets of Cleveland, Ohio.

■ ■ ■

I said goodbye to the Oral Roberts Bible, placing it back into the cardboard box, exchanging it for what I first assumed to be a fight program. The cover of the magazine read *Drew Bundini Brown: The Master Motivator.*

"Explain this one to me," I asked Drew III, realizing the entire program was dedicated to the subject of Drew Bundini Brown.

Drew smiled as if he were suddenly reunited with an old friend.

"They had those programs made up to sell before fights. This was toward the end of Ali's career, probably the second Spinks fight," Drew answered, peeling back yet another layer of his father's unique brand of street entrepreneurship.

The program featured over twenty pages of photographs and endorsements from those who knew Bundini best. Some of the messages were personalized, not unlike the messages one might receive in a high school yearbook. Other entries served as firsthand testimonials to Bundini's talents as a motivator. As I flipped through the pages, I found the usual suspects, testimonials from key members of the Ali entourage: Angelo Dundee, Ferdie Pacheco, Wali "Youngblood" Muhammad, Luis Sarria, Gene Kilroy, and Abdul Rahman (head of Ali's security). A few of Bundini's boxing comrades, both rivals and associates, were kind enough to offer their praise as well: Sugar Ray Robinson, Larry Holmes, Ken Norton, George Foreman, Jimmy Ellis, Ray "Boom Boom" Mancini, and Willie Pastrano were just a few of the names that caught my attention. Bundini's famous friends from other walks of life also made appearances in the program, like pioneering Black race car driver Willy T. Ribbs, former Los Angeles Dodger Don Newcombe, and expressionist painter LeRoy Nieman. George Plimpton, ever the comedian, began his entry by stating: "There is no telling how far Bundini Brown might have gone in life had it not been for his association with Muhammad Ali."

Skimming the pages, I began to obtain a clearer sense of how Bundini impacted those closest to him. It was apparent that he inspired those around him, made them feel like better versions of themselves, made them laugh, gave them renewed energy. As we finished our morning coffees, I read several of the entries out loud to Drew as we sat at his kitchen table. Each endorsement brought back old memories, transporting Drew to a vivid and fantastic past. There were stories of encounters with Diana Ross, Mickey Mantle, Jim Brown, and Kareem Abdul-Jabbar. The company Bundini had kept, it occurred to me, the human beings from various walks of life that he impacted and was impacted by, was implausible to say the least.

Located directly in the middle of the program was a two-page endorsement by a figure that I had not anticipated to find within the pages of *The Master Motivator*, Hall of Fame promoter Don King. His entry, much to my surprise, was the largest and most detailed entry of the entire magazine. On the left side of the page was a large portrait of King sitting behind his desk, hands clasped, dressed in a gray suit and striped tie, his hair famously reaching to the heavens. On the right side of the page was King's endorsement, a full-page story that read as follows:

> Bundini Brown accepted me as a friend from the very start of my career in boxing. For that, and his many words of wisdom, he will always be my friend. He's part of history and certainly played a major role in my career. I will never forget when Teddy Brenner was trying to sign Ali for a fight at Madison Square Garden. When Brenner came to the door, I jumped into the bathroom to hide. Herbert Muhammad, Ali's manager, was in the tub, taking a bath. Teddy was making a pretty good pitch and Ali was starting to listen. "You can sign your own contract in New York," Teddy told Ali, as he handed him the pen. Snatching the pen from Ali's hand, Bundini hollered, "Don't sign anything until Herbert reads it." The bottom line is that Brenner didn't sign Ali, I did. Drew Bundini Brown's value to Ali for over twenty years as a motivator, friend, cornerman, and confidant, cannot be measured. Their relationship was unique and Ali may have never attained his legendary heights without the colorful, ever caring, Bundini by his side. The catchphrase that became so much a part of Ali—"Float Like a Butterfly, Sting Like a Bee," was a Bundini original. Bundini has been a smashing success in his life as a father, friend, and philosopher, and indeed, the master motivator. I will always love him.

As I read King's endorsement aloud, I could sense that Drew Brown III was ready for me to turn the page, both literally and metaphorically.

"I seriously doubt that my father said that part about Herbert Muhammad. The truth is that Don King wasn't giving the complete scene. When Teddy left, my father went into the bathroom with Ali and said to give this fight to Don, you always talk about uplifting Black people, now do it. Daddy was the reason Don promoted one of the greatest fighters ever; it put Don King on the map," Drew said to me, a delayed reaction of sorts.

In the HBO film *Only in America*, based off Jack Newfield's Don King biography, Bundini is certainly positioned as such. Reading King's words, I was instantly taken back to the filmic portrayal of the bathroom scene described in the entry. Portrayed by actor and comedian Bernie Mac, Bundini serves as a key piece to the Muhammad Ali puzzle in director John Herzfeld's 1997 biopic.

In one of the key scenes in *Only in America,* King attempts to use the commonly known friction between Bundini and the Nation of Islam to his advantage.

"Bundini, you're Ali's trainer. Herbert is never around. He's always opening up this ministry and that. Man gets a third of Ali's salary and where is he? Two days before the fight," King, played by actor Ving Rhames, says to Bundini midway through the film.

"Your loyalty deserves full applicable recognition, baby. But how you living? Float like a butterfly, sting like a bee—that's your line. But who knows it? Herbert treats you like a damn poor stepchild. Now, I know what it's like to not get the respect you deserve. Just tell Ali that he needs a full-time manager, not a full-time minister. Let him know who is looking out for him, brother," King adds, sliding Bundini a paper bag full of cash.

Drew Brown III denies that any substantial money ever came his father's way from Don King.

"Once again, a Hollywood movie added a scene that never happened. Daddy didn't shoot heroin and he never got a bag of cash from Don King," Drew said to me, his narrative energy returning to a fevered pitch.

I repositioned myself at the kitchen table, returning the booklet to its rightful place. Don King's relationship to Bundini, for me, was an important, and often overlooked, component to the story of how "The Rumble in the Jungle" came to fruition.

"What did your father say to Ali, on King's behalf?" I asked cautiously.

At certain points during our weekend together, I could feel Drew slipping into his father's vernacular and cadence. When asked to quote his father, such would always be the case.

"Here is a Black promoter. Give him a chance. If he can come up with the $10 million, give him this one fight! Then you can go back to Arum or whoever. But, you can't say one thing and do the other. You can't say white people are the devil and deny a Black man an opportunity like this. Words are cheap so it's time to put your money where your mouth is," Drew said, sounding just like his father.

At the time, it almost felt as if I were receiving the news from Bundini himself. In considering Bundini's argumentative personality, I was reminded that, until this point in history, there were no prominent Black promoters, such as Leonard Ellerbe or Al Haymon, in the sport of boxing. The sport had long been populated by poor immigrants and minorities but had always been controlled by rich white promoters. Boiled down to their most basic elements, both Don King and Bundini Brown were survivors, rhetoricians of the streets who possessed an unteachable ability to read people and situations, instantly sizing up motivations and vulnerabilities. Bundini, according to his son, knew exactly who and what Don King was.

"My daddy had been around hustlers all his life. He always took the side of the underdog, who this time just happened to be Black," Drew argued. Yet his father was impacted by King's work ethic just the same.

King's argument, despite the shaky ethos of its rhetoric, was a good one. He was able to snatch what would later become one of the biggest fights in boxing history away from veteran promoter Bob Arum because, as Bundini's response suggested, King was able to fully recognize the symbolic void his presence would fill in the sport of boxing. Ali and Bundini, both free spirited in their own right, were intrinsically driven by their passions.

The story of Don King's unlikely rise to the top of the boxing world is described best by the controversial promoter's famous slogan, "Only in America." King's ascension reminds us of our predisposition to rags-to-riches myth building, our affinity for underdog stories. King, in many ways, serves as a living testament to the capitalist bootstraps narrative woven into the fabric of the American culture. In the spring of 1951, Don King, the son of a blue-collar factory worker, graduated from John Adams High School in Cleveland, Ohio. After graduation, he briefly attended Kent State University before dropping out. Turning to the streets, King ran an illegal bookmaking outfit out of the basement of a record shop. Life on the streets of Cleveland proved dangerous. Just a few years after his high school graduation, King shot and killed a local street hustler named Hillary Brown, who was attempting to rob one of his gambling houses. The shooting was ruled a justifiable homicide. Thirteen years later, in 1967, a violent altercation occurred between King and his former employee, Sam Garrett, at the Manhattan Tap Room in Cleveland. Garrett, who allegedly owed King $600, was beaten and stomped to death outside of the bar. King was convicted of manslaughter and would serve three years and eleven months in an Ohio prison. At thirty-six years old, his life seemingly amounting to nothing but disaster, King entered prison with absolutely no prospects. His prison stint is perhaps best described by one of the lines in Herzfeld's film: "I made time serve me," King brags.

After being released from prison in Marion, Ohio, in 1971, King reconnected with his old friend Lloyd Price, a popular R&B singer known for his Billboard hit "Personality." Price had a long-standing friendship with Muhammad Ali, dating back to Ali's teenage days hanging around music clubs in the West End of Louisville, Kentucky. Price first met Ali when he was a Golden Gloves amateur, and their friendship had continued throughout Ali's professional career. The singer was also close with members of the Ali entourage, most notably Gene Kilroy and Drew Bundini Brown. Price first became familiar with Kilroy and Bundini on separate occasions, at the Birdland nightclub in New York City, long before Ali became the heavyweight champion of the world.

Inspired by the magnetic spell Ali–Frazier had cast over his fellow inmates, King set his sights on the sport of boxing. Shortly after his release, King barricaded himself into Cleveland area assistant district attorney Clarence Rogers's office, demanding to be connected with Ohio's biggest boxing promoter, Don Elbaum. After much debate, Rogers gradually realized that King would not relent until being patched through to Elbaum, who was in Buffalo, New York, for a fight card. When the call was made, King sprang into action.

"He told me there's a Black hospital out here in Cleveland, Forrest City Hospital, that's going under. We've got to save it. I want to do a boxing exhibition to raise money for the hospital. I want to bring in Muhammad Ali for the show. He's the only man who can save it," Elbaum said to me, rehashing the conversation that would serve as King's introduction to boxing.

"The idea was to match a few local fighters who could attract a crowd. Ali's ten-round exhibition was going to be the main event," Elbaum added.

At the time, King had absolutely no idea how a fight promotion worked. As the pieces came together, Lloyd Price worked his connections to arrange a meeting between Don King and Herbert Muhammad, who was, in many ways, the gatekeeper to Muhammad Ali's future and finances. While incarcerated, King had made good use of the prison library. He returned to society verbally equipped to do battle with even the smartest Ivy League lawyers. Once King was able to secure a phone conversation with Ali, the former prison inmate was able to get the Champ's support for the so-called charitable cause.

After successfully orchestrating the charity exhibition event, King took to promoting small Ohio area fight cards. His time in the lower rungs of boxing would not last long. By 1974, King was brought in as a consultant to Video Techniques, a closed-circuit firm that promoted the Foreman–Norton championship fight. King's true coronation, however, would not come until the announcement of Ali–Foreman.

"That fight is what really started Don King. My daddy got him the fight. There may never have been a Don King without my father. But remember, my father never let him forget it either," Drew said to me.

The conditions were right for King's takeover. By the mid 1970s, the Nation of Islam had lost much of its sway in American culture. The organization continued to be embattled by public scandal, including bad publicity driven by a *New York Times* investigation that suggested the organization was turning to illegal means to recoup their depleted funds. Elijah Muhammad grew increasingly ill. Ali, now in his early thirties, was desperate to reclaim his title and place atop the sport. King, keen at sensing opportunity, was able to successfully pitch the fight to both George Foreman and Muhammad Ali, promising each fighter $5 million apiece. According to legend, Foreman and Ali would sign blank pieces of paper that would later become contracts.

As King's Bundini testimonial suggests, both Teddy Brenner and Bob Arum worked tirelessly to secure an Ali–Foreman fight at Madison Square Garden. Partially because of his lack of credibility, King and his associates were given only a few days to secure a down payment of $100,000 to both fighters. To come up with the money, King and his business partner Hank Schwartz were forced to get creative.

"Scrambling, Schwartz identified a British investor willing to give him $200,000. That bought him a little time. King and Schwartz also received $500,000 from an organized crime figure from King's hometown of Cleveland, according to an FBI memo," Ali biographer Jonathan Eig writes.

King was eventually able to secure the fight thanks to the vast personal wealth of military dictator and president Joseph Mobutu, the notorious ruler of the totalitarian nation of the Democratic Republic of Congo (which he renamed Zaire in conjunction with his rise to power). President Mobutu promised the $10 million up front, only if King agreed to stage the event in his country. Until this point, King had not intended to hold the fight outside of the United States. King's greatest achievement, one could easily argue, was reshaping the narrative of hosting Ali–Foreman in Zaire, despite the nation's reputation as a murderous dictatorship, a poor African country known for socioeconomic exploitation and routine political executions.

King was able to successfully dictate the Ali–Foreman "Rumble in the Jungle" narrative as a "symbolic Black happening," the most famous Black athlete in the world returning to the motherland to reclaim his crown. This was mostly because King's symbolism spoke to the imaginative sensibilities of both Ali and Bundini. In the end, it would be Ali, much more than King, who would frame the way we continue to view the bout even today. Despite all of the logistical, and perhaps moral, issues that came with hosting the fight in such a location, both Ali and Bundini clearly drew strength and inspiration from King's vision.

Beyond the symbolism, though, nothing about the bout made sense. The closed-circuit television would have to be flown to Zaire. The soccer stadium that would host the fight had no parking lot. The fight would need to be staged at four o'clock in the morning to accommodate American closed-circuit audiences. Americans who could afford the trip to Africa to see the fight would need to undergo a host of vaccinations beforehand. King, with the help of Ali, was able to frame the bout in romantic terms.

"I fought in many European countries, but it is a greater feeling fighting in a Black country. I am fighting in Africa because I am fighting in my homeland. America is not my original homeland. My original homeland is Africa. After 400 years of being separated, me and thousands of more American Blacks will be returning after 400 years," Ali stated to the media in the prefight announcement.

Thousands of American Blacks or whites would, of course, not be on their way to Zaire. For Ali, the idea, crafted in romantic imagery that spoke to his inner passions and motivations, need not have been grounded in the socioeconomic realities of the event itself. Bundini, Ali's chief motivator, clearly recognized the appeal.

The location of Ali–Foreman, despite its poetic significance, proved more than inconvenient for Bundini. When the fight was originally announced, Bundini did not believe that he would be able to attend.

"Until 'The Rumble in the Jungle,' Bundini was never able to work the fights that were hosted abroad," Kilroy told me. "He would work with Ali in the gym, but he had to stay home when it was time to travel to the fight. He couldn't get a passport because he didn't have a birth certificate or any of the proper documentation. That was until [I] talked to Teddy Kennedy and got him a passport. The [Foreman] fight was too important to leave Bundini behind," Kilroy confided in me.

A few weeks into Muhammad Ali's Deer Lake training camp, Bundini received the good news that he would be able to travel to Zaire with the entourage. This surprise turn of events, for Bundini's son, who was entering his first semester as a full scholarship student at Southern University of New Orleans, opened the door for what could potentially be a life-changing adventure.

"My father called me and said that Gene was allowing him to bring me along to Zaire. He wanted to know if I had school. Of course, I did. I told him that I'd talk to my professors and arrange to make up any work that I would miss," Drew III recalled.

"Give me the number of your teacher. I'll call and find out if you can go," Bundini flatly responded.

"Daddy, we don't have teachers, we have professors. This isn't elementary school—we don't need permission to miss class," Drew argued.

"I didn't ask you that. Boy, give me your teacher's number," Bundini replied.

Sensing that he could manipulate the situation to his favor, Drew gave his father the office phone number of Dr. Wilson, his economics professor.

"Dr. Wilson was a big boxing fan. He was thrilled when he learned that I was Bundini's son. He was a fan of my daddy. I held an A in his class, so I was confident this might work," Drew said to me.

"Most parents would see a trip to Africa as an educational experience. They would see the educational value in the trip, forget the boxing match," Drew continued, sounding if he were trying to convince me as much as he had tried to convince his father.

The following day, Bundini phoned Dr. Wilson from Deer Lake. "Yes, Mr. Brown. Your son told me about the trip this morning," Dr. Wilson stated. "I think it is a wonderful opportunity for Drew. I will make sure that he has everything he needs to complete his schoolwork," the professor added.

"I didn't ask all that. Does he have school?" Bundini interrupted.

"Well, yes, Mr. Brown. We have school during those dates but I am allowing Drew to make up his work. I will give him the readings and assignments ahead of time," Dr. Wilson said, a little surprised by Bundini's simple inquiry.

"Thank you very much. That's all I needed to know," Bundini replied before hanging up the phone.

When Drew Brown III arrived to Economics class the following morning, his professor relayed the exchange to him. A feeling of disappointment washed over the frustrated college student; he had already begun to brag to his friends about the trip.

"Boy, you lied to me. You have school," Bundini scolded his son over the phone later that evening.

"Daddy, this might be the only chance I ever have to visit Africa," Drew pleaded.

"This ain't more important than college," Bundini responded.

"Daddy, I can make up the work. Dr. Wilson is cutting me a break. This is a once-in-a-lifetime opportunity. I'm in college, I've done everything you've asked," Drew said, sounding like a little boy being sent to his room.

"You're gonna get an education, Buddy Drew. And you're gonna make something of yourself. You'll go to Africa. But you'll do it on your own," Bundini said, calling a halt to the debate.

In his Atlanta kitchen, Drew Brown III flipped through the laminated pages of a scrapbook. Enclosed were ticket stubs, autographs of famous celebrities his father had collected for him over the years, and newspaper clippings from his glory days as a SUNO basketball player.

"Did his prediction come true?" I asked. "Did you ever get to go to Africa on your own?"

A warm smile returned to Drew's face.

"Daddy was right," Drew nodded in agreement. For a moment, Drew Brown III was not the son of boxing's greatest hype man. Not to me. He was just a son, a man who in growing older and wiser was continuing to come to terms with the idea of his father.

The boxing fan in me felt sorry for the first-generation college student who could have easily been ringside in Kinshasa, Zaire, on October 30, 1974, a night that would forever change the course of boxing history—one that would catapult Muhammad Ali into the legendary status he now occupies in the minds of fight fans.

Win, lose, or draw, this was to be Ali's final bout. In interviews and press conferences leading up to the bout, the boisterous challenger ardently suggested that he was going to "whup George Foreman," reclaim his title, and move on to his future as an ambassador for Islam.

"It was not only a matter of [Ali] trying to get back what belonged to him: apart from Ali's impetus to regain the championship was his relationship with the Black Muslims and the assumption that when he finished fighting he would become a minister. He could be fully reinstated in the movement only after he gave up prizefighting, because in his religion no sports were allowed," George Plimpton writes in *Shadow Box*, rehashing a conversation with his good friend Bundini in Africa. According to Plimpton, Bundini played on these aspirations leading up to the Foreman fight.

"He want the championship so he can fish for Allah, so he can keep his mouth open and talk for the Muslims," Bundini told Plimpton.

"So that's what I remind Ali of sometimes in the corner—when Angelo has taken the stool down and the bell's just about to ring to start the round: I pat him on the trunks and I tell him that the other fellow is trying to close his mouth, take the thing away that make people listen, his championship, and I place my hand on him and I feel his body harden," Bundini added.

In essence, Bundini's approach serves as a textbook example of situational audience analysis, the process by which speechwriters craft arguments designed to meet the ideas, attitudes, and beliefs of their intended audience. Considering Bundini's antagonistic relationship with the Nation of Islam, I found Plimpton's passage striking and wanted Drew's assessment of how accurate the passage might be.

"Remember I told you that my father kept a small wallet-sized picture of Elijah Muhammad in his jacket," Drew said to me. "If things were going bad in a fight, he would take it out and show it to Ali. He'd tell Muhammad to remember who he was fighting for," Drew recalled, vouching for Plimpton's assessment.

■ ■ ■

Apart from Ali's prefight promises, there were many reasons to believe the Foreman bout would be Ali's last. With a record of forty wins and no losses, thirty-seven wins by way of knockout, Foreman held every measurable advantage. He was the bigger, stronger, and younger man. Ali's only noticeable advantage was that he, unlike Foreman, clearly drew inspiration from Africa, or at least the idea of Africa that he and King so brilliantly crafted for viewers. During his training preparations in Africa, everywhere Ali went the people chanted "Ali, *bomaye*," a phrase that translates to "Ali, kill him."

A master of controlling the narrative, Ali began his psychological campaign by playfully nicknaming Foreman "The Mummy," slow-swinging and predictable, intellectually inferior. Ali quickly learned that he could shape how Foreman was perceived by the citizens of Zaire, who, at first, assumed the champion was white. The people of Zaire were perhaps the only people on Earth who didn't view Ali as an underdog. Citing Foreman's pet German Shepherd as evidence, Ali sought to connect the champion with the Belgian oppressors of the African people. In interviews, he framed Foreman as a colonialist, positioning his own impending victory as symbolic to Black people all over the world. As was the case with Frazier, Ali was able to position Foreman as somehow less of a Black man than himself. In Africa, George Foreman, the boxer who had once captured an Olympic gold medal for the United States, proudly waving a miniature American flag around the ring after his victory, suddenly found himself in an unfamiliar role, that of the villain.

Just days before the original fight date, Foreman was cut above his right eye during sparring, forcing the bout to be postponed an additional six weeks. Fearing that he might not return, President Mobuto refused to grant Foreman the permission to seek doctors outside of Zaire. When the postponement was announced, rumors circulated that Ali's team had sought the services of Mobuto's witch doctor. Foreman was a cursed man, Ali led audiences to believe. In my conversations with Foreman, it became clear to me that during his extended time in Zaire, friendly faces, outside of the members of his team, were few and far between.

"In Zaire, I saw a look in Bundini's face that I hadn't seen in all my time with him earlier," George Foreman said to me. "When I first saw him, he looked at me and said, 'the real champion is back . . . the real champion is back to reclaim his throne.' He looked me right in my eyes. And, I said to myself, in Drew's mind there will always be one champion, Muhammad Ali."

Curious as to whether the champion felt betrayed by Bundini's turn, I asked Foreman to clarify his emotional response to the exchange.

"I considered Drew my friend. So, I excused it," Foreman replied, his tone of voice shifting.

In Zaire, Foreman felt ambushed. As the weeks passed, he began to feel the psychological effects of Ali's home-court advantage.

"You should have never come to Africa," Ali repeatedly scolded the champion leading up to the fight.

Despite Ali's sizable rhetorical advantages, the task of standing up to Foreman's power remained daunting. Ringside commentator Howard Cosell all but eulogized Ali at the beginning of the television broadcast. Before the fight, the mood, by all accounts, was tense, solemn even.

In *Shadow Box*, George Plimpton, who was covering the fight for *Sports Illustrated*, paints the picture of a tense and nervous locker room. According to Plimpton, an argument ensued between Ali and Bundini less than an hour before Ali exited the locker room.

"Look how much better this one looks," Ali allegedly said to Bundini, who, by Plimpton's assessment, was visibly disappointed that Ali had not chosen to wear the robe and trunks he had designed with Everlast.

Ali instead elected to wear the robe given to him as a gift by Zaire's controversial political figurehead. Such matters, as made evident by the first Norton fight, were extremely important to Bundini.

"Look how much better this one looks," Ali repeated, as Bundini, clearly disappointed, refused to look into the mirror. What came next, by Plimpton's estimation, was a shocking act of cruelty. When Bundini refused to answer, Ali slapped him across the face, "a stinging sound that echoed the locker room walls," Plimpton writes.

"You look when I tell you!" Ali shouted.

Bundini's glassy eyes remained fixed. Ali then slapped his cornerman a second time, even harder than the first. Plimpton described what happened next as follows:

> Bundini stood with his feet together, swaying slightly, still holding his robe and looking at Ali. He kept refusing to look in the mirror. I was stunned. I had seen it happen before, and while I had some vague notion that any outburst with that huge drama so close at hand was acceptable (Normal Mailer did not seem surprised at all), it seemed so gratuitous, and shaming, with everyone standing around, that I loathed Ali suddenly. Bundini seemed such an odd target—his concern and love for his fighter was almost pathological. In the ring he never took his eyes from him—a singleness of interest like a parent's staring at a three-year-old—and sometimes he cried seeing Ali hit by a sparring partner's punch.

Plimpton's assessment of Ali's attempt to smooth things over with Bundini is equally telling. After a few minutes of silence, Ali calls to his cornerman.

"Hey, Bundini!" Ali shouts.

Bundini offers no reply.

What comes next, according to Plimpton, was a much kinder, more patient explanation of why he chose the robe given to him by Zaire's president. Bundini's robe, in the end, was not selected. Ali's explanation, at first, does little to de-escalate the situation. The locker room remains low on energy. After a few moments, Ali enters the bathroom area, perhaps for his prefight prayer. When Ali returns, he does so as if he were entering the Sonny Liston weigh-in.

"Bundini, we gonna dance? Ain't we gonna dance, Bundini? You know I can't dance without you," Ali shouts, his demeanor completely shifted.

"All night long," Bundini responds, leaping to his feet. Not another word of the robe or the altercation is uttered.

The apology, for Plimpton, came in the form of an unspoken, innate recognition that both men had a job to do, a common goal that required distractions to be blocked out. Their relationship, perhaps like all partnerships, can be described as an often-imbalanced combination of admiration and disappointment in each other.

"We're gonna dance, Champ," Bundini shouted as the entourage exited the locker room.

Much to the surprise of the boxing world, and certainly to Foreman, Ali did not dance. When the bell rang, Ali rushed Foreman, electing to stand flat-footed and exchange. Ali landed almost all of the telling blows in the first round, his superior hand speed and defensive skills allowing him to successfully pull off the kamikaze strategy. Ali's intention, unbeknownst to Angelo Dundee and Bundini Brown, was to sock the playground bully in the mouth early into the fight, letting Foreman know that he did not possess any measure of fear or respect for him.

When Foreman did gain control of the fight in the subsequent rounds, cornering Ali onto the ropes, the champion was overanxious in his pursuit. Using a defensive strategy that he would later famously name "the rope-a-dope," Ali leaned back, using his forearms to block punches, occasionally offering quick counterpunches. Leading up to the fight, Foreman had gone two consecutive years without having to fight past the fourth round. All of Foreman's key victories had come by early knockouts. Ali, no longer able to dance and glide around the ring as he had done as a young champion, was betting on Foreman expending all of his energy in the early rounds.

"There was no conversation about rope-a-dope. My daddy had no idea what was going on. He and Angelo were screaming themselves crazy, telling Ali to get off the ropes," Drew Brown III assured me.

As the rounds progressed, Ali's trash talking increased.

"Is that all you got, George? Is that all you got?" Ali famously taunted, attempting to water any seeds of doubt that might have grown in Foreman's mind during his time in Zaire. By round six, Ali's rope-a-dope counterpunches were beginning to show their effectiveness, even wobbling George at times. Countering with wild right- and left-hand hooks, often in succession, Foreman launched nothing but knockout blows. The fatigue that appeared on Foreman's face was both mental and physical.

With only moments left in the eighth round, it happened: Ali landed a sharp right hand to Foreman's head, bouncing off the rope, as if he had suddenly returned to 1964. The challenger followed up with a series of neck-snapping punches that caused Foreman to stagger, stumble, and eventually spin headfirst to the canvas in a circular motion. Like many of the fallen trees Ali had cut down in the forests of Pennsylvania, Foreman's large frame jarred the canvas upon impact. The unbeatable George Foreman was stretched out on the canvas for the first time in his career, straining his neck upward as if to survey his own condition.

Moments later, Bundini would climb through the ropes, tears flowing down his face, leading a raucous mob into the ring in celebration.

In pulling off the improbable upset, Muhammad Ali had fulfilled Bundini's prefight prophecy, a divinely inspired redemption story that serves as the apex of the champion's mythos. On the surface, the bout had nothing to do with Ali's political exile, his place in the world as a civil rights ambassador.

Had Muhammad Ali lost the bout, kept his word, and retired from boxing, perhaps Don King's Zaire narrative would never have captured our imaginations. Listening to Drew Brown III speak of his relationship with his father, seated at his kitchen table, surrounded by his father's keepsakes and personal possessions, I tried my best to think of the leading characters as nothing more than human beings, the fight as nothing more than a sporting contest.

Despite having all the details, the full picture so to speak, I admittedly struggle, even today, to think of Ali's accomplishment as anything other than an act preordained by the gods. It is only in the minor details, the personal stories excluded from the books, movies, and television programs, which have long popularized the event, that I am capable of thinking of the participants as mortal men.

After the fight, Bundini visited Foreman's locker room, once again risking suspension. With the championship returned to where it truly belonged, at least in Bundini's mind, he could talk peacefully with George. In an attempt to comfort his friend, Bundini assured Foreman that he would be champion again one day, but on Shorty's time, not his own. Twenty-two years later, at the MGM Grand Arena in Las Vegas, Bundini's postfight prediction would come true. Bundini would not be alive to see Foreman recapture the heavyweight title he lost in Kinshasa, Zaire. If he had been alive, Bundini would have no doubt labeled the unlikely victory a divine happening, *God's act.*

"The only bad thing I can say about Bundini was that he was never in my corner. But then that too would be an inaccuracy because deep down I knew he loved us all," Foreman once wrote.

10

Everyone Sees but Only a Few Know

I t is perhaps the most iconic image of Drew Bundini Brown. His brows are furrowed, his eyes menacingly fixed upward. Bundini's long right arm is stretched toward the enemy, the sleeve of his white cardigan falls well short of the gold watch dangling about his wrist. Earlier in the day, in Drew Brown III's Atlanta house, I had held that very same wristwatch in my hands. The focal point of the photograph is the position of Bundini's middle and index fingers, seemingly forming the shape of a "V." Muhammad Ali, his mouth slightly agape, revealing the contour of his mouthpiece, is, for once, playing second fiddle to Bundini.

Boxing writers have long mistaken the gesture to symbolize "V" for victory. The image certainly works that way. Just as Neil Leifer's portrait of Muhammad Ali standing over the vanquished Sonny Liston continues to capture our imagination—boxing's version of King Arthur standing over a slain dragon—Bundini's "victory" photograph provides viewers with what appears to be a moment of true and honest triumph. For those of us who grew up idolizing Ali, this is how we remember his enigmatic cornerman.

"That might be my favorite shot of your father," I said to Drew Brown III, admiring the framed black-and-white portrait hanging in his home office.

Below the image, an inscription read: "Everyone Sees but Only a Few Know," one of Bundini's oft-quoted sayings. Drew studied the photograph, remaining silent, cupping his chin as he took in his father's passionate expression. For a moment, he resembled a patron of the Museum of Modern Art in Midtown Manhattan.

"This was taken before the fifteenth round of the Ali–Spinks rematch," Drew said, turning to me. "Daddy was shouting across the ring at Leon. That's who he was directing that gesture toward," he clarified.

Because the photograph had always been one my favorites, I suddenly felt embarrassed for having no knowledge of its context. There was a story lurking behind those long, outstretched fingers, I imagined.

"Do you have any idea what your father said to him?" I asked.

Drew cracked a devilish grin, stretched his own long ropey arm in my direction, mimicking his father's symbolic gesture. Throughout our weekend together, when preparing to quote his father, Drew, like any good method actor, suddenly went into full character. The body language and vocal delivery was just as important to Drew's performance as the words themselves. The impression was uncanny.

"You may kick his ass. But you won't beat the both of us," Drew Brown III shouted, echoing the walls of his office, his outstretched fingers symbolizing the bond between his father and Muhammad Ali.

"The saying, underneath the picture," I continued. "What does it mean?"

Drew's smile returned. He liked having pieces to my puzzle. I could sense it. Anytime I asked a question that Drew took to be relevant, he would suddenly come alive. His posture would straighten, his eyes turn one shade brighter.

"Everyone sees but only a few know," he repeated, his reflection showing itself in the glass casing of the framed poster. "Everyone sees the glitter and glamor of winning, the glory of being champion of the world, or anything else in life, but only a few know what it really takes to be a champion, to be successful. Only a few know about the extremely hard work, the never-ending hard work that it takes to become that champion or successful person," Drew said, his voice eerily similar to that of his famous father.

Muhammad Ali was well aware of the sacrifices that come with being champion. Winning back the title was not the hard part. Keeping it was the true Sisyphean task.[1] One could argue this is indeed the hidden tragedy of Muhammad Ali's second run as champion. It wasn't that Ali was unwilling to make the sacrifices necessary to be great. The tragedy lies in the fact that he did.

After becoming the second man in history to successfully recapture the heavyweight championship of the world, Muhammad Ali reeled off ten consecutive title defenses, five coming by way of knockout. In defeating fighters like Chuck Wepner, Ron Lyle, Joe Bugner, Joe Frazier (for a second time), Jean-Pierre Coopman, Jimmy Young, Richard Dunn, Ken Norton (for a second time), Alfredo Evangelista, and Earnie Shavers, Ali firmly cemented his place in boxing history as the division's greatest champion. Ali's second reign was made possible not by blinding speed or fast-twitch reflexes, but rather by his supreme level of mental toughness, a legendary ability to endure. Often employing the rope-a-dope style that won him back the title against Foreman, Ali suffered far more physical punishment than was the case in his first go-round. The fights would be closer, the damage irreversible. Despite his diminished physical skills, obvious to anybody who was watching, Ali's second title reign lasted longer than his first.

As a result of finally being granted a passport, Bundini was able to work Ali's corner for every bout of the final part of Ali's career. Bundini traveled with Ali for bouts in Malaysia, Germany, the Philippines, Puerto Rico, and the Bahamas. He and his son were also present for Ali's controversial bout with Japanese professional wrestler Antonio Inoki, often seen as a precursor to the popularity of modern mixed martial arts.

"The fight, itself, was terrible, but visiting Tokyo was an amazing experience," Drew told me, pointing out his large afro in a newspaper clipping that featured a photograph of Antonio Inoki kicking Ali in the shins.

Even in the Tokyo exhibition, playfully ruled a draw, Ali endured punishment, being repeatedly kicked throughout the fifteen rounds. As a result of the punishment, he would later be hospitalized for blood clots and muscle damage to his legs.

The defining moment of Ali's second title run would come via his rubber match with Joe Frazier, an epic demonstration of intestinal fortitude famously called "The Thrilla in Manila" by promoter Don King. When the fight was announced to the world, scheduled for October 1, 1975, in Quezon City in the Philippines, the consensus was that both men were far from their athletic primes. Their 1974 rematch had been entertaining but it didn't compare to the original. While Ali had, at times, looked vulnerable in his second round of title defenses, most pundits viewed Ali as the fresher of the two combatants. In the promotional buildup to the fight, in a fashion typical of the previous Ali–Frazier bouts, Ali often toed the line between playful taunts and inappropriate insults.

"Who'd [Frazier] every beat for the title? Buster Mathis and Jimmy Ellis. He ain't no champion. All he's got is a left hook—got no right hand, no jab, no rhythm. I was the real champion all the time. He reigned because I escaped the draft and he luckily got by me, but he was only an imitation champion. He just luckily got through because his head could take a lot of punches," Ali taunted, once again looking to diminish Frazier's credibility.

For their third and final meeting, however, Ali's verbal jabs increasingly became more potent and personal than ever before. Playing off a rhyme that fit with the "Thrilla in Manila" title Don King had given the bout, Ali took to bragging that he was going to "Get the Gorilla in Manila."

"What will people in Manila think? We can't have a gorilla for a champ. They're gonna think, lookin' at him, that all Black brothers are animals. Ignorant. Stupid. Ugly," Ali said to reporters, repeatedly thumping his fists alongside a rubber gorilla that he claimed resembled his longtime boxing rival.

While the incessant trash talk wore on Foreman, perhaps even providing an edge for Ali, it served as nothing but motivation for Frazier. Years after their third bout, in a conversation with Ali biographer Thomas Hauser, Frazier outlined his disdain for Ali's prefight antics, particularly the gorilla moniker.

"I hated Ali. God might not like me talking that way, but it's in my heart. I hated that man. First two fights, he tried to make me a white man. Then he tried to make me a nigger. How would you like it if your kids came home from school crying, because everyone was calling their daddy a gorilla?" Frazier bluntly stated.

Bundini, according to his son, had no hand in the gorilla schtick.

"There was a dark side to Muhammad Ali. It first came out in the bout with Floyd Patterson. Then it came out with [Ernie] Terrell. He really wanted to hurt and punish those guys because they refused to call him by his Muslim name. My father wasn't involved in either of those fights. You can see the different side of Ali in those fights. Frazier brought that side out in Ali as well. None of that gorilla junk was devised by daddy. With Frazier, my father had no control or input over the trash talk. In the case of Liston, some of that was my daddy. But not with Frazier. Joe clearly brought out that dark side of Ali," Drew confided in me.

Curious about whether his father expressed any measure of disapproval, I asked Drew to clarify how his father felt about Ali's gorilla taunts.

"Hell yes, daddy recognized the double standard. How are you going to claim to be an ambassador for Black people and then call another Black man a gorilla? My father didn't think any of that made sense. To be honest with you, it went against all of my father's teachings but he didn't let it affect his job or performance," Drew argued.

The prefight trash talk, as was often the case for Ali, carried over into the ring. Before the official introductions, in a somewhat clowning gesture, Ali made his way to center ring and lifted the oversized trophy awaiting the winner and carried it back to his corner. When the crowd booed, Ali pretended to cry, seizing the moment as if he were a professional wrestler playing the role of heel. In round one, however, there would be no clowning. Ali would stagger Frazier with pinpoint combinations, administering a one-sided shellacking of his longtime rival. When the bell sounded, calling a halt to the action, Frazier tapped Ali on the behind as he turned to make his way back to the corner. "I'm not going anywhere," the gesture likely signaled. Rounds two and three were more of the same. Ali's hand speed and superior footwork befuddled Frazier, who pressed forward regardless. Before the opening bell of the fourth round, Ali pumped his fists toward the crowd like a conductor signaling to an orchestra. "Ali! Ali! Ali!" the Filipino crowd cheered. At first, it appeared that Ali was on his way to completely outclassing Frazier. But as the playful tap at the end of round one signified, the challenger was just getting warmed up.

As the bout progressed, Frazier kept coming. By the middle rounds, Frazier's relentless pressure began to shift the complexion of the fight. In round six, a crushing left hook sent Ali's mouthpiece tumbling to the canvas. What, in the early stages of the fight, resembled a one-sided affair gradually turned into a back-and-forth war. Effectively cutting off the ring, cornering Ali with increasing regularity, Frazier pounded away at Ali's head and rib cage, mixing hooks and uppercuts into his arsenal. Ali was fading. Heading into the championship rounds of the fight, Frazier appeared to be on his way to a second victory over his longtime rival.

"Ali was on the verge of quitting," former heavyweight contender and Bundini pupil James "Quick" Tillis once said to me, reflecting on Frazier's mid-round comeback. "Ali was gone in that last Frazier fight. Bundini was a big part of him winning that fight. Keeping his spirit up in that fight. We would talk about that fight. Bundini would get that spirit in you. All the things he told Ali, he told me."

In the eleventh round, Ali found his spirit. The champion's work rate suddenly increased and, like any good drama, the plot would turn in the final act. Throughout rounds eleven, twelve, and thirteen, Ali blistered Frazier with stinging jabs and whipping lead right hands. The champion landed combinations at will, staggering Frazier on a number of occasions. Frazier somehow walked through the punches, demonstrating an unyielding resolve. As the fight progressed, both men began to show the effects of the sweltering heat—the arena did not have a working air conditioner. The swelling around Frazier's eyes gradually increased. Heading back to his corner after the fourteenth round, the challenger was cut above the left eye and was bleeding profusely from his nose. Both men, however, appeared to be on the brink of collapse.

"Joe, it's over. I don't want you going out for the next round," trainer Eddie Futch famously called to Frazier.

As the Philadelphia legend tried to protest, getting up off the stool to demonstrate his willingness to continue, Futch turned to the referee and waved his arms in surrender. According to Wali "Youngblood" Muhammad, Ali was, at the very same time, asking trainer Angelo Dundee to cut off the gloves—again. Dundee, legend has it, ignored his fighter's request. Moments later Ali would be declared the winner by technical knockout. The champion had outlasted his rival, but only by seconds.

Moments before the bell sounding the beginning of the fifteenth round was about to ring, Bundini patted Ali alongside his chest, not unlike the bedside parent of a sick child. Wali Muhammad leaned over the ropes, expressing his concern. Dundee, it appears, was the first to recognize that Frazier's corner had stopped the fight. Dundee tugged at Ali's left arm, as if to conjure his fighter off the stool. "You just stopped Smokin' Joe Frazier—it's time to celebrate," Dundee's gesture suggested. Ferdie Pacheco was the first to climb through the ropes, hugging Ali as Ali momentarily mustered the strength to stand on his feet, extending his right arm in the air in a brief victory salute. Tears flowed down Bundini's face as he made his way through the ropes, only to find his fighter collapsed back onto the stool from exhaustion. Wali Muhammad, removing a green towel from Dundee's shoulder, began to fan Ali, who was in desperate need of oxygen. Don King, Rahman Ali, and a host of cameramen, media personalities, and well-wishers rushed into the ring to congratulate Ali, who remained seated on the stool, arms resting on his bent knees, seemingly unable to lift his head. As cameramen jockeyed for position, in something of a mob scene, Bundini could be heard shouting, "Leave him alone!" It was a chaotic and sudden end to a vicious night of ebb-and-flow action.

During their forty-one rounds together, Muhammad Ali and Joe Frazier exemplified the true essence of the term *nemesis*. Each man's style was the binary opposite of his archenemy; neither man could fathom the idea of relenting to the other. In their first fight, which continues to be one of the biggest promotions in boxing history, winning was everything. In their third fight, winning was something of an afterthought. Both had proven themselves to be all-time greats. Neither man was a loser.

"He is the greatest fighter of all times, next to me," Ali told the ringside commentator, his voice little more than a whisper.

"This is too painful. Too much work. I might have a heart attack or something. I want to get out while I'm on top," Ali said when asked about his future in the sport. Neither man would ever be the same.

"My father respected Frazier," Drew Brown III said to me. "In fact, he once told me, without Joe Frazier, the world would never know how great Muhammad Ali truly is."

"The Thrilla in Manila," in many ways, marks the symbolic end of Muhammad Ali's pugilistic brilliance. Joe Frazier would never again win a professional boxing match.

Listening to the postfight interview, watching Ali struggle to stand erect, nobody in the arena, or watching in the United States on closed-circuit television, could have possibly imagined he would defend his championship six additional times. Those six title defenses would mark a steep decline in Ali's ring performances. As his skills slowly began to deteriorate, the fights became increasingly ugly. Against the much less talented Jimmy Young, Ali was clearly out of shape. In his bout with Alfredo Evangelista, the action was nearly nonexistent. Against Ken Norton, in their third fight, Ali was fortunate to edge out a razor-thin decision victory. Following the bout, Ali would exit the ring to a steady chorus of boos from the crowd. Norton would shed tears of disappointment.

While the aesthetic beauty of Ali's ring performances gradually changed, the makeup of Ali's entourage began to shift as well. On September 2, 1976, less than a month before his third fight with Norton, Ali would file for divorce from Khalilah. Ali's affair with Veronica Porché was, at this point, well known to the American public. Porché, at eighteen years old, had traveled to Zaire to work as a "poster girl" for the Ali–Foreman fight. Upon meeting in Zaire, Ali and Porché quickly began a relationship. Their affair was, without question, one of the prominent tabloid subplots going into the "Thrilla in Manila." Ali would marry Veronica less than a year after his divorce from Khalilah.

Partially because of his marital problems, and partially because of his declining health, Ali struggled to maintain his focus and conditioning. After a pitched battle with Earnie Shavers in Madison Square Garden on September 29, 1977, another close but unanimous decision, Ali's longtime fight doctor Ferdie Pacheco would leave the entourage on his own accord.

"The Shavers fight was the final straw for me," Pacheco later said, citing Ali's damaged kidneys as the reason for his departure.

In hindsight, Pacheco's exit proved to be the correct move. Cracks were beginning to form in the thin ice upon which Muhammad Ali skated.

■　■　■

A few months before Ali's victory over Earnie Shavers, Drew Brown III graduated cum laude with a bachelor's degree in business administration with a minor in economics from Southern University of New Orleans, becoming the first member of his family to get a college degree. During three consecutive scholarship years at SUNO, Drew demonstrated flashes of brilliance on the basketball court. While Drew's dreams of playing in the NBA were slim, his father scored him a tryout with the Boston Celtics. Drew got himself a tryout with the Harlem Globetrotters.

"I knew my basketball skills were not at a professional level. I'd learned that at New Mexico State. But, with the Globetrotters, I thought I'd found a way. It felt perfect. Me matching with the Globetrotters and me getting it on my own. This was the first time that I really took training seriously—I worked very hard," Drew said.

"I was warned in the beginning to not do tricks. I was told to play straight basketball at the tryouts. I didn't listen. I was the fanciest ball player at the tryouts," Drew recalled.

Despite initial success at tryouts, the pairing would not be. Humility, as is often the case for recent college graduates, would come before success.

Drew's first post-college job was that of a door-to-door salesman, selling water purification systems in New Orleans, a task that required him to learn how to handle rejection continuously. Drew's second job would come with WGNO, an independent television station in New Orleans. Building off his experience at the station, Drew would secure a job with a Texas-based firm that produced souvenir programs for high-level boxing matches.

By early 1978, Drew was reveling in his new life. He was a college graduate, a young husband and father, making steady money and becoming a fixture in the Las Vegas fight scene at Caesars Palace. When Muhammad Ali granted Drew's company the rights to produce the official fight program for his upcoming February bout against Leon Spinks, Drew was elated to tell his father the good news. When Bundini answered the call, however, Drew was shocked to find his father inconsolably distraught.

"Herbert said I can't come in until fight week, three days before the fight!" Bundini shouted, once again feeling mistreated by the Black Muslims.

"I'm with Ali because Shorty sent me," Bundini continued, fearing his absence would impact Ali's performance.

"My father believed that Herbert Muhammad was trying to cut corners, trying to save Ali money. The Champ was starting to have financial problems and they didn't see Spinks as a serious fight. At least that's what Daddy believed," Drew told me.

In hindsight, Bundini's assessment of the situation appears to be, in many ways, an accurate one. In *Muhammad Ali: His Life and Times*, biographer Thomas Hauser outlines the mounting financial difficulties that plagued Ali toward the end of his career.

"During his career, Ali made tens of millions of dollars. . . . All totaled, Ali's ring earnings surpassed the combined earnings of every heavyweight champion who had come before him. Moreover, he'd been well-situated to take advantage of numerous business ventures and endorsement opportunities. By 1979 when Ali retired, most of the money he'd earned was gone. Much of it had been generously spent and used to pay taxes, but a lot had been lost to bad deals, exploitation, and outright theft by people he'd trusted," Hauser writes.

In early 1978, research suggests, Ali's physical condition was in no better shape than his financial condition. Knowing what we now know of Ali's unfortunate fiscal situation, one could easily argue that the reason the Champ continued fighting was because maintaining the quality of life he had grown accustomed to required him to do so. Fighting the vastly inexperienced Leon Spinks, on the surface, appeared to be nothing more than a quick money grab.

Leon Spinks looked the part of an underdog. From his unkempt afro, to his undersized frame, to his missing front teeth, Spinks was, in every way, the polar opposite of the physical specimen that was Muhammad Ali. And even though Leon Spinks, as well as his brother Michael, had captured an Olympic gold in the 1976 summer games, no one viewed the twenty-four-year-old boxer as a legitimate threat to Ali's crown. With only seven professional bouts' experience to Spinks's credit—one of those fights resulting in a draw with journeyman Scott LeDoux—Bob Arum and Top Rank had to exercise their creative imaginations in marketing the fight. The promotional angle was simple, playing off Ali's desire to rewrite the record books. Defeating Spinks would provide Ali his fourth victory over a U.S. Olympic gold medalist—Floyd Patterson, Joe Frazier, and George Foreman being the other Olympic champions Ali had beaten. When the fight was announced, very few sportswriters bought the story line. By all estimations, Ali's handlers were looking for an easy tune-up after his war with Shavers the previous year. Despite the creative promotional angle, the fight was a hard sell. Ali–Spinks did not possess box-office stardust.

As the weeks went by and Bundini didn't receive an invitation to training camp, Drew Brown III, working on securing advertising for the Ali–Spinks fight program, found his father increasingly heartbroken. Bundini often phoned his son to express his frustration.

"They want to cut the budget but Champ knows I'm the nutmeg that makes the cake taste special!" Bundini shouted.

For the first time since Ali's first tussle with Ken Norton, Drew's father would not be by Ali's side as he prepared for battle, waking him up in the morning for roadwork, calling those famous poetic lines during sparring. The time away from boxing, as was usually the case, was not good for Bundini. Working for Ali curbed many of Bundini's bad habits, particularly his drinking. When cast off on his own, old demons resurfaced.

Calculating Bundini's worth to Ali's training regimen is also difficult to quantify. Ali's training camp for the first Spinks fight was nothing short of abysmal. Some reports suggest Ali arrived at Deer Lake at just under

250 pounds; the Champ would officially weigh in at just under 225 pounds, the heaviest weight of his professional boxing career.

When the Ali entourage finally assembled in Las Vegas, Drew worried that his father would cause a scene. At fifty years old, Bundini had grown tired of being let go and then brought back into the fold. Appeasing the king, despite all the perks that came with being a member of the royal court, was no easy job.

"Ali probably fired Bundini twenty times during his career. Typically, it didn't last long. Bundini would call me crying and I'd talk to Ali and he would be right back in the gym. Sometimes Ali would fire him and he would just come back anyway," Gene Kilroy told me. When Drew greeted his father at the Las Vegas Hilton, however, he could sense a change in his demeanor. This had been no ordinary leave of absence, a simple cost-cutting business decision.

"I could tell he was bitter. He was still hurt. Daddy seemed more interested in his souvenir business than anything and that wasn't like him. Something was different. He sat by the damn phone waiting for it to ring and it never did. Over the next couple of years, the fights got longer and longer apart. And the paychecks got smaller and smaller. It hurts me to say this but the magic wasn't there anymore. They had finally broken my father's spirit and he tried to numb the pain with Chivas Regal," Drew told me.

During the weeklong buildup to Ali–Spinks, much of Bundini's focus had nothing to do with boxing.

"My father initially told me he had a scored a business deal. We were going to meet with these lawyers in the lobby of the Las Vegas Hilton. Daddy wanted me to read the contract before he signed," Drew recalled.

Three days before the opening bell, Bundini and his son met with two lawyers who introduced themselves as representatives of Herbert Muhammad. As Bundini greeted the two men, he was presented with several legal documents.

"Here is the contract that we agreed upon," one lawyer said to Bundini. Drew, at this moment, had no idea what was going on.

"Daddy, it seems, had agreed to sign a contract that waived his legal claim to the slogan [Float Like a Butterfly] for one fight. Daddy had trademarked the slogan a few years earlier. This new contract would enable Ali's team to produce and sell the paraphernalia for Ali–Spinks and would, in return, grant my father with $25,000," Drew said.

The responsibility of reading and reviewing the contract fell to his college-educated son. Drew read the contract with shaky hands.

"I was standing there in the lobby, trying to read the contract with everyone looking over me and watching. I saw the word *perpetuity* and started to get nervous," Drew added.

Amid the noise and confusion of the Las Vegas Hilton lobby, the young college graduate suddenly felt a wave of panic. His father was about to be scammed.

"Daddy, if you sign this they will take *Float Like a Butterfly* from you forever. They are trying to rip you off," Drew said, handing the contract back to his father.

The lawyers scrambled, verbally falling over each other, in an attempt to counter his estimation of the legal document.

"Mr. Brown, we didn't realize that was in there. This is news to us," they clamored, attempting to save face.

Bundini did not need a second opinion. Tears forming at the corners of his eyes, Bundini ripped the contract into as many pieces as he could possibly muster before turning and heading toward the hotel lobby elevators.

"I don't have to take care of you, Shorty will!" Bundini shouted as he stomped away. Hotel guests, unaware of what they had just witnessed, gawked at the exchange as if it were a car accident.

Drew followed his father into the elevator and up to Muhammad Ali's hotel suite. Bundini banged on the door until it was answered. Storming into the room, Bundini went looking for Ali, who was asleep in bed.

"Daddy had me in tow like I was seven years old, seemingly wanting to show me what that contract really signified. Pulling me into the bedroom, Daddy swung open the door and pointed his finger straight at Ali. The Champ sat up in bed, confused," Drew recounted.

"If they are doing this to me, imagine what they are trying to do to you," Bundini argued.

Drew never forgot the incident. The expression on his tired face, when reliving those memories, told the story of a son's disappointment. The altercation had been a bad omen, shifting the mood.

"Ali asked for clarification. My father repeated the phrase. The next thing I remember was Ali jumping out of bed naked, chasing after us. That's the one thing I remember the most. My most vivid memory of that day. My father looking down at Ali in the bed, saying those words. Ali believed he was different than Joe Louis because he paid his taxes after every fight. Ali believed he was different than Sugar Ray because he only invested in Black businessmen. My father told him there are no Black lawyers and white lawyers. He believed there was only good lawyers and thieves. They were both headed for trouble and I think Daddy could sense it," Drew added.

Bundini, in refusing to sign the contract, would lose out on an opportunity for quick money. Three days later, Ali would lose his heavyweight championship. Spinks, in just his eighth professional fight, would pull off one of the biggest upsets in boxing history.

■   ■   ■

In the early moments of the fight, Ali connected with crisp jabs and pinpoint right hands. By the fourth round, however, it was obvious that the champion was sucking wind. Laying on the ropes, attempting to invite the younger man to punch himself out, inactivity cost Ali rounds on the scorecards. Spinks, on the other hand, was in the best condition of his life. The challenger frequently cornered Ali, launching a nonstop barrage of punches, aiming at nothing and everything all at once. Spinks's aggressive style overwhelmed Ali for much of the fight. The champion wasn't being battered and beaten, knocked around the canvas as had been the case in the final round of the first Frazier fight. Rather, Ali was consistently being outworked, an almost impossible notion to fathom during the prime of his career. As the fight wore on, the impending result became obvious to anyone who was watching. "Close the show, Champ," Bundini called to his fighter from ringside, to no avail.

In the fifteenth and final round, Ali would mount something of a comeback, pinning Spinks into the ropes and launching his own flurry. The effort would prove to be too little too late. In a fight that was, in all actuality, not as close as the official scores suggested, Spinks would win a split decision.

"My father was completely devastated to see Ali lose to Leon Spinks. But I could see a certain gleam in his eyes on the way back to the locker room," Drew recalled.

"You can't beat Shorty," Bundini mumbled to his son after the fight.

For the first and only time in Muhammad Ali's career, his championship was usurped by another man. Fighting through a serious rib injury, unbeknownst to the sporting public, Spinks had been the busier man for each of the fifteen rounds of action. He had also been the more prepared of the two, had gritted through the pain, and had willed himself to victory.

On February 15, 1978, Leon Spinks wanted it more. In defeat, Ali found a renewed determination.

"Allah showed me that I'm not a bad motherfucker," Victor Solano, Ali's friend and training camp stablemate, remembers a dejected Ali saying in the locker room after the fight.

"This is good. I deserved to lose," Ali continued.

Truly embarrassed by a performance for the first time in his career, Ali returned to Deer Lake, Bundini once again by his side, focused on regaining the heavyweight championship. Ali ate properly, limited his distractions, ran five miles a day, and sparred more than he had in previous years combined. His goal was to win back his title to become the first man in boxing history to win the heavyweight championship three times over; he would then retire from the sport. Bundini, according to his son, also approached the second Spinks training camp with a renewed vigor.

"Everyone believed that training camp was going to be the last one. There was no question about it. This *was* it," Drew said.

The second Spinks training camp, according to Drew, took on the feeling of a family reunion. Each member of the entourage stepped up their game in a collective effort to ready Ali for his final shot at redemption.

Leon Spinks, on the other hand, quickly found himself blinded by the limelight, sidetracked by the pleasures and temptations that come with being the heavyweight champion. Shortly after dethroning Ali, the young St. Louis native was arrested for cocaine possession—temporarily placing the return bout in jeopardy. The relatively quick turnaround between the first fight and the rematch, just under seven months, would ironically favor the older man.

■ ■ ■

For Drew, the announcement that the rematch would be held in New Orleans had special meaning. New Orleans was Drew's second home. It was the city where he had attended college, met his then-wife Laurie, and where Laurie had given birth to their six-month-old daughter, Taryn. Although Drew worked in Las Vegas, securing ads for boxing programs, the Big Easy was his family's home. The rematch, scheduled for September 15, 1978, at the New Orleans Superdome, would, like his bar mitzvah many years prior, reunite Drew's new world with his old one. The location provided Laurie's family, most of whom resided in New Orleans, an opportunity to see big-time boxing up close and personal.

"My father was a boxing fanatic. His idol was Sugar Ray Robinson. He was very excited that Ali was going to fight in New Orleans," Laurie said to me, reflecting on the announcement. Little did Laurie know, Bundini was about to give her father one of the most memorable experiences of his life.

The morning of Ali's rematch with Spinks, Drew and Laurie met with Bundini at Ali's hotel headquarters.

"Angel, where's my baby?" Bundini shouted to Laurie, wearing a puzzled expression.

"She's with my parents. They're going to babysit for us tonight," Laurie replied.

Bundini, eager to see his first grandchild, Taryn, would have none of it.

"Think they want to come out to the fight? I want to see my baby, she gives me energy," Bundini proposed.

"I think we could probably talk my parents into it," Laurie sarcastically responded, little hesitation in her voice.

On the day of the most anticipated boxing match in the history of the Big Easy, hours before the opening bell, Bundini somehow arranged for a hotel room to accommodate Laurie's parents. When Lynne and Lawrence Guimont arrived at the hotel, baby Taryn in tow, they were greeted by Bundini, Drew, and Laurie in the lobby, a warm exchange filled with hugs and smiles.

"Hey, there goes Uncle Ray," Drew shouted, interrupting the greeting.

"It was Sugar Ray Robinson and a bunch of boxing guys with him. He was in town to see Ali. My father was completely awestruck," Laurie recalled.

Drew, to no avail, urged his father-in-law to approach his boxing idol.

"I can't go over there," Lawrence bashfully replied.

To this response, Bundini all but dragged Laurie's father across the hotel lobby.

"It was honestly one of the highlights of my father's life. He got to meet his idol," Laurie said to me.

Sensing the significance of the meeting, Bundini invited Lawrence to attend an after-party with Sugar Ray and Muhammad Ali.

"My father, the post office worker, got to hang out with Muhammad Ali and Bundini and Sugar Ray after the fight. I have this vivid memory of him walking through the hotel with those guys, like a real member of the entourage. It almost makes me cry just thinking about how happy it made him. Bundini could drive me crazy at times but I will always love him for being so kind to my father that day. He could also be a saint," Laurie remembered.

"For the Spinks rematch, my father was back to being his old self. His spirit was back. He was a Drew again," Drew III told me.

Moments before the opening bell, Spinks stood in his corner, bouncing up and down on his toes, alone. The pressures of being heavyweight champion had, in just over six months, reduced Spinks as a fighter. Before exiting the ring apron, making his way down the steps, Bundini leaned over the top rope, across Ali's left shoulder, and gestured toward the young champion.

"You might kick his ass, but you'll never beat the both of us!" Bundini shouted at Spinks.

The nutmeg had returned to the recipe and the cake tasted better than ever. In the Big Easy, Ali and Bundini danced for the final time.

The fight itself was not easy on the eyes. Both Ali and Spinks took turns looking sluggish. Relying on his much-improved conditioning, Ali glided around the ring, using his superior lateral movement to avoid Spinks's awkward flurries. In the rematch, there would be no more rope-a-dope. Instead, Ali would work to keep the fight at the center of the ring, consistently tying up his younger opponent when the fight moved into close quarters. The result of Ali's persistent holding would be a point deduction in the fifth round.

Ali's second tactical adjustment was to flurry at the end of the rounds, particularly in the final ten seconds. In close rounds, or rounds where both combatants offered little to no action whatsoever, Ali outworked Spinks in the final moments, attempting to sway the judges in his favor.

"Daddy came up with the perfect solution to a bad round. Always close the show in the last ten seconds! That is when the judges pick up their pencils. He told Ali that. Today, they give that ten-second warning but my father was, in some ways, the pioneer of that concept," Drew remembered.

Spinks attacked, swinging wildly, but not with the same fury or intensity of the first fight. If it had been any other challenger, had the stakes not been so high, the crowd might have booed the action. Instead, the 60,000 fans in attendance cheered relentlessly. Every time Ali landed a punch, significant or otherwise, the crowd came alive.

"The atmosphere was unbelievable. It was as if New Orleans was dragging their hero to the finish line," Drew recalled.

The lively New Orleans crowd, perhaps more inspired by the historical significance of what was taking place than the actual fight itself, provided an appropriate soundscape to the high drama of the night.

When the final bell rang, Bundini awkwardly climbed over the top rope, as if there were no other way to enter the ring. As was almost always the case, Bundini was the first to greet Ali. Minutes later, Ali would be granted a unanimous decision victory that would rewrite the record books. Before exiting the ring, Ali blew kisses to the capacity crowd, as if to say farewell. The cosmic balance of the boxing universe had been restored. Muhammad Ali was once again champion of the world.

If his life were a fairy tale, the Spinks rematch would have been a fitting ending to the story. Muhammad Ali's career, an epic demonstration of bravery against impossible odds, was always more Beowulf than Cinderella.[2] The happily-ever-after would last only two brief years. Boxing's king would eventually soldier on in search of new dragons to slay. Epic poems, unlike fairy tales, do not have happy endings. Such would be the case for Muhammad Ali, an aging warrior whose self-belief knew no boundaries.

■　■　■

In the end, Don King scored his long-awaited, painfully symbolic revenge. After successfully promoting, and in many ways salvaging, "The Rumble in the Jungle," King's master plan was to gain promotional and managerial control over Ali, supplanting Bob Arum and Herbert Muhammad, respectively. At first, it appeared the controversial promoter just might pull it off. After dethroning Foreman, Ali agreed to give King another try. Ali's first title defense, promoted under the banner of Don King Productions, was a success only in that the legendary mismatch inspired writer and actor Sylvester Stallone to invent the character Rocky Balboa. The event, pitting the newly crowned champion against journeyman Chuck Wepner, in King's hometown of Cleveland, Ohio, was, by all accounts, a financial disaster.

Marking Wepner as a hard-drinking, everyday man with a puncher's chance, King employed the same "Great White Hope" formula that he would later make famous in the Larry Holmes–Gerry Cooney megafight. In the case of Wepner, however, the mismatch was so great there was no betting line. The fight lost money and closed-circuit-television numbers were abysmal. When Ali returned to the ring against dangerous puncher Ron Lyle, just a few months later, Bob Arum was back in the promotional driver's seat.

After the Wepner debacle, Don King struggled to find his way back into Ali's inner circle. While King was granted the opportunity to co-promote the third Ali–Frazier fight with Bob Arum, he was unable to fully capitalize on the blockbuster in Zaire. With Ali proving loyal to Arum, King set his sights on Herbert Muhammad.

"Don tried a hostile takeover of Muhammad Ali and it failed. He was relying on the flunkies he was paying off. He underestimated the bond between Ali and Herbert, the religious piece. That's why, to this day, orthodox Muslims don't like Don King. He tried to cheat the messenger's son," Bahar Muhammad candidly told investigative journalist Jack Newfield for *The Life and Crimes of Don King*.

Whether or not Bundini was one of the so-called "flunkies" Bahar Muhammad is referring to is unclear. In the HBO film *Only in America*, based off Newfield's book, Bundini serves as the dramatic stand-in. Drew Brown III, on the other hand, denies this version of the events.

Based on Bundini's rocky relationship with Herbert Muhammad and the Nation of Islam, it is plausible to suggest Bundini actually preferred King's message and took issue with the Nation of Islam's choice to back a white promoter over a Black one. As a result of King's desperate attempt to remove Herbert Muhammad from the equation, Ali distanced himself from King after his victory in Manila. Now on the outside of the Ali entourage, King began to craft his Plan B.

If King couldn't have the champion, he would sign up all of the worthwhile contenders, particularly the division's emerging crop of young talent.

When the Ali–Spinks rematch was announced in spring of 1978, the World Boxing Council stripped Spinks of their version of the world title. By defeating Ali, Spinks had earned both the WBC and WBA belts. In *The Life and Crimes of Don King*, Jack Newfield outlines the behind-the-scenes boxing politics that surrounded the WBC's decision: "[Don] King called José Sulaimán, the president of the World Boxing Council, one of the comic regulating authorities, based in Mexico City, and convinced him to strip Spinks of his title for the crime of giving Ali an immediate rematch, instead of fighting number-one contender Ken Norton [Don King's fighter]. By stripping Spinks without due process or a fair hearing, Sulaimán created a second version of the heavyweight title, a great advantage to King, who had all the other contenders under contract."

King's heavyweight roster now included proven veterans Ken Norton and Earnie Shavers, as well as newcomers Tim Witherspoon and Larry Holmes. The decision to strip Spinks of his WBC title, unpopular at the time, would, in hindsight, mark the beginning of a new era in the heavyweight division.

On June 9, 1978, Ken Norton would face off with the WBC's number-two contender, Larry Holmes, both fighters signed to Don King Productions, for the vacant WBC title. The fight would not disappoint. In an epic contest of skill and will, Holmes would take his first step toward writing his own legacy, shedding the label of sparring partner. The same could be said for King, who now had a much younger heavyweight champion under an exclusive promotional contract. In becoming the WBC heavyweight champion, winning a spirited fifteen-round split decision over a man Ali had twice defeated, Holmes would, however, not receive immediate acclaim. At first, Holmes would struggle to gain mainstream respectability. Ali–Spinks II was for the true championship of the world, according to public opinion. Ali's immediate retirement following his victory over Spinks would momentarily eliminate any chance of Holmes obtaining the lineal title. After defeating Norton, Holmes successfully defended his WBC crown seven times, all by way of knockout. Those wins, despite the champion's dominance in the ring, did little to make the boxing public forget about Ali. Holmes struggled to find a suitable rival, a Liston, Frazier, or Foreman who could catapult him into superstardom. Defeating Alfredo Evangelista and Earnie Shavers, both of whom had already lost to Ali, did little to bolster Holmes's legend.

While Holmes struggled to obtain crossover success, Ali struggled to adjust to life after boxing. First came an invitation from President Jimmy Carter to serve as an ambassador for the United States, an ill-fated attempt to convince other countries to support the United States' proposed boycott of the 1980 Moscow Olympics, a reaction to the Soviet invasion of Afghanistan. Ali's travels would take him to Moscow, India, Kenya, Liberia, and Senegal. In the minds of some critics, Ali looked like a political puppet. The fighter who bravely stood up to the American political machine was now being used to promote the American agenda. When pressed on the political issues, Ali sometimes struggled to outline the purpose of his travels. Shortly after Ali returned to the United States, rumors swirled that he was eager to return to the ring. Those rumors would soon prove to be true.

In March of 1980, Bob Arum announced that Ali would end his two-year retirement and return to face WBA champion "Big John" Tate in a bout scheduled for early summer. Three weeks after the announcement, Tate would be knocked out by Mike Weaver. Arum's plan took an additional hit when Ali, only days into returning to Deer Lake, was severely cut above the lip in sparring, delaying any immediate return to the ring. With Tate out of the picture and Ali publicly committed to a return to boxing, promoters flocked in Ali's direction. Arum could offer Ali a bout with Weaver but Don King could provide the former champion with a shot at the title. King's $8 million offer for an Ali–Holmes bout came complete with a built-in story line. The bout could easily be sold as a showdown between the student and his teacher, the former sparring partner and his legendary master. King sold Ali on the historical significance of the match, an opportunity to win the title for an unthinkable fourth time. King understood that Ali was broke and needed money.

There are multiple reasons why Muhammad Ali ended his two-year retirement from boxing, none of which have anything to do with any pent-up disdain toward Larry Holmes. Most critics point to Ali's mounting financial difficulties. When asked why Ali took the fight, Wali "Youngblood" Muhammad, in the ESPN 30 for 30 documentary *Muhammad and Larry*, suggested "greed" was the primary factor.

"Greed. They showed him that money," Muhammad contends.[3]

In my conversations with Drew Brown III, I was struck by his take on Ali–Holmes. "Fame," Drew said to me, his voice full of certainty. Fame was the true reason Ali returned to the sport of boxing.

"Muhammad Ali was absolutely addicted to fame," Drew insisted. "The lights. The crowd. When you are the Champ, everything revolves around you. Everyone is working for a common cause. Your cause. Ali never did drugs. He didn't drink. But he was a junkie for fame. Ali would sign every single autograph. He was generous with fans. I would never deny his generosity. But Champ was addicted to the attention that came with celebrity. He loved the feeling of being loved. He didn't want the show to be over any more than the fans."

The same could perhaps be argued about Drew's father, who was undoubtedly at his best when working by Ali's side. The two-year hiatus from boxing had been equally unkind to Bundini. Unfortunately, Bundini's son, at the same time, was struggling with his own personal issues. Drinking had ruined Drew Brown Sr.'s life, it had done the same for Drew III's parents. The disease was now beginning to wreck his life as well. The family, for a brief period of time, was in utter disarray.

"When Daddy would get low, he would stop coming around. We wouldn't hear from him for months. He didn't want his family to see him struggle," Drew said to me.

Ali's comeback fight against Holmes was the lifeline Bundini had been praying for. He was, as one might suspect, elated to return to work, his old life.

"My father was broke. He was struggling. What would you expect him to say when the Champ called him?" Drew added.

Looking back on the fight, it is almost impossible to imagine anyone believing the thirty-eight-year-old Muhammad Ali could defeat a prime Larry Holmes, particularly after a two-year layoff, with no tune-up fight to test or sharpen his skills. Today, we recognize Holmes as the Hall of Fame champion he would later become. We've seen what Parkinson's disease would do to Ali's body in the coming years. Aside from the obvious allure of another big paycheck, one last dance in the spotlight, Ali's team was, in many ways, agreeable to the fight because they were blind to the realities of the situation, largely because of their unique relationship to each man. They'd watched Ali handle Holmes in the gym for half a decade, they'd grown accustomed to thinking of Holmes as Ali's hired hand. Their overconfidence, the result of a remarkable career of logic-defying upset victories, was an unfortunate by-product of their past.

"Yes. My father said he thought Ali could win, but deep down in his heart he knew what was coming," Drew told me.

Returning to proper fighting shape, in the end, would prove next to impossible for Ali. In the two years since his victory over Spinks, his mental and physical health had rapidly begun to deteriorate. The severity of his physical condition leading up to the Holmes fight continues to be a topic of controversy and debate among boxing scholars.

In Jonathan Eig's best-selling biography *Ali: A Life*, Veronica Porché suggests that she began to notice slurring in Ali's speech leading up to the Holmes bout. She had also noticed that Ali's thumb had begun to twitch on occasion. While Ali often complained of insomnia, he paid little mind to his other physical ailments. Those closest to the Champ believed his ailments were nothing more than typical side effects from a long career in boxing. Three months before the bout, in an attempt to demonstrate his physical readiness, Ali would undergo a three-day examination at the Mayo Clinic. The two reports that emerged from the examination remain controversial to this day. Dr. John Mitchell concluded that "[Ali] is in excellent general medical health with no evidence of renal impairment or chronic or acute medical illness." When the Nevada State Athletic Commission refused to make the Mayo Clinic report available to the press, controversy ensued. Leading up to the bout, Ali's health became an unfortunate subplot for promoter Don King.

After the Ali–Holmes bout was signed, King held the typical prefight press conference, an extravaganza of trash talk and hyperbolic posturing. Playing off the shape of the champion's head, Ali nicknamed Holmes "The Peanut." As expected, there was plenty of talk regarding Holmes's former duties at Deer Lake, Pennsylvania.

"I knew exactly what they were going to say before they even said it," Holmes said to me. "The trash talk didn't concern me because I already knew what they were gonna say. You're a sparring partner. You ain't no real champ. The real Champ is back," Holmes continued, chuckling, doing his best to mimic Ali's unmistakable cadence.

While Ali was eager to fuel King's promotional flame, some members of the entourage felt uncomfortable goading Holmes. In the ESPN 30 for 30 documentary *Muhammad and Larry*, Bundini clearly expresses discomfort about forwarding the teacher vs. pupil narrative. "What you want me to say? Larry don't give a damn about the Champ? Champ don't give a damn about Larry? That what you want? I hope you're happy with yourself," Bundini scolds one reporter.

In the end, Ali–Holmes would produce no fireworks or indelible memories. There were no knockdowns, cuts, or wild exchanges. After the completion of nine humiliating rounds, trainer Angelo Dundee stopped the bout, screaming to referee Richard Green, "I'm the chief second and I say the fight is over!"

Bundini, his face contorted in disappointment, begged Dundee for "one more round."

Ali had not won a single moment of the fight.

Throughout the night, Holmes landed his telephone-pole jab at will, and dug hard right hands into Ali's kidneys and rib cage. Ali plodded around the ring, attempting to dance, occasionally showboating. Despite the enthusiasm Ali exhibited in the ring before the official announcements—Ali called for fans to boo Holmes and was repeatedly restrained by his corner—his demeanor completely changed after the opening bell. This was more than a mismatch. This was public torture. This was a beatdown. As the rounds progressed, Holmes began to gradually press the action, landing telling blows to the head and body. Ali offered little to nothing in return. Holmes's conundrum was obvious. The champion wanted to make Ali quit. He wanted to inflict just enough punishment to stop the fight, without injuring or knocking out his tired and weakened friend.

"After all these years, how would you define your relationship with Muhammad Ali?" I asked Holmes.

"He was my buddy. Ali was my buddy," Larry Holmes replied.

■ ■ ■

In defeating Muhammad Ali, becoming the true lineal champion of the division, Larry Holmes experienced one of his saddest moments in boxing. In his corner, in front of the entire world, Holmes began to cry. The champion was not alone in this sentiment. For Black America, Ali was a walking personification of pride and power, an enduring champion born amid the Civil Rights Movement. For others, Ali was a symbol of protest against the Vietnam War, the oppression of poor and colored people. In boxing, he was the most handsome, articulate, and artistic champion the sport had ever seen. Holmes, despite taking no punishment whatsoever, would suffer plenty, particularly in the court of public opinion. Holmes dedicated his life to boxing, reigned as heavyweight champion of the world for twenty successful title defenses, placing him behind only the great Joe Louis in the history books. His reign would be, at the time, the longest individual heavyweight title streak in modern boxing history. Despite all the highlight victories that made up his Hall of Fame career, and there were many, Holmes would never fully escape the shadow of Ali's enduring legend. Defeating a thirty-eight-year-old version of Ali, a man who was beginning to show the signs of early onset Parkinson's, Holmes did little to win over the masses. The victory, in many respects, had the opposite effect. After the fight, Ali would be taken to a Las Vegas hospital. In true fashion, Don King would pay him $1.17 million less than the contract stipulated.

In September of 1981, less than a year after Ali–Holmes, "Drama in Bahama" was officially announced, a ten-round nontitle bout that would pit a thirty-nine-year-old Muhammad Ali against little-known Jamaican-Canadian heavyweight Trevor Berbick, who sported a modest record of nineteen wins, two losses, and one draw. The announcement was met with very little enthusiasm from the American public. Heralded as a "last hurrah," the bout would take place at Nassau Coliseum in the Bahamas, partially because no athletic commission in the United States would touch it.

"Ali fooled us before the Holmes fight. But the Berbick fight was different. Everyone knew that he was going to get his ass kicked. Daddy knew. Angelo knew. The rest of them did too. It was a matter of people wanting to be there by Ali's side. Ali was having financial trouble at the time. Champ wanted every single one of them there," Drew said.

For even the most die-hard Ali fans, the match made little to no sense. Ali's health, following the Holmes fight, was the only true story line. Some within the Ali camp argued that Ali's embarrassing performance against Holmes was connected to a misdiagnosed thyroid problem as opposed to old age. Berbick, little known to mainstream audiences, offered no additional angle or story line, other than the fact that his limited skills might provide Ali with an opportunity to score a victory in the final bout of his career.

Upon arriving at Deer Lake, Pennsylvania, for the final training camp of Ali's career, Bundini worked with other members of the team to collect money to purchase a surprise gift for their soon-to-be-retired boss.

"It was going to be their final camp together so everyone pitched in, with the idea of buying a plaque with the engraved names of Ali's entourage, in alphabetical order. They were going to have it put up at camp as a remembrance of all they had accomplished at Deer Lake," Drew said.

When Bundini made his way into town, he mistakenly ordered a gravestone. The good-natured mistake couldn't have been a more accurate one.

■ ■ ■

Resting atop Drew Brown III's bookshelf in his Atlanta home was a framed copy of Muhammad Ali's famous "Last Hurrah" *Sports Illustrated* cover, from the October 13, 1980, issue reporting on Ali's comeback defeat to Larry Holmes. Drew had, no doubt, framed the magazine cover because his father was so prominently featured in the picture. Otherwise, the image is one that most Ali supporters would like to forget.

"I've always had a difficult time watching Ali–Holmes. I don't think I have ever watched the Berbick fight, aside from the highlights," I said to Drew. Surprisingly, Bundini's son suggested he had never watched the Berbick fight either.

The image on the magazine cover, after listening to Drew's stories, was more troubling than might have otherwise been the case. These had been dark days for the Brown family. Leaning through the ropes, his left hand resting on Ali's shoulder, Bundini whispers into the ear of the battered champion.

"What's the story with your father's ring?" I asked, pointing out the NBA championship–style ring on his father's hand.

"That's his heavyweight championship ring. Ali gave it to him. At the end, my father was down on his luck. He was forced to hock the ring because he was broke," Drew answered.

In the photo, the red ring rope rests just below Bundini's chin, the famous bald strip shining atop Bundini's head. Both men display the physical evidence of old age.

Studying the sad expression in Ali's puffy eyes, I was reminded of Percy Bysshe Shelley's "Ozymandias," a poem where the speaker stumbles upon the ruins of a once-powerful king. Pretensions of greatness blind even the most powerful kings of their own inevitable decline, Shelley warns.

"This was a bad time in our family," Drew injected. "Even in those Spinks fights, my father could sense it was all coming to an end. Everyone around Ali was scrambling to get that final dollar," Drew continued, placing the magazine back on the shelf.

To be heralded as great, to be recognized as not only great but perhaps the greatest of all the greats, is a feeling that hardly any human being will ever get the chance to experience. Hubris is not the by-product of greatness, I thought to myself. Rather, it is often the driving force behind acts of greatness, a blind and foolish and perhaps necessary brand of internal belief.

What had begun as a simple inquiry had eaten up all of my final morning in Atlanta. It was now less than three hours until my departure to Albany, New York.

"We should probably make our way to the airport," I said to Drew, returning my host to the present.

While I was in the guest room, collecting my carry-on bag, Drew Brown III removed the framed portrait of Ali and his father from the wall, undid the back of the frame, and rolled it up.

This was his parting gift to me.

Drew Brown III with his "big brother" Muhammad Ali in
the mess hall at Deer Lake. *Courtesy of Drew Brown III*

Drew Bundini Brown poses with a young boy during a press conference in New
York City in 1974. Bundini believed in a higher power called "Shorty," a God
who looks out for the little guy. *The Ring Magazine via Getty Images*

Drew Bundini Brown urges on Muhammad Ali during his fight against hard-punching Earnie Shavers at Madison Square Garden on September 29, 1977. *Getty Images*

Bundini shadows Ali in the gym at Deer Lake before his rematch with Leon Spinks. *Courtesy of Jeff Julian*

Deer Lake, Pennsylvania, 1978: Drew Bundini Brown wraps Muhammad Ali's hands as he prepares for Ali–Spinks II. *Courtesy of Jeff Julian*

New Orleans, 1978: "You may kick his ass, but you won't ever beat the both of us," Bundini calls out to Leon Spinks just before the fifteenth round of the Ali–Spinks rematch. *Courtesy of Drew Brown III*

New Orleans, November 1979: Muhammad Ali at the grand opening of Drew Brown III's nightclub "Bundini's." *Courtesy of Drew Brown III*

Drew Bundini Brown and Angelo Dundee express concern during Ali's fight with former sparring partner Larry Holmes at Caesars Palace in Las Vegas on October 2, 1980. *AP Photo*

Muhammad Ali, Drew Bundini Brown, and James "Quick" Tillis, "The Fighting Cowboy." Bundini trained Tillis during 1984 and 1985. *Courtesy of Drew Brown III*

Drew Bundini Brown, Drew Brown III, and
Drew Brown IV. Bundini was a proud father
and grandfather. *Courtesy of Drew Brown III*

New Orleans, 1978: Drew Bundini Brown and his granddaughter, Taryn. *Courtesy of Drew Brown III*

The iconic rocks at Deer Lake were painted with the names of team members, legendary champions, and notable Ali opponents. Bundini's rock features his famous line, *Float like a butterfly, sting like a bee. Courtesy of Jeff Julian*

ALI'S STAFF

HOWARD L. BINGHAM
DREW "BUNDINI" BROWN
ANGELO DUNDEE
JIMMY ELLIS
GENE KILROY
WALI MUHAMMAD
ABDUL RAHMAN
LUIS SARRIA
LANA SHABAZZ

JAMES ANDERSON

A re-creation of the tablet Drew Bundini Brown purchased as a retirement present for Muhammad Ali in 1978. On June 3, 2016, Mike Madden, the son of football coach John Madden, bought the Deer Lake property to restore and preserve it as a historical site. "Fighter's Heaven" opened to the public in 2019. *Courtesy of Jeff Julian*

11

The Fighting Cowboy

The life of James Theodore Tillis is best described as a contradiction. Born and raised in a small neighborhood in North Tulsa, Oklahoma, the predominately Black section of town, his is a story both typical of its surroundings and extraordinary just the same. Like many Oklahoma boys, Tillis was the product of the prairies, riding horses at the tender age of eight, eventually competing in local rodeos. His grandfather, Peter Hawkins, was a Black cowboy who made his living breaking horses. Lassoing calves would later become his grandson's specialty. While cowboying was Tillis's first love, the young wrangler also excelled at organized sports. In high school, Tillis was a standout fullback, also played baseball, and was a member of the wrestling team. For the man who would one day come to be known as "The Fighting Cowboy," it was a dubious path to challenging for the heavyweight championship of the world.

The seed was planted the night Cassius Clay shocked the world by lifting the heavyweight crown from Sonny Liston.

"Oh, Mama, I want to be just like him!" the seven-year-old version of James Tillis called to his mother.

"You can be anything you want to be, James," Rose answered. "But, shut up now . . . we trying to listen to the fight," she added, adjusting the volume on the radio.

The roots began to form at O'Brien Park Recreation Center in Tulsa, Oklahoma. Under the tutelage of trainer Ed Duncan, Tillis amassed an impressive amateur record of ninety-eight wins to only eight losses, winning three state Golden Gloves and four AAU titles. Tillis would, of course, have to leave the Oklahoma prairie to pursue his career in professional boxing.

The flower began to grow and eventually bloom in Chicago, under the direction of manager Jim Kaulentis and promoter Ernie Terrell. In the Windy City, Tillis quickly earned a reputation as one of the top heavyweight prospects in the sport, garnering the collective attention of the boxing world, including Muhammad Ali.

The "Fighting Cowboy's" first face-to-face encounter with "The Greatest" was, in typical Ali fashion, teasing and playful.

"I was getting ready for my fourth pro fight at DePaul University in Chicago [February 28, 1979]. Ali came into the dressing room before the fight. Ali was my idol. I wanted to be like him. I was awestruck," Tillis recalled.

"Is you a champ or a chump?" Ali shouted upon approaching Tillis, playfully slap-boxing with the twenty-two-year-old as he attempted to tie the laces of his boxing shoes.

"You got a baby face. But I know the truth. Us baby-face boys can fight," Ali teased after the impromptu slap-boxing match had ended.

Later that night, Tillis would knock out a journeyman from Cleveland, Ohio. Seated ringside, Ali must have liked what he saw in the slick boxer. After the bout, Ali invited Tillis to train at his secluded boxing wonderland in Deer Lake, Pennsylvania.

"We became friends right from the start. From then on, we were tight. They brought me to Deer Lake. I sparred with Ali five times. Went ten rounds with him. He was very helpful to me in my early career. Because of Ali, I became close with Bundini and Angelo," Tillis reflected.

During his time at Deer Lake, Tillis was able to witness, firsthand, the complex relationship Ali shared with his personal motivator. The young boxer instantly gained an appreciation for Bundini's unique approach. Listening to Tillis relive those memories, I was struck by the manner in which he described the experience, something akin to being the pupil of a spiritual guru. Tillis clearly viewed Bundini as the catalyst to Ali's mental strength, a teacher who removed spiritual and mental darkness from the minds of his pupils. For Tillis, Bundini was more than a boxing trainer.

"When Bundini would get to talking like that, he'd make the hairs on your arms stand up. Wasn't one time that I was around them that it didn't give me a thrill. He was Ali's spirit man. He really loved Ali. You could see it. Ain't nobody else in the game was like him. Bundini focused on the spirit," Tillis suggested.

In our conversations, Tillis went out of his way to highlight the authority in which Bundini spoke to the Champ. Bundini did not mince words when he felt Ali was not giving his best effort in the gym.

"[Bundini] would cuss Ali out. You better believe it. He kept Ali grounded," Tillis argued.

Early into his time at Deer Lake, Tillis formed a strong bond with Ali's entourage, a deep admiration for the way in which the unit conducted business.

Befriending Ali and Bundini changed the young professional in more ways than one. Until visiting Deer Lake, the boxer had been known in the media as James "Quick" Tillis, a nickname that had followed him around since 1973. The moniker "The Fighting Cowboy," on the other hand, first began with a poem crafted by Ali and Bundini, something of a parting gift. The poem went as follows:

He don't float like a butterfly or sting like a bee
Cause he ain't Ali
He's the fighting cowboy
He rides 'em, ropes 'em, brands 'em, and corrals 'em
He's the fighting cowboy, ol' dude!!! Yahweee!!

Watching Ali and Bundini perform the poem, just as they had done in their rendition of "float like a butterfly," was one of the true high points of Tillis's young life. The greatest fighter–trainer duo of all time, at least by Tillis's estimation, had given him an original battle cry, with a moniker to match. The young fighter felt he was destined to become the next heavyweight champion of the world.

It would be a career rife with both flashes of promise and moments of befuddling disappointment, a seismograph chart of ups and downs. Tillis would win the first twenty bouts of his professional career, fighting mostly in the Chicago area, before losing a controversial decision to Mike Weaver in his first heavyweight title fight.

For the biggest fight of his career, Tillis would employ the services of Angelo Dundee. Before the Weaver fight, when Tillis had mentioned the possibility of adding Bundini to the mix, Dundee had advised his fighter against the move.

"I think Drew's drinking problems were beginning to get out of hand at that point. It was nothing against Drew, but I think he was in a bad place at the time. That's all that was. I remember my father trying everything in the book to motivate Tillis. He even pulled a hair out of his chest in the corner," Jim Dundee said to me.

In hindsight, Tillis expressed regret for acquiescing to Dundee's advice. For Tillis, having Bundini in his corner might have made the difference in what became a close decision loss.

"I wish I would have had Bundini when I fought Mike Weaver for the championship. Angelo was in my corner for that fight. Angelo was a good fitness man. I like Angelo. I ain't putting Angelo down or nothing. But he didn't have soul. I wish Bundini would have been there," Tillis told me.

The controversial loss to Weaver was followed up by bounce-back wins against Jerry Williams and Earnie Shavers, those victories followed up by back-to-back technical knockout losses to Pinklon Thomas and Greg Page. Even in defeat, Tillis showed flashes of greatness. In the Page fight, for example, Tills dropped Page in the second but gradually faded and was stopped in the eighth. While some boxing pundits continued to view the twenty-seven-year-old fighter as a legitimate contender, others wrote him off as nothing more than a pugilistic litmus test for young prospects.

When "The Fighting Cowboy" and Angelo Dundee mutually decided to part ways after the loss to Page, Tillis began to mull over the possibility of bringing Bundini on board as his head trainer. In the fall of 1984, at a crossroads in his career, faced with the opportunity to square off against undefeated heavyweight prospect Carl "The Truth" Williams, Tillis finally made the call. Bundini had not stepped into a boxing ring since Ali's humiliating loss to Trevor Berbick.

"Since Ali had retired, my father was left unemployed with no real options, even though Daddy was only fifty-two years old," Drew Brown III reflected.

Bundini accepted the challenge of revitalizing Tillis's boxing career. Tillis, above all else, was his friend. Life had taught both men the importance of getting back on the horse.

■   ■   ■

While Bundini struggled to adjust to life after Ali, the early 1980s were also a time of flux for his son. The disappointment Drew III experienced as a result of his failed New Orleans nightclub was countered by the joy his family experienced by the arrival of a fourth-generation Drew. On July 19, 1979, Laurie gave birth to Drew Jacques Brown IV, the couple's second child. The boy's name served as a tribute to both of Buddy Drew's grandfathers. With no money to invest and no business reputation to fall back on, once again feeling the added pressure to become the father and provider he never had, Drew III put aside his entrepreneurial dreams. Combing through the job ads in the *Times-Picayune*, a job advertisement for the Offshore Drilling and Exploration Company caught the young father's eye. The pay wasn't great but Drew III was focused on continuing to provide for his family.

"I saw the ad in the paper for an offshore drilling company in the Gulf Coast. My friend Craig and I both went to the interview. Because I had a college degree and he didn't, I got paid twice as much to work as a safety engineer. It was one of my first realizations that Daddy was right, college did make a big difference," Drew said to me.

As a safety officer, Drew worked seven days a week, forty miles out in the Gulf of Mexico, before returning to shore for a solid week of leave, a cycle that would repeat itself twice a month. The *Ocean Traveler*, the oil rig to which Drew was assigned, is best described as an emotional desert, the polar opposite of the luxury suite the young college graduate had enjoyed during his time at Caesars Palace. Constructed of metal and steel, coated with deep-gray paint, the physical environment was built for function rather than comfort. Simply put, there were no recreation activities or all-access nightclubs on the *Ocean Traveler*. Work was the only way to occupy one's mind. Drew's daily routine consisted of checking fire extinguishers, a couple of safety lines, and making sure everyone was wearing a hard hat. When his shift was complete, Drew took a shower, ate, and went to sleep. The mundane routine, a mind-crushing mixture of boredom and seclusion, was a blessing in disguise for the young father.

Looking back on what was, at the time, one of the truly humbling experiences of his work life, Drew said the following: "I needed the radical change in lifestyle that [the job] offered. First, we would have to leave home in the wee hours of the delta mornings and drive to the Gulf shore in Houston. That eliminated the all-night drinking and partying I had been doing. Once I got to Houston, I had to take a helicopter ride to the rig."

In October of 1980, Drew watched Larry Holmes's somber dismantling of Muhammad Ali, a bout that would be the Champ's last on American soil. Witnessing the end of Ali's mythic era had a sobering effect on Drew, who had grown up thinking of Ali as a big brother.

At twenty-six years old, and with his wife Laurie back working at D. H. Homes, the same department store in which the couple had met years ago, Drew began to view his life as a series of failures. Drew longed for a career to call his own.

"Get yourself a profession," Bundini urged his son, never one to entertain complaints. "You went to college, boy. Find something you can do well and enjoy. Find a profession that nobody can take from you," he argued.

"But Daddy, I don't know how to transform all this negativity into a positive," Drew cried.

"Show up, wake up, and pay attention. Shorty's got you. Shorty don't make mistakes," Bundini responded.

In hindsight, the fatherly advice would indeed prove useful. The answer Drew was looking for amid the troubled waters of the Gulf Coast, the unpredictable currents of his own life, would both literally and figuratively fall from the sky.

During the spring of 1981, two separate incidents would change the trajectory of Drew Brown III's life. The first would come in the form of a tragic accident. As a crew of men worked to make sludge for the drilling hole, a rig located over the workers' heads hauled one-hundred-pound bags of cement on a pallet, a routine procedure. This day, however, one of the pallets would break, and before anyone could react, a worker was buried underneath the falling materials. "I thought he was crushed to death," Drew remembered.

Transported off the oil rig by a medical helicopter, the victim would suffer a broken back and multiple internal injuries. As the safety inspector, he was required to accompany the victim to the hospital. Shaken up by the incident, Drew began to pray for a better life.

A few days after the accident, Drew's salvation emerged from the clouds, ripping through the suspended white, a sonic boom born of speed, power, and impressive force, impossible to ignore. The military jets flying missions above the oil rig reminded Drew of the fighter planes he had seen in Israel as a boy. When Drew made it back to shore the next week, he and a co-worker engaged in a casual conversation about the air missions. The conversation quickly turned to the topic of airline pilots.

"They only work a few days a month," Drew's friend suggested. "Pilots have it made. It's like a hidden country club. They make all this money and have all this free time, flying all over the world," he urged.

On Drew's next shore leave, he visited a U.S. Air Force recruiting office in downtown New Orleans.

Unaware of the U.S. Armed Services' inability to diversify their recruiting efforts, Drew was shocked to find his ambitions met with enthusiasm and encouragement.

"They treated me like gold. There were so few Blacks signing up for the Air Force in those days. I was a college-educated Black man so I definitely fit the bill. My only disappointment would come in learning that I would not be able to begin Air Force training for another sixteen weeks," Drew recalled.

The young dreamer was unwilling to endure another three months in the Gulf.

"Try the Navy. There are no Black pilots in the Navy. Man, they can get you in much faster," a local recruit suggested to Drew in the hallway, sensing his impatience.

"They showed me scenes from this movie, *Sea Legs*. It had action-packed footage of navy jets flying on and off aircraft carriers. I was sold! But I never thought *that* was what I was going to do. I was just trying to make it to a career as an airline pilot," Drew said to me, chuckling at his own youthful exuberance.

When Drew arrived home later that evening, he proudly announced to Laurie that he was joining the Navy and becoming a pilot.

Because of his own negative experiences, one might assume Bundini was, at first, skeptical of his son's newfound Navy ambitions. When Drew broke the news, in April of 1981, however, his father was ecstatic.

"Go get 'em, Sneezer," Bundini proudly said.

"When I was a little, I wanted to go to Annapolis because of Daddy. Ironically, here I was, joining the Navy, just like he did," Drew said to me.

A week later Bundini mailed his son a letter of recommendation written and signed by none other than literary giant George Plimpton, who wrote that Drew was "a most engaging young man—bright, a fine athlete . . . and it gives me great pleasure to recommend him for your branch of service."

The letter, unsolicited by Drew, was Bundini's way of helping.

After securing a second recommendation letter, written by his old economics professor Dr. Wilson, Drew completed the necessary physical examination requirements. He quit his job on the oil rig and readied himself for a life in the sky.

To fulfill his dream of becoming a jet pilot, Drew would first have to become a naval officer. In late spring of 1981, he entered officer candidate school at the Naval Air Station in Pensacola, Florida, a prestigious sixteen-week program. When Drew arrived in Pensacola, he instantly felt the magnitude of his undertaking.

"I was the Navy's answer to Jack Johnson, Jackie Robinson, and Joe Louis. The other candidates were much younger, shorter, and, of course, white. They came from prestigious schools such as Harvard, Yale, Cornell, and Dartmouth. They came from aviation schools, they had dreamed of doing this their entire life. None of [them had] even heard of Southern University of New Orleans," Drew recalled.

After the introductory session began, candidates listened to a series of speeches from the base captain and the lieutenant in charge of the academic program. At the end of the information session, the lieutenant said calmly, "Now I would like to introduce you to someone who you are going to become very intimate with. Your drill instructor, Gunnery Sergeant Stephen W. Clark." From the back of the room walked a white man who stood well over six feet tall, weighing in at a solid 200 pounds.

"He was wearing those black government-issue eyeglasses, carrying his hat underneath his arm, and when he reached the front of the room, he turned about-face, and—bam!—he looked like Moses. I had never seen a bigger, stronger, meaner, more serious person in my life," Drew recalled.

The bellowing voice of Gunnery Sergeant Stephen W. Clark would mark the end of Drew Brown III's fantasy. A daunting task awaited. Later that day, Drew was issued fatigues casually referred to as "poopie suits," and silver-painted helmets called "chrome domes." Holding those artifacts in his hands, alone in his assigned room, the reality set in. This experience would be far more daunting than the kibbutz in Israel, far more challenging than a training camp at Deer Lake. The next morning, at 4 a.m., Drew Brown III's life changed forever.

"Get up, you sonuvabitches, get up! Get your brown-stained underwear off, and get out here in the hallway. Now!"

Within minutes, Drew found himself standing, alongside fifty other men, naked and confused.

"You didn't do it fast enough. Get your asses back in bed. And get back out here like *real men*. I'm telling you: Half of you sissies ain't makin' it today. Now move!" Gunny Sergeant Clark screamed.

"I remember him calling me a big Black sonuvabitch. Those first seven days of AOCS training turned out to be the hardest 168 straight hours of my life. By comparison, basketball practice at SUNO seemed like a picnic. The hell of living under Gunny Clark's bootheels was, by far, the worst. We dug ditches. We ran miles upon miles on the beach, all while carrying our heavy, antiquated M-1 rifles until they felt like a third arm. No matter what we did, Gunny Clark remained true to form. He didn't just order us to run. He ran right alongside us. Within four days, half of that class of poopies quit," Drew recalled.

On August 21, 1981, perhaps for the first time in his life, Drew Brown III experienced a pure sense of self accomplishment. He had stayed the course. He had not given in or given up. After completing the program, he was no longer merely Bundini's son; he was no longer cloaked in the shadow of his father's legacy. He was commissioned Ensign Drew Timothy Brown III, an officer of the United States Navy.

"My daddy had told me many times, 'Son, you'll have many fathers in life,' and I had always hated hearing that. But in Gunny Clark, I discovered another father figure. He broke me down and built me back up. Gunny was my father, my grandfather, my Bubba, and my mother all wrapped into one. At the ceremony, when our class stood and began to file one by one past Gunny Clark, I made sure that I was last. Each ensign gave him a silver dollar, received the GS's salute, and exchanged handshakes. When my time came, Gunny Clark popped me the finest marine salute. I handed him two silver dollars, one from me and one from my daddy, and he returned his salute. Tears swelled up in my eyes when he called me 'Sir,'" Drew recalled.

After the ceremony, Gunnery Sergeant Stephen W. Clark granted the young officer a few moments of his time. He wanted to assure that Drew understood his methodology.

"Drew, you're going to go through a lot, being Black in the Navy," Gunny Clark said. "And that racism is the nature of the beasts you'll be around. You'll always have to work twice as hard. That's why I called you a 'big Black sonuvabitch' that first morning. Right from the start, I wanted to know if that prejudice garbage would turn you away. And if it would, then I wanted your ass out," Gunny Clark continued.

"Because of those sixteen weeks, Gunny Clark prepared me for the rest of my new life," Drew said, paying homage to the drill instructor who, in many ways, served as a stand-in for his own father.

The coronation would take place on a beautiful Pensacola afternoon, the sky clear, the commissioned officers dressed in their freshly pressed naval uniforms, an ensemble complete with white ceremonial gloves and ensign shoulder boards. Laurie, Taryn, and Drew IV posed with the newly commissioned naval officer, beaming with pride. It had been a morning of parades, marching bands, and inspirational speeches.

Pensacola would serve as a fitting location for Drew Brown III's rebirth. The state of Florida had long played a prominent role in the Brown family narrative. It was the backdrop to his family's history. It was the site of Bundini's national debut as a cornerman, the victory that changed the trajectory of his life as a trainer. Yet the Brown family's most famous Floridian would be noticeably missing from this picturesque occasion.

Hesitant to attend the ceremony, out of fear that his 1942 incident of "bad conduct" would somehow be held against his son, denying him commission, Bundini did not attend Drew's graduation ceremony. Earlier that day, Drew received the following telegram from his father:

To: *Timothy Brown III, Ensign, U.S. Navy*
From: *Drew Bundini Brown, Jr.*
Congratulations, Son. I'd be proud to shine your shoes.

During the ceremony, Drew kept the telegram in his back pocket, keeping his father's spirit close by. As a young boy, Bundini had shined the shoes of the commissioned officers making their way into town from Naval Air Station Sanford. As a steward, he had served commissioned officers dinner, waited on them as if he were a second-class citizen. On that warm Florida day, in the same humid terrain where Bundini's own improbable journey had begun, Drew Brown III's victory was his father's.

After being commissioned, Drew entered primary flight training at the Naval Air Station in Corpus Christi, Texas. The two-year program consisted of a curriculum of intense self-directed study and performance-based skills training, all before he was assigned to an actual aircraft carrier. In Corpus

Christi, Drew would cut his teeth on the propeller-driven WWII T-28, the so-called "flying dinosaur of the sky." In March of 1982, under the supervision of Lieutenant Craig Luigart, Drew would complete his first successful flight behind the controls. By early 1983, Drew was being trained in the TA-4J Skyhawk, made famous by the Blue Angels during the Vietnam War.

"After my initial training on the T-28, we had to make a choice: jets or helicopters. I listed jets as my first choice, thinking *what the hell, might as well try.* The day I received my orders, I was overtaken by pride. I was on a mission to become one of the top one percent on the planet. I was going to become a bad-ass jet pilot," Drew said.

Bundini was equally proud of his son. During the summer months of 1982, he traveled to San Diego to witness his son fly for the first time. Dressed in all black, a matching cowboy hat on his head, Bundini approached the naval air station runway as if he were strolling into Madison Square Garden for yet another Joe Frazier fight.

"I land the jet and I see my father standing on the runway, at military parade rest, with machine guns drawn on him. I open the cockpit and I hear him screaming, 'That's my boy! My boy, the jet pilot!' So I waved at him, in hopes of letting everyone know that he was my father," Drew recalled.

"When I finally made it down to my father, he said, 'Boy, keep your damn hands on the steering wheel," Drew added.

"Daddy, there is no steering wheel," the young pilot corrected his father.

For the next two years, the picture-perfect family moments would be few and far between. As was the case with his father, Drew experienced his fair share of racism during his time at Naval Air Station Meridian.

"I would call my father when I had a problem. I felt extreme racism during my training in the pursuit of my gold wings. At times, it felt like nobody wanted me to make it. But I would call my father and he would always set me straight," Drew recalled.

"Sure, I made some mistakes. . . . But Daddy, if I was a white student . . ." Drew attempted to complain.

"Boy, did I hear you say that you made some mistakes?" Bundini interrupted. "Are you crazy? You sitting here telling me that your instructor is being hard on you? It's your Black ass that is flying in the sky, boy. If that is racism then racism is only going to make you a better pilot. When

they talk to you like that, you'd better answer with 'thank you, sir,'"
Bundini scolded his son, ever the motivator.

Drew Brown III would earn his gold wings on August 25, 1983. Soon
thereafter, Drew's accomplishment was featured in a *Jet* magazine article
titled "Navy 'A Family Affair' for Ali's Ex-Aide Bundini Brown and Jet
Pilot Son." In the article, Bundini gushes with pride, swelling his proverbial chest. "From the root to the fruit is what I call it," Bundini told
reporters.

By January 1984, Drew III, Laurie, and their children, Taryn and Drew
IV, settled into their new home in Virginia Beach, Virginia, where Drew
was stationed at the Naval Air Station Oceana as a member of the Replacement Air Group (RAG) to receive training on the all-weather attack bomber,
the A-6E Intruder.

While Drew began his extensive training in Virginia, Bundini was on
the other side of the country, back in the gym with James "Quick" Tillis,
in Los Angeles, California.

Despite the moment of good fortune for the Brown family, the fall of
1984 would, however, mark a time of grim reality for the family's most
famous extended family member, Muhammad Ali.

On September 20, 1984, a few weeks into Bundini's first training camp
with Tillis, news broke that Ali, recently hospitalized at the Columbia
Presbyterian Medical Center in New York City, had been diagnosed with
"Parkinsonism." The press rollout suggested the forty-two-year-old former
champion, three years removed from his loss to Trevor Berbick, suffered
from minor symptoms of Parkinson's disease, a degenerative brain disorder.
The original diagnosis was optimistic.

"He's not in any danger. It is not a fatal disease," Dr. Martin Decker,
a diagnostic radiologist who served as one of Ali's physicians, urged the
Associated Press via a media conference call.

"You don't die from what he has and I feel very optimistic that what
he has can be controlled by medication," Decker added.

For Bundini and other members of Ali's inner circle, the news was
hardly shocking. For almost ten years, friends and family members had
taken note of the gradual decline in Ali's health. At first, Ali began to
suffer from unpredictable fatigue. Next, his hands began to shake with
slight tremors. As the years passed, the Champ's speech began to slow
and eventually slur. The early signs of Ali's verbal struggles can clearly

be seen in interviews leading up to both the Larry Holmes and Trevor Berbick fights. When the news broke, Bundini was saddened but not surprised.

"I distinctly remember one time at training camp, Bundini saying to Muhammad, 'Stop playing, Champ. Stop that.' He saw Muhammad's hands shaking, noticed the tremors," Victor Solano said to me.

Despite Ali's retirement and declining health, he and Bundini remained in steady contact. "You think you're bad, Champ? You're afraid to fly on a plane and now my boy is a jet pilot," Bundini often teased Ali, doing his best to treat the Champ as if he were not sick.

"He would stick with Muhammad. Like with the Parkinson's. When Ali and Bundini would get together, they couldn't stop talking at times." George Foreman confided in me. "There at the end, Bundini knew there was something wrong. And he endured it like no one ever. One night I was with them and I watched Bundini encourage him. Talking and talking. It went on for hours. Five hours. Bundini tried to lift his spirits. Nobody in his corner could have endured it. Not Angelo. Nobody. But Bundini endured. He knew Muhammad needed him,"

■　■　■

On October 10, 1984, James "Quick" Tillis (30-4, 23 KOs) climbed through the ropes to face Carl "The Truth" Williams (15-0, 12 KOs) at the Atlantis Hotel and Casino in Atlantic City, New Jersey. Dressed in a purple cornerman's jacket with white trim, with the outline of the state of Oklahoma embroidered on the back, Drew Bundini Brown followed his new pupil around the ring, buzzing in his ear. For all intents and purposes, the Tillis–Williams bout was designed to be a showcase for the undefeated prospect.

"A lot of people in the boxing industry, including myself, think that [Williams] could be a throwback to a guy that came along twenty-five years ago, a quarter of a century ago, a guy by the name of Cassius Marcellus Clay," the announcer called as Williams shadowboxed in his corner before the ring introductions.

Largely because of his phenomenal eighty-five-inch reach, the longest in boxing, many pundits believed Williams had the tools to become heavyweight champion. Tillis, durable and battle-tested against some of the division's best, was to be a barometer of Williams's progress. At the time, Williams was ranked sixth by the World Boxing Association.

"[Tillis] now has a new outlook on life. He has a new manager and a new trainer and he says he is the best shape in his life," the announcer commented, noting Bundini's presence in the Tillis corner.

At first, Tillis appeared to be a new man. One minute and twenty-five seconds into the first round, Tillis dropped the undefeated Williams with a brilliant right hand to the chin. The punch instantly buckled Williams at the knees, sending him sprawling to the canvas. Down for the first time in his professional career, Williams struggled to regain his composure. A few moments later, after action resumed, another left-right combination would send Williams tumbling to the canvas. Sensing his opponent was in serious trouble, Tillis rushed Williams, backing him into the corner with a flurry of punches. In a surprisingly veteran move, Williams held on, bear-hugging his opponent, conceding the rest of round one. Tillis was unable to finish the job.

While Tillis would carry the second round, the momentum of the fight began to shift in the third as Williams began to physically recover from the near catastrophe. As the rounds progressed, Williams began to bounce on his toes, snapping his long jab and solid right hand with ease. By the fifth round, Tillis was visibly out of gas. During the second half of the fight, he occasionally landed lead right hands but was unable to follow up with any measure of ferocity. Slow to get up from the stool at the beginning of each new round, taking deep breaths and wearing an uneasy expression on his face, Tillis appeared to be a man attempting to survive rather than take hold of the fight. By the end of the tenth and final round, Williams appeared to be in complete control of the fight. When the results were read, Williams would be awarded a close but unanimous decision victory.

A few months later, on December 15, 1984, Bundini once again served as the head trainer for Tillis in his bout against Bashir Wadud (11-11-1) at Genesee Theatre in Waukegan, Illinois. In something of a tune-up fight, Tillis easily outpointed Wadud. Tillis had performed well enough in the Williams fight, almost scoring a miraculous first-round knockout, to get another television opportunity. The Wadud bout, for Bundini and Tillis, was about getting another mark in the win column as his team awaited a more lucrative opportunity. That opportunity would come in the form of a very familiar name.

On May 20, 1985, Tillis (31-5, 24 KOs) stepped into the ring to face Marvis Frazier (13-1, 8 KOs), the son of Smokin' Joe Frazier, in the televised co-feature to the Larry Holmes (47-0) vs. Carl "The Truth" Williams (16-0) IBF heavyweight championship title fight. Broadcast as an NBC Sports special, the fight card took place at the Lawlor Events Center on the campus of the University of Las Vegas at Reno. The first heavyweight championship fight card to take place in Reno since 1910, when Jack Johnson beat Jim Jeffries, NBC played up the nostalgia. Promoters even went as far as to dust off the actual scales that were used in the Johnson–Jeffries fight. This same sense of nostalgia was equally present in the co-feature. As referee Joey Curtis offered his prefight instructions, the irony was inescapable. To Curtis's left, dressed in a burgundy Everlast cornerman's jacket, stood the great Smokin' Joe Frazier, chief second to his son Marvis, who was, at least in the physical sense, the spitting image of his father. To Curtis's right, applying Vaseline to the forehead of heavyweight contender James Tillis, was the imposing figure of Muhammad Ali's former hype man, Drew Bundini Brown. Calling the fight at ringside were broadcasters Marv Albert and Ferdie Pacheco, Ali's longtime fight doctor. The topic of Bundini's role in the Ali–Frazier rivalry was unavoidable.

Joe Frazier placed the guard into Marvis's mouth. Bundini wiped Vaseline along the face of Tillis. The old rivals were back at center ring for what would be the final time. Dressed in his trademark white cardigan, Bundini glared at Frazier as if the bout were between him and the former heavyweight champion.

"We beat the root, now we gonna beat the fruit," Bundini had called during the weeklong promotional buildup to the fight.

Moments before the bell rang, the combatants themselves were relegated to a secondary role.

"You are going to be hearing the voice of Drew Bundini Brown, who has never been known for keeping quiet in the corner. I had a punctured eardrum from standing on the right side of him," Pacheco joked.

Lost amid the nostalgia of the night was the significance of the matchup for both heavyweight contenders. A loss would likely relegate Tillis to journeyman status, typecasting the Oklahoma native as nothing more than a stepping-stone opponent. To this point in his young career, Frazier's only disappointment had come via a first-round knockout loss to Holmes. A victory would serve as a step toward redeeming his fractured reputation.

When the opening bell rang, Tillis quickly took control of the fight, gliding around the ring, stinging Frazier with a sharp jab and a quick right hand. As Tillis began to land with ease, Bundini became increasingly vocal.

"Bundini is shouting, 'Go to the basement when the elevator comes down,'" Marv Albert said to Pacheco, all but begging his colleague for a translation.

"That means 'punch to the head when the guard comes down,'" Pacheco laughed, clearly enjoying his ability to provide viewers with an insider's perspective.

"Put that Sugar Ray Robinson on 'em . . . that's what I'm talking about," Bundini continued.

In the second round, Tillis did just that, rocking Frazier with a solid left-right combination, backing him into the corner. As Tillis pummeled Frazier into the ropes, Joey Curtis stepped in to administer a standing eight count. Saved by the bell, Frazier returned to his corner on unsteady legs.

"I'm alright, Pop," Marvis assured his father.

In the third round, Bundini feverishly urged his boxer to close the show.

"I want to point out that we do not have a microphone on Bundini Brown, that is the voice you are hearing," Albert assured viewers.

"Try standing next to that for fifteen years," Pacheco added.

As Tillis continued to carry the fight, the subject shifted to his new trainer.

"There is no question that a man like Bundini can spur a lazy fighter like Tillis to fight," Pacheco argued.

"[Bundini] just keeps you going. He keeps your blood hot. He's invaluable in the corner as a cheerleader. Nobody like him," Pacheco mused.

Albert, clearly more interested in Pacheco's insight than Tillis's beating of Frazier, continued, with the questions.

"Did Ali pay any attention to him?" Albert asked.

To this, Pacheco replied, "Well, he was a big part of the Ali circus. The Ali mystique."

Meanwhile in the ring, Frazier's legs began to return. Tillis, who appeared to be gassed from all of the energy he spent in the first two rounds, began to slow his punch output. In the rounds that would follow, Tillis began to fade. Bundini shouted at the top of his lungs from ringside.

Albert commented to his colleague, "Bundini is using so many code words . . . I wonder if [Tillis] understands all of it."

In the fourth round, NBC placed a small box in the lower left corner of the shot, just as they had done during the second Ali–Norton fight, televising Bundini as he urged on Tillis from ringside.

"You got the firepower . . . fire your guns!" Bundini can be seen shouting.

In between rounds five and six, the NBC cameras captured Bundini in all of his desperate glory.

"You worked too hard . . . got up too many mornings . . . get that spirit in you . . . you ain't no ordinary man, don't fight like one . . . get mad!" Bundini called to his fighter.

As the rounds unfolded, Bundini increasingly became the focal point of the broadcast and coverage, stealing the show, so to speak.

"Hit 'em like he spit on you, hit 'em hard . . . good shot cowboy . . . that's what I'm talking about cowboy . . . c'mon cowboy . . . come out riding that horse, cowboy," Bundini pleaded. Tillis would land a big right hand in the seventh, a whipping uppercut in the eighth but the effective aggressiveness would belong to Frazier, who outworked his tiring opponent in the closing rounds.

In the tenth and final round, both combatants appeared to be completely gassed, a smattering of boos could be heard from the 12,000 fans in attendance. The official scorecards would read 98-91, 97-91, 96-92, all in favor of Frazier.

After the fight, in a segment titled "Corner Story," NBC aired a montage of Bundini snippets. For perhaps the first time in his boxing career, Bundini had completely stolen the spotlight from the two combatants in the ring. Often credited as being the inventor of the famous boxing phrase "stick and move," the Bundini highlight reel was a fitting send-off.

"Pop shot him. He's drunk. You can mug him now," Bundini shouts after Tillis in the first clip, footage from the end of round one.

"You trying to hit a home run. Load the bases up first," Bundini calls to Tillis after the second.

The vignette of sound bites, shown in chronological order, serves as the only focused documentation of what it was like to experience a Bundini Brown corner.

"Get your spirits about you. This is our birthday and we ain't gonna have no miscarriage," Bundini urges in the late rounds.

"What's wrong with you? We been doing roadwork. You ain't got no spirit. Don't go back to the old stuff. Get that spirit. Think about your momma. Do this for your momma," Bundini pleads before the tenth and final round.

"Colorful man, a true poet of the street," Ferdie Pacheco reflected after the highlight reel was complete.

Pacheco's characterization was spot on. With his hand on the fighter's shoulder, wearing a facial expression that clearly demonstrates he is visibly shaken by the loss, Bundini made his way through the ropes and down the three wooden steps. It would be the last time he would ever work a professional boxing match.

In our interview, I shared the NBC sound bites with Tillis, in hopes of discovering what it was like to have a trainer who spoke his own language, one deeply rooted in metaphor and parable.

"Oh, yes. I remember all that. Bundini got close with my momma, he knew that would motivate me," Tillis laughed.

Much to my surprise, "The Fighting Cowboy" insisted that the NBC cameras missed all of the good lines.

"He'd say, 'Ray Charles,'" code for sneaking a hard right hand behind a blinding jab. "He'd say, 'ride the horse, cowboy. Wrangle him down,'" code for cutting off the ring and cornering an opponent against the ropes, Tillis told me.

Listening to Tillis give his best Bundini impression, it was clear he enjoyed the linguistic banter.

"I loved it when he would talk like that to me. Bundini was just great to be around. I miss him," Tillis reflected.

In the end, Bundini's three-fight tenure with Tillis, two near upset victories and a meaningless tune-up fight, left both the boxer and trainer wondering what could have been.

"I trained really hard for those fights but got really tired every time," Tillis said to me. While Tillis showed flashes of brilliance, those performances were likely impacted by undiagnosed food allergies. After Bundini's unofficial retirement, Tillis would continue his boxing career with unanimous decision losses to Gerrie Coetzee and Tyrell Biggs. As the familiar pattern continued, Tillis became increasingly concerned about his health. After visiting a physician, Tillis discovered that a plethora of food allergies were impairing his conditioning. While dietary changes cleared up the issue, the damage to his ring résumé had already been done. "The Fighting Cowboy" was no longer considered a contender. With a record of thirty-one wins and eight losses, and at twenty-nine years of age, Tillis couldn't have possibly known he had yet to give his most memorable performance.

On May 5, 1986, Tillis traveled to the Glens Falls Civic Center to face an undefeated slugger fighting out of Catskill, New York, a feared puncher with sixteen consecutive victories, all by way of knockout. With his dietary issues finally cleared up, Tillis was able to turn back the clock for one last memorable performance. At the end of the night, "The Fighting Cowboy" would become an answer to one of boxing's best trivia questions. Who was the first man to go the distance with "Iron" Mike Tyson?

What many contemporary boxing fans forget about Tyson–Tillis, however, is how close the Oklahoma native came to beating Tyson that night in Upstate New York. Had Tyson not scored a knockdown in the fourth round, a round he was losing, the bout would have been scored a majority draw. Two of the three judges scored the fight six rounds to four in favor of Tyson. Throughout the night, Tillis had confused the younger Tyson with sharp lead right hands, impressive footwork, and veteran ring generalship.

Looking back on his performance against one of the heavyweight division's most feared punchers, Tillis couldn't help but to daydream of a legendary career that never quite took shape, a career with Bundini Brown in his corner.

"When I worked with Bundini, I was always in top shape. He had my mind in the right place. He was good about getting you focused and getting your mind off negative stuff. It was just that the allergies were a big problem we couldn't overcome. If I had Bundini for the Tyson fight, I might have won," Tillis lamented.

While the two friends would not be able to capture heavyweight championship glory, Tillis, to this day, continues to view the year he spent working with Bundini as one of the most significant chapters in his life. Time spent with Bundini always led to adventure. Keeping in mind the larger cultural context of their time together, one could argue that the duo's most significant collaboration did not happen in a boxing ring.

■　■　■

Directed by the legendary Stephen Spielberg, *The Color Purple* brought Drew Bundini Brown and his "Fighting Cowboy" toe-to-toe with Hollywood heavyweights Danny Glover, Oprah Winfrey, and Whoopi Goldberg. Based on Alice Walker's Pulitzer Prize and National Book Award winning novel by the same name, *The Color Purple* is a coming-of-age drama set in rural Georgia. Spielberg's film, a rare departure from his summer blockbuster formula, leans heavily on themes of domestic violence, incest, pedophilia, racism, and sexism, providing viewers with a powerful glimpse into the life of Black women during the early twentieth century. Bundini's cameo would mark his fifth appearance in a feature film.

"Gale Jacobs, my lawyer, said some movie guys called. I was in training camp [for the Frazier fight] with Bundini in Los Angeles. They wanted Bundini because they knew he could talk good. Bundini brought me along too," Tillis remembered.

Bundini and Tillis show up in Spielberg's film during a scene set in Harpo's, a rowdy juke joint where music, dancing, gambling, drinking, and infidelity are on the menu. As was the case in Bundini's reoccurring role in the *Shaft* franchise, his presence adds a certain measure of credibility to the film. A precursor to the social scene that would one day unfold during the Harlem Renaissance, juke joints were historically found on the outskirts of southern towns, often in dilapidated buildings, barns, or private homes. These were illegal social spaces, a product of Jim Crow laws that barred Blacks from white establishments, the cultural by-product of an era where plantation workers and sharecroppers sought release from the adverse circumstances that surrounded their everyday lives. Harpo's can easily be read as a makeshift version of the Harlem jazz joints Bundini frequented as a young man, an atmosphere he attempted to recapture in his own failed night club, Bundini's World.

In the scene, Bundini plays the role of an unnamed patron who is mesmerized by the beauty of Shug Avery's sultry jazz tune. Dressed in a sparkling red gown, pearl earrings, and a feathery headdress, Shug, with her sexually suggestive routine, rouses the men in attendance as they dance to the music and drink from their flasks.

"Girl, I'd drink your bathwater," one patron calls, dripping with sweat, shoulder-to-shoulder in a mosh pit of transgressive exuberance.

"You can catch a fish without a hook, girl," Bundini grins, dressed in a suit and tie, a tilted driver's cap on his head, wearing a million-dollar smile that lights up the screen.

"I remember Daddy once telling me that he was going to do a Spielberg movie, this was the height of *Star Wars*. I forgot about it, to be honest.

Three years later, I was in a movie theater, watching this great movie, not realizing it was a Spielberg film. Can you imagine my surprise, midway through the movie, when my father's face occupied the entire screen? I stood up in the theater and shouted, 'That's my daddy!' I shouted it as loud as I could. Shorty had given me a little present," Drew Brown III recalled.

Playing the role of Henry "Buster" Broadnax, the extramarital lover of Sophie (played by Oprah Winfrey), James Tillis appears in the second half of the juke-joint scene. Following Shug Avery's performance, Sophie takes a glass of moonshine into her possession and places herself on Broadnax's lap.

"I want to introduce ya'll to my friend, Henry Broadnax his name, everybody calls him Buster. He's a good man with a family," Sophie says in a flirtatious voice.

"How ya doing? How ya feel?" Buster replies.

In the crescendo to the brief scene, Sophie is whisked away by her husband, who has been eavesdropping on his wife. Broadnax, who had come to the juke joint clearly looking for romantic action, finds himself the odd man out.

"First time I've ever been knocked out without throwing a punch," Broadnax says in defeat, playfully shadowboxing.

"Bundini coached me on my lines," Tillis told me. "He was like, 'Nah, Quick, say it like this here.' And I was like, 'Dang, he's good.'"

Receiving overwhelmingly positive reviews from movie critics, *The Color Purple* was a knockout at the box office, raising $142 million with a budget of only $15 million. Despite having only minor cameos in the film, both Bundini and Tillis were both grateful to be part of a film of such magnitude, if only for one day.

"I can promise you me and Bundini had 'em rolling on the set. There was a supernatural thing about him. People just loved being around Bundini. I don't have the words for it but he was a supernatural man," Tillis assured me.

"Bundini was a hell of a trainer and a hell of an acting coach," the Oklahoma slugger added.

While it is unclear as to whether Bundini fancied himself a drama coach, one can easily infer that he was, in some aspects, bitten by the acting bug. Bundini would follow up his appearance in *The Color Purple* with an appearance in the 1987 grindhouse-style action comedy *Penitentiary 3*, a continuation of the story of Martel "Too Sweet" Gordone, a reoccurring role made famous by blaxploitation star Leon Isaac Kennedy. The plot of the film series centers on the story of a troubled former boxer framed for murder and sent to prison, forced to compete in an underground fighting league to secure parole.

While the first film in the franchise was well received in the world of blaxploitation films, the third installment of the franchise can hardly be mistaken for a cinematic masterpiece. *Penitentiary 3* is clearly a B film. Bundini's presence in the movie, an odd cinematic mixture of comedy and gore, deserves to be recognized, however, if for no other reason than the role demonstrated a more ambitious acting gig than was the case in *The Color Purple*. In his sixth appearance on the silver screen, Bundini plays a trash-talking prison inmate named Snug. Despite the film being the least impressive notch on his Hollywood belt, it is in *Penitentiary 3* that we begin to see Bundini's range as an actor. This time around, Bundini's role in the film was far greater than a cameo. With the proper management, a more strategic and well-thought-out career path, Bundini might have made a post-boxing career in Hollywood, serving up cameos and small roles in movies and television. Perhaps he could have followed his old 5th Street pal Ferdie Pacheco into the announcer's booth.

"Imagine my father calling fights," Drew III said to me, pointing to the career paths of trainers turned commentators such as Gil Clancy, Emanuel Steward, and Teddy Atlas. "Nobody could talk like my daddy. It could be the worst fight ever and he would have had you glued to the television set, waiting to hear what he was going to say next," Drew added. NBC's coverage of the Tillis–Frazier bout does, in many ways, support Drew's thesis. Bundini's colorful instructions were *the* story of the fight, as made evident by NBC's Bundini highlight reel.

Unfortunately, Bundini would never have the opportunity to reinvent himself, to explore the true depths of his talents and celebrity. *Penitentiary 3* was released in theaters on September 4, 1987. Twenty days later, Bundini would be gone.

12

**From the Root
to the Fruit**

His favorite song was "Nature Boy," his favorite rendition by jazz vocalist Nat King Cole. Bundini shed tears every time he heard the song, regardless of the context. On my Southwest Airlines flight home to New York, I listened to the song several times, my earbuds transmitting the story of a mystic search for truth, a vagabond's perilous journey through life. The song instantly struck me as a Bundini self-portrait.

"There was a boy, a very strange, enchanted boy / They say he wandered very far, very far, over land and sea," the song begins.

On our return drive to Hartsfield-Jackson Atlanta International Airport, I had asked Drew Brown III for a playlist that would bring me closer to Bundini. Music had been important to Bundini's life and I wanted to be as close to him as possible.

"'Nature Boy,' that's Daddy's song. Play that one and Daddy will be right there," Drew assured me.

The Rolls-Royce pulled up to the curb of the designated drop-off area located outside the Southwest terminal. The suicide doors, effortless in motion, swung open. Scrambling to collect my carry-on bag, I swallowed my pride, recognizing that I was simply no good at entering or exiting luxury vehicles. More than likely, I never will be.

Drew, like his father, was a hugger. He was tall and boisterous, a commanding personality. When Drew expressed affection, however, he suddenly shrunk down to my size. He wore his emotions openly, honestly.

"When you write, be free. Free is the best feeling in the world, Dr. Snyder. Just let it come," Drew instructed me, his embrace loving and affectionate.

Above the clouds, peering out into the blue, I played his father's favorite song on repeat, learning something new with each listen.

When I was a young boy, growing up in Willoughby Trailer Park in Cowen, West Virginia, I never imagined visiting Atlanta, let alone being ushered around the city in a Rolls-Royce, especially one driven by a Navy jet pilot, the son of Drew Bundini Brown. Muhammad Ali had been my father's boyhood hero, Bundini one of his favorite sports personalities. Feeling nostalgic, my thoughts turned to my own life's journey. As child, I would lay in the grass, looking up to the sky, admiring the white contrails jet engines would leave in their wake, chalk marks along a blue canvas. There were no airports within two hours of my small mountain town, certainly no Rolls-Royce dealerships. In becoming a college graduate, not to mention a college professor, I realized my father's ambitions. Drew's father carried a spit bucket, mine carried a dinner bucket. College would save us from such fates. Our fathers were from the streets, survivors who had great expectations for their sons. Education was the pathway, they imagined. We are first-generation college students, Drew and I, attempting to symbolically right the wrongs of our fathers' pasts. We are the sons of flawed and loving men, dreamers and schemers, their imaginations boundless.

"I'm not successful because I have a Rolls-Royce," Drew said to me on our way to the airport. "I'm successful because my kids can do things I can't. I'm successful because they've grown up to be better than their father. That's the lesson Daddy taught me," he added.

Like their father, Drew's Brown III's children have accomplished great things. It would be next to impossible to argue that Drew has been anything less than a spectacular father. His daughter, Taryn, a graduate of the University of Texas and Tulane Law School, is an associate attorney in New York City working with a company owned by the New York Yankees. His son, Drew Brown IV, a graduate of the University of Texas and Tufts University School of Medicine, is an orthopedic spine surgeon in Tampa, Florida. Both Taryn and Drew played college basketball at the University of Texas.

"My children are my biggest victory in life," Drew III reminded me throughout the weekend. On the plane ride home, I closed my eyes, imagined Bundini saying those same words in reference to his own son.

Back in Albany, underneath the clouds, my wife, Stephanie, and son, Huntington, were no doubt already at the airport, awaiting my arrival.

"The greatest thing you'll ever learn / Is just to love and be loved in return," the final lines of Bundini's favorite song go.

Until hearing those lyrics, it hadn't occurred to me, not until then, that Drew Bundini Brown's life story had the happiest of endings.

■　■　■

The first day he entered Howie Steiner's Main Street Gym in downtown Los Angeles, located on 3rd and Main, Victor Solano fell in love with boxing. A few weeks into his new life as a pugilist, Victor spotted an elderly Black man attempting to get a drink of water from the rickety fountain, unable to properly do so because he was wearing boxing gloves. Victor had noticed the elderly gentleman making the speed bag sing the previous day.

"You look kind of familiar. You used to box, back in the day?" Victor asked the man, assisting him with the water fountain.

"Yes, I did, son. Yes, I did," the old man replied.

Little did the thirteen-year-old boy know, he had just met the great Sugar Ray Robinson.

After the chance encounter, Victor Solano and Sugar Ray Robinson struck up an unlikely friendship. Victor would fetch water and juice for the former champion, gloving him up and assisting with workouts. As Solano's amateur career progressed, Robinson became something of a mentor to Solano. The turning point in the boxer's young life, however, would come when Robinson informed the fifteen-year-old Solano that Muhammad Ali was going to be training at the nearby Olympic Auditorium. Uninvited, Victor traveled to the facility in hopes of meeting and learning from Ali, who at the time was still in exile. Not only did Solano get to meet Ali, he ended up in the ring with him.

"It only lasted about a round and a half," Solano said to me, laughing at his teenage audacity. "I maybe hit him a few times," he suggested.

After the workout, Solano waited around to thank Ali for his graciousness. At the time, he had no idea that a lifelong friendship was about to begin.

"After the workout, he literally gave me his number. Two numbers, actually. One in Chicago, one in New York, I think. We would stay in contact. Then, in 1971, I moved to Washington, D.C., and told him that

I had moved closer. He invited me to Cherry Hill, with Belinda and Rashida, and Janella, and Maryum. I was only twenty years old when he first invited me to their home," Solano remembered.

After moving to the East Coast, Solano joined Ali and his entourage at "Fighter's Heaven" in Deer Lake, Pennsylvania. Solano was present for many of Ali's most important training camps, including his pre-Africa preparations for George Foreman. When Ali married Veronica Porché in 1977, Solano's home city of Los Angeles became the couple's new home base. Victor moved back to California shortly thereafter, and he and Ali grew closer as the years went by.

When Ali and Solano relocated to California, Drew Bundini Brown did the same. The move, according to friends and family, was the beginning of hard times in Bundini's life.

"When Bundini moved to California, he started calling for money all of the time. He would call and I would send him a couple of hundred. He would always call and ask but he would never call and say thanks," Gene Kilroy told me.

"I would tell him, 'Hey, you called asking for money not too long ago but you didn't call for thanks.' Then he would start, 'I don't have to thank you. I'm your friend. You know it went to a good cause—me.' Bundini would have me so turned around that I felt bad for even mentioning it. He was going through some tough times out there," Kilroy added.

"Daddy didn't want his grandkids to see him like that. He didn't want me to see him like that either. So he would disappear for periods of time," Drew Brown III said. "I was in the Navy, living in Virginia Beach, when my father was going through those hard times."

Very little has been written about the circumstances surrounding Bundini's death. Even less has been written about his final years in Los Angeles. What has been written, however, paints a grim picture. The pervasive notion is that a ratty motel room, located near downtown Los Angeles, living quarters only a meager step up from homelessness, served as the setting for the final chapter of Bundini's life. He was broke, alone, and suffering from depression, writers have suggested. In my conversations with Solano, however, he clearly looked to push against this depiction.

"Drew lived at a couple of different places. One near Fremont and one in Hollywood. The one in Hollywood was a two-story motel. It had fluorescent lights. I remember Drew's room was upstairs. The first apartment [in Fremont] was downstairs. Both rooms were clean. I remember his room had red carpet. When we would go pay his rent, Muhammad would hand me the money and I would go pay. He would always sit with Drew while I paid. It was not filthy. All of this stuff saying he was destitute isn't true. Ali loved him unconditionally. He wasn't alone. At the time, we had Ali coming to the gym to work out [as a method of combatting Parkinson's]. Drew often came with us. We knew he was hitting the bottle pretty hard. Ali talked to him about it. There may have been other drugs but we didn't see it. Sometimes there would be empty Seagram's bottles on the table or under the bed. I remember seeing a Bible on the nightstand. But Muhammad made sure the maids would clean. We would pay for the week, probably $200 to $250 a week. Sometimes we would bring Drew to the gym with us. When we picked him up, he'd always be outside, cleaned up, waiting on us. He was always punctual."

"You can't write that after boxing was over with, Drew's life ended sadly. You can't say that, Todd. It would anger me!" Solano pleaded. "Muhammad was there to show his loyalty. Drew showed his loyalty to Muhammad while he was alive and Muhammad tried to return the favor, even though the disease was beginning to take over. Muhammad was helping take care of him in Los Angeles. He was doing it to show his appreciation for Drew being there and taking the punches with him. Ali would tell me, 'Drew is my motivator.' He would always say that. Muham-mad made sure [Bundini] had a roof over his head, that he had food to eat. He would give the maids and the front desk workers an extra $100 bill and tell them to make sure Drew was eating."

"Anytime Muhammad heard that Drew was in trouble or something, we quietly—and I use the word 'quietly' because Muhammad helping Drew didn't please a lot of people, Ali's wife at the time, and others that are now gone. It didn't please them that Muhammad would give money to Drew. But Muhammad would quietly sneak off with me and we would check on him. I know there are people who probably feel Muhammad should have done more. But Muhammad did what he could. Muhammad's financial situation wasn't in the best shape at the time," Solano continued.

When I shared Solano's comments with Drew Brown III, he struggled to contain his emotions, offering the following assessment of his complicated personal relationship with the greatest fighter of all time: "I fell in love with Cassius Clay when I was nine years old. And he fell in love with me. We were like best friends for a period of time. From the beginning, I saw his love for my father and my father's definite love for him. With success, people change. It was hard for me to watch him take advantage of his friend, my father. Unknowingly and perhaps unwillingly, he allowed that to happen. But he always held a special love for me. He looked at me in a special way. He was fun, brash, full of life. My frustration came in him allowing my father to get to that point. It hurt. I've been through a lot. But in the end, I love my big brother."

On September 3, 1987, Drew Bundini Brown was found unconscious at the bottom of the staircase leading to his second-story Los Angeles motel room. Bundini was allegedly drunk, fell down the staircase, and suffered a variety of head and spinal injuries as he tumbled to the ground. He was alone at the time of the fall.

Bundini was found by a motel maid, who, after discovering his body, called for an ambulance. According to the paramedics, Bundini had laid at the bottom of the steps over ten hours before being discovered. His lungs were full of fluid, the damage to his spinal cord irreversible. He was taken to Good Samaritan Hospital in Los Angeles. Within hours of Bundini being transported, the bad news found its way to Muhammad Ali.

"We were at the gym. Someone had called and said that something happened to Drew. Me and Muhammad and Howard [Bingham] went straight down to the motel. Drew had already been taken to Good Sam. When we arrived at the motel there were many conflicting stories and reports. Confusion. It seemed to us like they were not saying exactly what happened. It was like somebody was trying to protect themselves. The maid said that Drew had been drinking. They said he had fallen forward. When they found him, his arms were under his chest. They said that because he was diabetic there was no circulation. That was the worst thing that could have happened to a diabetic. But I remember there was a detective that said he knew the area where the motel was at, and he had talked to me and Muhammad and told us that he was not sure if it was alcohol or drug related," Solano told me, continuing to grapple with his own emotions.

Later that afternoon, at Attack Squadron VA-35, located in Virginia Beach, Virginia, Lieutenant Drew Brown III was called into the office of Commander Lou Lalli.

"Commander Lalli told me the bad news and said that the situation was dire. And, at that point, we didn't know how much time Daddy had left. They gave me a jet to go to California. He gave me a jet to go see Daddy. I flew myself to California," Drew said.

When Drew arrived at the hospital, still dressed in his Navy flight gear, he was told by doctors that the fall had rendered his father a quadriplegic. Before entering the room, doctors warned Drew that his father lay in a Stryker critical-care bed, with a metal halo fixed around his head and neck. The bed moved in four directions, laterally, then side to side. The bed was designed to keep Bundini's bodily fluids moving. The fall had broken his spine but not his spirit.

"My father was quadriplegic, with a halo on his head, talking more shit than anybody that I've ever heard in my entire life," Drew recalled.

"We good, son. It's okay," Bundini whispered as Drew arrived at his bedside. Overcome with emotion, his son began to sob. Recognizing his anguish, Bundini attempted to comfort his boy.

"My feet moving, son?" Bundini asked.

"No, Dad. They aren't moving," Drew answered, tears streaming down his cheeks.

"Yeah, they are. We gonna be okay. I'll be riding a bicycle by the end of the week," Bundini chuckled.

The joke was humorous on multiple levels. Drew had never seen his father ride a bicycle.

"Where that cute blonde nurse at? Tell her to come back in here. I want to give her a little pinch," Bundini continued, attempting to lift his son's spirits.

"Daddy spent three weeks in the hospital. He died of pneumonia. It was the fluid in his lungs. At first, Daddy really believed it was going to be okay. He *believed* it. And I did too. But when they put the tubes down his throat, when they took away his ability to talk, things went downhill rapidly. At one point, my father looked at me, without saying a word, and spoke to me clear as a bell. 'Listen to me carefully, do not shut this machine off now because this might work but you will not let your father live like this, boy. Do you understand what to do?' That's what Daddy's look communicated to me. He didn't want to die, not that moment. But that look said everything I needed to know," Drew recalled.

One week before Bundini passed away, Muhammad Ali arrived at Good Samaritan Hospital to visit his old companion. Ali was accompanied by his close friends Victor Solano and Howard Bingham.

"I placed the call to Good Sam," Victor Solano said to me. "They told us Drew was not in good shape at all. They told us to be prepared. He was quadriplegic. They said it was going to be very difficult to see him that way. They said, for a diabetic, the lack of circulation is not a good thing. Things manifest pretty quickly. I told Muhammad, 'We have to go before it is too late.'"

When the trio arrived at the hospital, Solano witnessed something he had never seen before: Muhammad Ali turning down autographs.

"When we made it to Drew's room, Howard [Bingham] turned to me and said, 'I can't go in. I don't want to see him like that.' We got to the doorway, you could see Drew through this little window. Howard started shuddering. He walked away. He repeated, 'I can't go.' It kind of shocked me. This guy had done everything with Drew but it was clear that he couldn't stomach it," Solano remembered.

Ali and Solano entered the room while Bingham remained in the hallway. Inside the room, Drew was seated in the corner, resting in a visitor's chair. After exchanging pleasantries, Drew exited the room, leaving Ali and Solano to meet with his father privately. Bundini's son uncharacteristically ignored the presence of his world-famous big brother. The pain and disappointment he felt simply cut too deep.

"Muhammad quietly went up to Drew [Bundini]. I walked to Drew's right and Muhammad walked to his left. Drew opened his eyes and looked from right to left. He looked at both of us. His eyes shifting from left to right," Solano told me.

"Hey, Drew, you not doing so good?" Ali spoke softly into Bundini's ear.

Bundini tilted his head right to left, indicating his answer to the question. The former heavyweight champion lifted Bundini's hand and held it. Bundini attempted to speak but, because of the breathing tubes down his throat, was unable to do so.

"Quiet, Drew," Ali continued, asking a nurse for a towel.

The nurse handed Ali a damp washcloth from a bedside tray.

"My turn to wipe your sweat off," Ali said, patting Bundini's forehead gently.

Bundini attempted to smile. For a few minutes, Ali sat next to his cornerman and said nothing, occasionally applying the damp cloth to Bundini's forehead. Ali leaned in, positioning his mouth next to Bundini's left ear.

"Man, just think, you're gonna be up there in heaven with Shorty," Ali said. "You're going off to meet Shorty. And I'll be up there one day too. When you get up there, you're gonna see Jack Johnson, and Rocky Marciano, and all them great fighters up in heaven. And one day you are going to see me," Ali continued, his voice shaky.

Ali held his own hand to Bundini's cheek. He wanted his trainer to feel his physical presence. Bundini began to cry, heaving slightly. Ali stroked Bundini's hair, running his fingers through the bald spot. After a few moments of silence, Ali bent down and kissed Bundini on the forehead. Seated at the other side of the bed, Solano began to cry.

"We are going to pray for you, Drew. We all love you so much, Drew. Shorty is going to take care of you, Drew," Solano repeated before kissing Bundini on the forehead, just as Ali had done moments earlier.

After a few moments of stony silence, Ali arose from his seat. Solano did the same. Ali bent down one last time, leaning into Bundini's ear.

"Drew, can you hear me?" Ali asked.

Bundini once again tilted his head to indicate his response.

"Float like a butterfly, sting like a bee. . . . Rumble young man, rumble," Ali said, before adding the trademark ending to the slogan.

"I remember, he did it twice. Slowly. 'Ahhhhh. Ahhhhh,'" Solano told me.

With tears forming in the corners of his tired eyes, Bundini attempted to smile. Muhammad Ali turned and exited the hospital room. He would never see Drew Bundini Brown again.

"Out in the hallway, we couldn't find Howard. As we were looking for him this doctor came up to us and said Drew's condition was bad. He let us know that it wasn't going to get better. Then he said there is this teenage boy next door to Drew, he had this very rare case. If you touched his skin, it would literally fall apart. But the doctor told us he liked boxing and asked if Muhammad would go in there," Solano said.

"Where's this boy wants to box me? They said he looks like Joe Frazier. C'mon, boy," Ali shouted upon entering the room, playfully shadowboxing.

The boy instantly smiled.

"You have to get better. That's my order. And when you do, me and you have to fight. You get better and I'm going to get back in shape," Ali continued, unwilling to let the boy know that he felt deep sympathy for his condition.

"The doctor said he had never seen him smile. They were so happy that Muhammad visited with him," Solano recalled.

After visiting the boy, Ali and Solano glanced back into Bundini's room, peering through the hallway window.

"Drew's eyes were closed, he looked settled down. He was okay. I wanted his son, Drew Brown III, to know that his father was okay. He was surrounded by nothing but love, all the way to the end," Solano urged.

The hospital visit made a significant impact on Muhammad Ali, who at this point in his life had lost only a handful of people who were close to him, Malcolm X and Elijah Muhammad being the primary exceptions. Before leaving Los Angeles to embark on a goodwill tour in Pakistan, where he visited mosques, shrines, schools, hospitals, orphanages, and government offices, Ali, Solano, and Bingham also paid a visit to Sugar Ray Robinson, who was living out the final days of his life in Los Angeles, suffering the effects of Alzheimer's disease.

When Ali and Solano entered the living room of Robinson's home, the legendary fighter at first recognized only Solano.

"Ray, you've always been my main man," Ali said to the boxing legend. Robinson did not reply.

During the visit Ali, Solano, and Bingham talked mostly with Robinson's wife, Millie. Bingham, shook up over the day's events, forgot to bring film for his camera. Solano gave him the film out of his own camera so that Bingham could document Ali's final meeting with Robinson.

When it was time to leave, Ali briefly browsed Robinson's living room trophy case, admiring the championship belts, medals, and memorabilia. Solano recalls seeing tears in Ali's eyes through the reflection of the trophy case.

"I'm going to be like that someday. I know it. Just like that. I'm going to die just like that. I'm not going to know anybody. Just like that," Ali said to Solano after exiting Robinson's residence.

Sugar Ray Robinson would die two years later, on April 29, 1989, at the age of sixty-seven.

After Ali's visit, Bundini's condition deteriorated rapidly. Members of the Brown family were called in. In the coming days, only the breathing machines were keeping him alive. Drew Brown III's only solace came in the teachings he gleaned from his father as a young man, lessons on life and death.

"The first time I ever dealt with death was my Poppa Jack. He passed away in 1979. I was twenty-four years old. Poppa Jack was in the funeral home. I wouldn't go inside. Daddy took my hand and escorted me to the front of the synagogue to say goodbye to Poppa Jack. He held my hand like I was a little boy. Suddenly, I wasn't scared anymore. I cried and cried but I wasn't scared anymore because I had my daddy with me," Drew remembered.

On the way home from Jack Palestine's funeral services, Bundini turned to his son, his face tightening with stark seriousness.

"When I die, boy, you can chop me up into a thousand pieces and throw my ass into the Mississippi River because if you have a funeral I will not be attending," Bundini insisted.

"What are you talking about?" Drew asked his father, fighting back tears.

"Son, if I lost my finger, would you love me any less?"

To this his son shook his head in disagreement.

"Son, if I lost my hand, would you love me any less?" Bundini continued.

"Daddy, what the hell are you talking about?" Drew III responded.

"Son, if I lost both arms, would you love me any less? Both arms, both legs?" Bundini asked.

"Daddy, you aren't making any sense at all," his son puzzled, unable to recognize the point of his father's philosophical musings.

"When you get your hair cut, you leave some of yourself in the barbershop, right?" Bundini said, his eyes fixed like a hawk.

Drew III offered no response.

"I won't ever leave you, son. The body will go. But I won't," Bundini continued, touching his arms, tugging at his vest, his tie, and buttons along his black suit.

"All of this is just *stuff*. The spirit remains," Bundini stated.

At three o'clock in the afternoon, on Thursday, September 28, 1987, Drew Bundini Brown was pronounced dead. He was fifty-nine years old.

"I will never forget that day," Victor Solano said to me. "Drew died on my daughter's birthday. I've thought about him on that day every year since."

■ ■ ■

Drew Bundini Brown's funeral was held at New Bethel Church in Sanford, Florida. Bundini was laid to rest at nearby Page Jackson Cemetery. Reverend Robert Doctor spoke at the services, calling Bundini Muhammad Ali's "spirit coach," adding: "He had the gift of gab. The man could talk. Talk inspiringly, convincingly. He would walk with two champions, Sugar Ray Robinson and Muhammad Ali, and that's a lot for a man with a small gift."

Gene Kilroy, one of only two members of the Ali entourage to attend the funeral, served as a pallbearer and also spoke at the services. Florida native Abdul Rahman, formerly known as Captain Sam, was also in attendance.

"I was horribly sad. Bundini was the first one of our gang to die. When I told Ali of the news, Ali said, 'I feel like I've lost part of my body,'" Kilroy told me.

Ali, who was in Pakistan the day Bundini passed away, was unable to attend the funeral. The Champ did, however, send flowers and a card that read: "With deepest sympathy. *You* made me the greatest."

For a variety of reasons, the other members of the Ali entourage, scattered about the country, were also unable to attend. Angelo Dundee, for example, was in Springfield, Illinois, being honored as "Man of the Year" from an Italian American club.

"Everybody in the entourage cared about each other. I'm positive that everyone was deeply upset. It was a brotherhood. My father was very upset," Jim Dundee assured me. "Bundini was a huge part of his life. They spent over eighteen years together, in tight quarters. My father adored Drew and was heartbroken."

On the day of the funeral, news cameras lined the sidewalks of small-town Sanford. *Sports Illustrated* photographers set up their equipment across the street from the New Bethel Church. News of Bundini's passing sent a ripple throughout the sports world. The loss was felt particularly hard in the boxing community.

"I was very sad when I heard about what happened to him. Bundini was a good guy. Everybody that knew him, loved him," Larry Holmes reflected.

"I was devastated," George Foreman told me. "When I decided to make my comeback, he was one of the first people I called," Foreman added.

In early 1987, at the age of thirty-eight, George Foreman ended his ten-year retirement from boxing, reemerging from isolation as a jolly, bald, 300-pound reinvention of himself. After experiencing a life-altering episode in his locker room in Puerto Rico, following a bout with Jimmy Young, Foreman became a born-again Christian. He'd spent his time away from boxing doing God's work, he believed. When the comeback was announced, a dangerous endeavor according to most boxing experts, Foreman was making his living as a full-time pastor of a small church in Texas. The former heavyweight champion told members of the media that his return was an attempt to earn enough money to save his struggling youth and community center.

"I talked to Bundini about my comeback. He would give me advice on losing weight. He said. 'If you are for real, I'll come down and work with you.' I told him this is for real. Every few days he would call and say, 'You ready for me?' And then, after I won my first fight, I met with him and he was sickly. He wasn't healthy. So when I saw him like that, I saw his face and realized he didn't have the strength anymore to return to the corner. But I still called Bundini all the time as I prepared for my comeback. Bundini gave me energy and belief that I could do it," Foreman insisted.

On November 5, 1994, at the MGM Grand Arena, with trainer Angelo Dundee in his corner, George Foreman accomplished the unthinkable. Just five days shy of his forty-sixth birthday, he became the oldest man ever to win the heavyweight championship by knocking out the undefeated WBA/IBF champion Michael Moorer in the tenth round. With one crushing straight right hand, Drew Bundini Brown's prediction became a reality. Foreman was champion of the world again.

"Bundini should have been in my corner that night," Foreman confided in me.

At the funeral, Drew Brown III was joined by his wife, Laurie, and his children, Taryn (then twelve years old) and Drew IV (then ten years old). Partially because of their location, and partially because of Bundini's self-imposed isolation, the children had spent very little time with their grandfather in the years leading up to his death.

"It was the first major death in our immediate family," Drew Brown IV said to me. "I remember my dad asking me to kiss his cheek when we approached the casket. I didn't know this person. The rest of my memories come from my grandfather's tales of heroism and tragedy and, of course, clips from movies and documentaries."

Bundini's ex-wife, Rhoda, despite all the ups and downs of their turbulent relationship, made the trip from Brooklyn to Florida.

"Rhoda wasn't going to miss the funeral," Laurie recalled. "Deep down, she loved Bundini. They had been separated for some time but she still loved him. We all sat together at the funeral. Rhoda wore these gold lamé gloves. I commented on them and she said, 'This is my tribute to him, for Bundini.'"

The wrist-length metallic gloves sparkled in the Florida sunlight as Rhoda said goodbye to her Golden Glove champion.

All of the living members of the Brown family—cousins, aunts, uncles, and the like—were in attendance for a celebration of life that was, in many aspects, a hometown affair. Sunrise Funeral Home, owned by Frederick Alexander, Bundini's cousin, handled the arrangements. According to Drew Brown III, the funeral expenses were paid for by none other than boxing's most controversial promoter, Don King:

"I was in the Navy, I had a family, and I didn't have the money. I thought that when I called Don King and explained it to him, I believed in my heart, when I told him about the circumstances, he would say, 'No problem, how much?' That didn't happen. I had to plead for it. I had to ask for it to be borrowed. Not only am I going to give King the $5,000, I am going to ask if he wants to put interest on it. What's right is right, what's wrong is wrong," Drew III insisted, his body language suggesting he was back at Sunrise Funeral Home, if only for a moment.

All of Sanford, it appeared, came out to say farewell to their beloved son. Although Bundini was known as the Black Prince of Harlem, nowhere on Earth was his name bigger than in Seminole County, Florida. Still today, Sanford continues to take pride in their connection to Bundini. In 1992, baseball great Tim Raines, another Sanford kid who made it to the limelight, purchased and donated Bundini's scrapbooks to the sports collection at the local Sanford Historical Museum, where they remain on display to this day.

Drew Bundini Brown traveled the world as a teenager, voyaging from Central Florida to the ports of India where he earned his famous nickname. As a member of Sugar Ray Robinson's entourage, he saw all the glitz and glamour the United States of America had to offer. As Muhammad Ali's chief motivator, he traveled the world from Zaire to Malaysia, meeting some of the most powerful and impactful human beings of his generation. With his physical journey complete, his spirit finally set free, the little boy in the galvanized washtub returned to the place where the story began.

On October 4, 1987, Bundini's body, at his request, was buried next to his father, Drew Brown Sr., in Page Jackson Cemetery.[1]

■ ■ ■

In December of 1994, Rhoda Palestine visited Drew Brown III and his family in Virginia Beach, Virginia. She stayed with the family for two weeks. As was her custom, Rhoda brought the family four dozen bagels from Neptune Bakery, where Buddy Drew used to work after school.

"I remember the bagels. She would also bring pastrami from this place in Brooklyn [Irving Delicatessen]. My mom wasn't that big on sugar, so my grandmother would sneak me and my brother Swedish fish," Rhoda's granddaughter, Taryn Brown, told me.

During the visit, Rhoda experienced the side effects of a nasty chest cold. According to Drew, Rhoda was unfazed by the illness. When Rhoda returned to Brooklyn, however, she immediately became sick and was hospitalized. Her brother, Herbie, was by her side in the hospital, providing Drew with frequent updates on his mother's condition.

"For the past five or six years my mother had lost that bubbly self. She'd lost that spark. When she came to my house for that last visit, however, she was her old self again. Mommy was back. She knew she was going to die, I think. So she gave her son his old momma back one last time. She was the greatest mother on planet Earth. But, when untreated, the disease of alcoholism always wins. That's why they call it a disease," Drew argued.

"Rhoda passed while we were in Virginia. We never got to New York in time. It was completely shocking. It happened very quickly," Laurie said to me.

"Rhoda and I were very close. She would call me the daughter she never had. I grieved for so long. I'll never forget when we first met, she came to New Orleans when Taryn was born. Rhoda was a Jewish woman but she had this cool, writer, hippie side to her. She got off the plane and she had her hair parted down the middle, with two long braids. She was genius-level smart. So well read. She was instrumental in helping Bundini gain the level of literacy he did attain. Back when they were on good terms, she would help him with his rhymes. She would read over things for him. They were just two spirits that were so very much alike," Laurie continued.

When Drew Brown III was a teenager, he would often call to his mother, "Why can't you be normal?"

Young Drew longed for a traditional family but life had given him two of the most eclectic parents on Earth. Rhoda Palestine, like her offbeat husband, simply did not conform to contemporary standards of normalcy.

"Normal? Normal is boring," Rhoda would snap.

As a young man, Drew was inspired by his father's street-corner wisdom but found self-confidence in his mother's support. Because her son's birthday fell on inauguration day, Rhoda would often tell him, "You'll have your birthday party when you become President of the United States of America." The statement, for Drew, was not taken as a joke. His mother held an unwavering belief in his abilities.

"I could always sense that it was Rhoda that made Buddy Drew feel special. She built him up, convinced him that he was destined to do something great in his life," Rick "Cubby" Katz, Drew's high school friend, told me.

"Rhoda had this very warm and inviting presence about her. She was unlike anyone that I've ever met. She was ahead of her time. My most vivid memories of being with her and Buddy Drew are at dinnertime. Instantly, she made you feel like part of her family. As I got to know her, I began to think of her as a very special woman. She wasn't cookie cutter. She had this enlightenment about her, like Yoda from the *Star Wars* movies. She had this presence about her. She was deep, one of a kind. It was interesting watching the two of them interact. Buddy Drew had this big aura, his big energy, and Rhoda's favorite counter expression was always 'Don't be so heavy, Buddy,'" Katz continued.

During my fist evening in Atlanta, I noticed the tambourine next to Rhoda's urn. She was a dancer, a free spirit. I did not need to ask for clarification. The placement of the instrument made perfect sense to me. Life was Rhoda's religion and music the outward expression of her soul. To know Rhoda was to be impacted by her, even for those who only knew her for a brief period of time.

"I remember, when I was a little girl, we would stand in the sun and hold hands, to energize our batteries. I still do that when I'm walking down the street in New York. I will stand in the sunlight and recharge my batteries," Taryn Brown said to me.

"I do it to this day. We would all three charge our batteries together," Drew Brown IV added.

Much like Bundini, Rhoda's story is both inspiring and tragic. She was a woman who loved openly, yet lived by her own moral code. She could be wise and contradictory in the very same moment.

"I loved Rhoda. There is no denying she was brilliant. She had a great sense of humor. Everyone in the family loved her. But she and Bundini both had serious drinking problems. It was sad to see her like that in the later years," Irwin Levowitz, Rhoda's second cousin, said to me.

Losing both of his parents in a relatively short period of time forced Drew Brown III to confront his own struggle with alcohol.

"My father was drunk when he fell down those steps. My life started changing when I started falling down, drunk. I knew that my father would be so disappointed when I started falling down. I knew my mother expected better of me. If I died in a jet crash, great. But they didn't want me to be like them. This awful disease doesn't make sense. I was just like them toward the end. I was falling. Falling down drunk. My wife took a picture of me on the ground one time. That was my rock bottom. That picture was the beginning of the end," Drew said to me, struggling to get the words out of his trembling lips.

"My dad really believed that he just lacked self-control. My mother and father felt like, deep inside, they were just weak. These two mentally strong people felt weak. Bubba would say to them, 'Why are you doing this?' They thought they got free when they were drunk. But, in fact, it was the total opposite," Drew continued.

Things would get worse before they would get better. Drew Brown III's beloved grandmother, Mildred "Bubba" Palestine, would pass away in Brighton Beach in January of 1996, two years after Rhoda's death.

With his parents and grandparents gone, Drew's drinking spiraled out of control.

"That was the contradiction of my childhood, growing up with a motivational speaker who was struggling," Drew Brown IV reflected. "He was a motivator at heart. He coached all of our sports teams. When he wasn't in the Navy, he was as involved as he could be. But, there were also memories of the drinking, the fighting between my parents."

"The disease of alcoholism was a major part of the reason for Laurie leaving. In all outside appearances, I achieved the *Brady Bunch* family I had longed for. Despite my loving and well-meaning intentions, some of my actions didn't show that. Since I was three years old, sitting next to my Daddy on the bed, when he was packing to leave, my lifelong mission was to get my parents back together. It succeeded and then it blew up. I didn't want my children to go through that type of struggle," Drew III reflected .

Alcoholism cost Drew Brown III his marriage to Laurie Guimont, but not their friendship. The couple would divorce but continue to play an active role in the lives of their children.

In early 1998, driven by the fear that he would one day find himself at the bottom of a staircase, Drew Brown III entered treatment for the disease that plagued his family. At his first group therapy meeting, he was greeted by an old friend.

"They ended the meeting with the 'King Kong' prayer, the only prayer my father and I said together. You'll never know how much that meant to me. That was Shorty, my daddy's way of being there with me," Drew Brown III recalled.

■ ■ ■

In countless documentaries and interviews, Muhammad Ali referred to Parkinson's as a "trial," a test from Allah. The final thirty-two years of Ali's life, as was the case in many of his biggest bouts, served as a testimony to the champion's unyielding heart and determination. Parkinson's robbed Ali of the physical attributes that once made him famous but would not, in the end, take what made him *The Greatest of All Time*. It was Ali's spirit that set him apart from other fighters. His hands grew more unsteady, his voice weaker. Ali's energy varied from day to day. On good days, the former champion smiled and laughed with loved ones. Other times, Ali sat in complete silence.

"The last time we visited Ali, this was many years after my father's passing, the Champ whispered to me and said, 'How's your Daddy doing?' We never went back after that. He had become just like Uncle Ray," Drew Brown III said to me.

On August 25, 2008, Ali's manager, Jabir Herbert Muhammad, become the second member of the Ali team to pass away, as a result of complications from heart disease. Herbert Muhammad died at the University of Illinois Medical Center in Chicago, at the age of seventy-nine.

Four years later, on January 17, 2012 (Muhammad Ali's seventieth birthday), Buddy's Drew's pseudo-uncle, Walter "Youngblood" Muhammad, passed away at Calvary Hospital in the Bronx where he was in hospice care after a long battle with cancer.

One month after Youngblood's death, on February 1, 2012, Angelo Dundee died in his home in Tampa, Florida. Dundee, ninety years old, had attended Ali's seventieth birthday party the previous month.

On Friday, June 3, 2016, at the age of seventy-four, Muhammad Ali's legendary heart stopped beating. He had been transported to a hospital in Phoenix, Arizona, because of a respiratory illness the previous day. In New York City, Ali tributes were broadcast at Madison Square Garden, Times Square, and the Apollo Theater. My wife, Stephanie, and I happened to be in New York City that day, celebrating our tenth wedding anniversary.

Later that night, Mayor Bill de Blasio announced that a special tribute in lights would be projected to honor Ali. On a very special Harlem street corner, three images were displayed via alternating slides. The first image contained a famous Ali saying: "Life is short. We get old fast. It doesn't make sense to waste time on hating." The second slide was an artist's rendering of Ali standing over Sonny Liston. The final slide, a fitting crescendo to the tribute, juxtaposed overlapping images of a butterfly and a bee. The visuals were broadcast on the side of a large building on West 125th Street and St. Nicholas Avenue in Harlem, the former home of Ali's faithful cornerman, Drew Bundini Brown.

■   ■   ■

My wife and I emerged from Penn Station, pushing through the crowds, making our way to the taxi line outside of Madison Square Garden. Our taxi weaved in and out of traffic, our driver thumping his horn at other vehicles along the way. Stephanie was eager to meet the man who had occupied so much of my time over the past year; my conversations with Drew Brown III had become weekly affairs.

The occasion was a brunch in Midtown Manhattan, following Taryn Brown's baby shower. The former Texas Longhorns basketball star was expecting her first child, a baby girl. This would be my first opportunity to see the entire Brown family interact with each other.

As Stephanie and I entered the restaurant, we were immediately greeted by Drew Brown III, dressed in pink, a visual celebration of his first grandchild.

"Hey, Grandpa," I called, teasingly.

"Don't call me Grandpa. It's Big Poppa Drew," he insisted, with that famous Bundini smile on his face.

My wife and I then exchanged hugs with Drew's second wife, Katrina. In Atlanta, I was instantly drawn to her. From her southern drawl, to her impressive knowledge of hip-hop culture, Katrina was my kind of person. She was quick to laugh, the kind of woman who didn't let you take yourself too seriously.

"I was cleaning the house one day, moving things around, and I found this postcard signed by Muhammad Ali, addressed to Drew's grandmother, Bubba. The postcard was signed Cassius Clay," Katrina said to me.

"I almost threw it in the trash. I told him, 'Drew, you can't be leaving stuff like this around,'" she laughed.

Now celebrating their eighteenth year of marriage, I found Drew and Katrina Brown among the happiest couples I had ever met. After the Navy, life had directed Drew to Memphis, Tennessee, where he worked as a pilot for FedEx. The couple met shortly after Drew was forced to take medical leave from his job, because of back problems that, no doubt, stemmed from his days landing attack jets on aircraft carriers. At the time, Katrina worked in the area as a hairdresser, owning her own salon, another reason she and I instantly connected. My own mother was a hairdresser, my father's boxing gym was, at one point, located in the back room of her beauty shop in Cowen, West Virginia. Beauticians are excellent talkers, I've come to learn.

"Give me the story of how you guys came together," I asked early into the reunion brunch.

The story of Drew and Katrina's first encounter was a uniquely Bundini occurrence.

"Drew and I met at a party, hosted by a mutual friend. I saw this guy walk through the party. He was this handsome, older guy. He walked through a couple of times. He told a joke and I didn't laugh. Crickets. I was ready to leave the party, so I tried to ease out," Katrina said. Out on the front porch, Drew Brown III, as persistent as his father, tracked down the beautiful hairdresser who caught his eye. He'd instantly fallen for Katrina and, within seconds of meeting her, had envisioned a future with the two of them together. Like his father, Drew is often driven by feeling rather than reason, Katrina's story suggested.

"Not heeding my father's advice to avoid the word *never*, I'd told anyone that would listen that I would *never* get married again. 'Use the word *never* and you'll end up doing it,' my father would say. As soon as I saw Katrina, she looked like one of those movie actresses in black-and-white films, underneath the spotlight. I instantly knew I was going to marry her," Drew Brown III interrupted.

"Out on the porch, Drew starts in with the interview. 'Are you married? Did you go to college? Tennessee State. Cool. What did you study? Agricultural science? Cool. What kind of work do you do? How much money do you make? Do you invest? How much? Do you like tall men? Do you swim? Do you drink? No, that's good. I'm a recovering alcoholic.' Who says that? The whole thing was bizarre. I'm thinking, who does this? To my surprise, I answered every question. Then he ends the interview by telling me that he is moving. I'm thinking he's moving downtown. The next state. No. He's like 'I'm packing up, getting ready to move to St. Thomas in the Virgin Islands.' After telling me all of this, he asks for my number. I gave him the number and he called me at seven o'clock in the morning. That tenacity, that's his Daddy's side," Katrina laughed.

Drew Brown III wasn't lying. He would indeed move to St. Thomas in the coming months. Little did Katrina know, she would be coming with him.

The next to arrive at brunch was Taryn Brown and her husband, Nick. Taryn, seven months pregnant, wore a flowing sundress. I had interviewed Taryn over the phone just three days prior to the baby shower. I found her personality warm and bubbly, her demeanor open and inviting.

"I didn't grow up with many good memories of my grandfather," Taryn warned me. "But, as I've grown older, I've come to understand that many of my father's philosophies and life lessons actually came from my grandfather," she added.

Like any good parent, Drew Brown III loves to brag about the accomplishments of his children. At our brunch in Manhattan, the subject of Drew's children dominated our conversation. My favorite Taryn story centered around a typical moment of high school disappointment. During her freshman year, Taryn didn't make the high school cheerleading squad. When Drew III came home from a flight, he found Taryn crying in her bedroom.

Placing a basketball in her hands, he said the following: "If they won't let you be a cheerleader, let's make them cheer for you."

In typical Bundini fashion, the father and daughter turned a negative into a positive, disappointment into opportunity. Despite having never played the sport in any organized fashion, Taryn went on to become a Memphis area high school basketball star, earning a scholarship to the Lady Longhorns basketball team at the University of Texas. Taryn would go from being cut from the cheerleading squad to having her jersey retired and hung in the trophy case.

During her career at the University of Texas, Taryn was part of some milestone moments for the program. While in law school at Tulane, Taryn worked as a legal intern for the New Orleans Saints and the New Orleans Hornets, paving the way for her career in corporate law in New York City.

Next to arrive at the table was Drew Brown IV. He was tall and thin, with soft eyes and his father's smile. While Drew also played basketball at the University of Texas, for two seasons, I could sense he had a slightly different demeanor. In Taryn, I found one side of her father. In Drew IV, I found another.

Before joining St. Lucie Medical Center, in Tampa, Florida, Drew Brown IV lived in Hawaii for ten years. Big wave surfing, aside from performing spine surgery, was his passion.

"It is high stakes with high rewards and you need the same serenity and calm in the arts of surfing and surgery. Surfing in Hawaii is a hierarchical sport. There is a pecking order. You wait your turn. Surfing is dangerous and you learn what it takes to be accepted as part of the crew," Drew IV stated.

In chatting with Drew IV, it occurred to me that he, like the Drews before him, gravitated toward water. For members of the Brown family, water has always served as something of an escape.

"When I was young, if it was raining, I would go sleep in the rain. I have always been very connected with the ocean or any body of water. It has been a trend with the Drews. We all felt that deep connection with that life source," Drew IV said.

There was a peacefulness about Drew IV that I found intriguing. I wondered how much of it came from Rhoda.

"In medicine, it is a lifelong journey. It also has a hierarchy. You gain experience and you move up. Just as the ocean is extremely humbling, so is medicine. You think you have conquered one aspect and two obstacles arise. The ocean shows you how little you know. The human body and the ocean never stop," Drew IV stated, crafting a Bundini-like analogy.

The final guests to arrive at the table were Laurie Guimont-Guillaume and her husband, Warmoth. Old wounds had healed. Warmoth and Drew III spoke to each other with kindness and affection. Laurie and Katrina did the same. Everyone at our table laughed and shared stories. I was taken aback by the amount of love in the room.

After brunch, my wife and I said our goodbyes, hugging every family member as we made our exit. Out on the New York City pavement, Stephanie and I chatted briefly with Drew III and Katrina.

"I have to ask you one last question: What would your father have thought of me?" I asked Bundini's son.

Drew III smiled. He liked my question.

"He would have instantly given you a nickname. He probably would have given you a hard time. But, I can promise you this, when he heard you talk about how much you love your daddy, he would have cried," Drew III said to me.

As Stephanie and I made our way toward Columbus Square, raindrops began to fall. Unprepared for the rain, we ducked into a café, looking for both coffee and shelter.

Ten or fifteen minutes into our stay, a young Black man wearing a gray Muhammad Ali T-shirt walked through the door. I was suddenly energized. A silly little part of me wanted to stop the young man and test his Bundini knowledge. I wanted to interview him but said nothing. The young man purchased his coffee and headed back into the rain.

The idea of Muhammad Ali, it occurred to me, sitting in the coffee shop waiting for the weather to let up, has many interconnected parts. Part of what we loved about Muhammad Ali belonged to Drew Bundini Brown, regardless of whether we knew it or not. We are shades of our mothers and fathers, reflections of our family members. We are the places we go, the people we meet. We are shaped by the Bundinis we meet along the way, our teachers, coaches, wives, husbands, friends, and enemies.

"Do you know how you're going to end the book?" my wife asked.

My thoughts turned to a story Muhammad Ali's pal Victor Solano once told me.

"When Muhammad and I would go see Drew [Bundini], in Hollywood, Drew always wanted to say the right things. He wanted to talk about God," Solano insisted.

Each visit, Ali and Solano would find Bundini seated on the corner of his bed, looking toward the light of his window, lost in meditative silence.

"What are you doing, Drew?" Solano would ask.

"I'm talking to Shorty. I'm working all this out with Shorty. Getting it worked out," Bundini would answer. "Shorty is talking and all you have to do is listen."

Maybe this is how Drew Bundini Brown's story truly ends, not in a lonesome, rundown Los Angeles motel, but in an upscale restaurant in Midtown Manhattan, surrounded by love.

The lawyers tried to cheat Bundini out of the copyright to his most famous contribution to American poetry, and yet his granddaughter is now a board-certified corporate lawyer working in the sports industry. Bundini's spine suffered irreversible damage in his horrific accident, and yet his grandson is now an orthopedic spine surgeon. Bundini was kicked out of the Navy, yet, at one time, his son was the only Black Navy attack pilot flying off aircraft carriers in the Atlantic fleet. Bundini was robbed of his education, and yet his son is now an author and motivational speaker, delivering a message of how education and hard work are the keys to success, and, ironically, showing millions the realities of addiction.

"Maybe that's why it has taken so long for someone to write Bundini's life story," I thought as I watched the raindrops sprinkle along the coffee-shop window.

The story wasn't over.

ACKNOWLEDGMENTS

This book is dedicated to my wife, Stephanie, and my son, Huntington Jay. Living with a writer isn't easy. Thank you. I also want to thank my mother, Cheryl; my father, Mike "Lo" Snyder; my sister, Katie; and my brother-in-law, Zach Tonkin, for their unwavering support.

Next, I would like to thank my friend, Drew Timothy Brown III, and his wife, Katrina. Over the past year, I conducted over fifty recorded interviews with Drew and his family. I also visited Drew's home in Atlanta on multiple occasions. This book would not have been possible without his contributions, as well as the contributions of his extended family members: Willy Brown III, Claudia Brown, Ellen Brown, Irwin Levowitz, and Rick "Cubby" Katz.

During our time together, Drew shared with me intimate family photographs, handwritten documents, and countless other historical artifacts. Drew held nothing back. He welcomed me into his family and into his life. I will forever be in debt to Drew and Katrina for their hospitality. Buddy Drew, you will always be my friend. Shorty brought our worlds together.

Katrina, when we searching for a subtitle, you came through in the clutch. Thank you.

I also want to thank Drew's children, Taryn and Drew IV, as well as their mother, Laurie Guimont, for welcoming me into the family. I'm lucky to have met each of you.

Writing Drew Bundini Brown's life story was challenging because so many members of the Muhammad Ali entourage are no longer with us. Herbert Muhammad passed away in 2012; Muhammad Ali and his lifelong friend Howard Bingham passed away in 2016; Wali "Youngblood" Muhammad, Angelo Dundee, and Ferdie Pacheco each passed away in

2017; and Abdul Rahman passed away in 2019, before I could reach out to him for an interview.

I was, however, blessed with the opportunity to converse with many individuals who shared their lives with Muhammad Ali and Drew Bundini Brown.

First and foremost, I want to thank Gene Kilroy for being gracious with his time, digging deep into the recesses of his memories to ensure that Bundini's story was told with integrity. Gene, I hope that my work makes you proud.

I also want to thank Khalilah Camacho-Ali, George Foreman, Larry Holmes, James "Quick" Tillis, Earnie Shavers, Gerry Cooney, Tim Witherspoon, Marvis Frazier, Harold Hazzard, Victor Solano, Jim Dundee, Don Elbaum, Cassius Green, Al Bernstein, James "Smitty" Smith, Jeff Julian, and Rick Kaletsky for being kind enough to talk with me.

I want to thank the staff at "Fighter's Heaven" in Deer Lake, Pennsylvania, for granting me a private tour of their facilities. Thank you.

I feel obliged to acknowledge the support of two of my favorite boxing scribes, Thomas Hauser and Jonathan Eig, both of whom directly influenced this book.

I am, of course, in debt to all of the wonderful boxing writers and filmmakers whose work I cited in this book. I could not have written this story without your wonderful contributions to boxing history.

On the publishing end of things, I am thankful for Kyle Sarofeen and Andy Komack for believing in my talent. As a writer, I couldn't have asked for a better team. Thank you.

On the pragmatic side of things, I want to thank the good folks at the Starbucks on Troy-Schenectady Road in Latham, New York, where I wrote every single word of this book, particularly my friends Devesh Chandra, Roman Jaquez, and Bill Womer.

On the academic side of things, I am thankful for the influence of my colleagues at Marshall University, Ohio University, and Siena College, past and present. To Nate Leslie, *we did it again, my friend*. I love and miss you.

Last but not least, I want to thank Muhammad Ali and Drew Bundini Brown for changing the world for the better. We have never met in the physical sense, but, after this experience, I now feel as if the three of us are old friends.

I love you both and feel humbled to be connected to your legacies, if only in the most miniscule and vicarious of ways.

Todd Snyder

WORKS REFERENCED

Ali. Dir. Michael Mann. Perf. Will Smith, Jamie Foxx, Jon Voight. Columbia Pictures, 2000.

Ali, Hana. *At Home with Muhammad Ali: A Memoir of Love, Loss, and Forgiveness*. New York: Amistad, 2019.

Ali, Muhammad, with Richard Durham. *The Greatest: My Own Story*. New York: Random House, 1975.

Ali–Frazier: One Nation Divisible. Dir. Dave Anderson. Perf. Joe Frazier, Muhammad Ali, Liev Schreiber. HBO Sports, 2000.

Ali Rap. Dir. Joseph Maar. Perf. Kareem Abdul-Jabar, Khalilah Ali, Muhammad Ali. ESPN Original Entertainment, 2006.

Anderson, Dave. "Money Puts Dundee in Ellis's Corner." *New York Times*, July 25, 1971. https://www.nytimes.com/1971/07/25/archives/money-puts-dundee-in-elliss-corner.html

———. "Sports of the Times: Float Like a Bundini." *New York Times*, September 29, 1987. https://www.nytimes.com/1987/09/29/sports/sports-of-the-times-float-like-a-bundini.html

Bernstein, Al. Personal interview, February 12, 2019.

Boyd, Herb; with Ray Robinson II. *Pound for Pound: A Biography of Sugar Ray Robinson*. New York: Amistad, 2005.

Boyd, Herb. "Bundini Brown: Muhammad Ali's Sidekick, Trainer, and Collaborator." *Amsterdam News*, June 6, 2016. http://amsterdamnews.com/news/2016/jun/09/bundini-brown-muhammad-alis-sidekick-trainer-and-c/?page=2

Brown, Claudia. Personal interview, February 20, 2019.

Brown, Drew T., III. *You Gotta Believe!: Education + Hard Work – Drugs = The American Dream*. New York: William & Morrow Company, 1991.

———. Personal interviews, January 6–August 31, 2019.

Brown, Drew, IV. Personal interview, August 5, 2019.

Brown, Katrina. Personal interview, February 23, 2019.

Brown, Ruth, with Andrew Yule. *Miss Rhythm*. New York: Da Capo Press, 1996.

Brown, Taryn. Personal interview, March 25, 2019.

Brown, Willy, III. Personal interview, February 20, 2019.

Brunt, Stephen. *Facing Ali: 15 Fighters, 15 Stories*. Guilford, CT: Lyons Press, 2002.

Byrne, Jason. "Lynched in Longwood: The Brutal Killing of John West." *Medium*, June 6, 2017. https://medium.com/florida-history/lynched-in -longwood-john-west-8fa37a1661b5

Camacho-Ali, Khalilah. Personal interview, February 7, 2019.

Chung, Jen. "Photos, Video of NYC's Muhammad Ali Tribute in Harlem." *Gothamist*, June 5, 2016. https://gothamist.com/2016/06/05/muhammad _ali_nyc_projections.php#photo-1

Clay, Cassius. *I Am the Greatest*. Columbia Records, 1963.

Cole, Nat King. *Nature Boy*. Capitol Records, 1948.

Cooney, Gerry. Personal interview, February 6, 2019.

Don King: Only in America. Dir. John Herzfeld. Perf. Ving Rhames, Vondie Curtis-Hall, Jeremy Piven. HBO Films, 1996.

Edwards, Paul. *How to Rap: The Art and Science of the Hip-Hop MC*. Chicago: Chicago Review Press, 2009.

Eig, Jonathan. *Ali: A Life*. New York: Houghton Mifflin, 2017.

———. Personal interview, June 24, 2019.

Elbaum, Don. Personal interview, June 12, 2019.

Erdman, Corey. "Honey Boy Bratton: The Boxer Who Inspired Miles Davis and Muhammad Ali." *Vice*, March 29, 2017. http://fightland .vice.com/blog/honey-boy-bratton-the-boxer-who-inspired-miles-davis -and-muhammad-ali

Fletcher, Tony. *All Hopped Up and Ready to Go: Music from the Streets of New York: 1927–77*. New York: W. W. Norton & Company, 2009.

Foreman, George. Personal interview, February 15, 2019.

Frazier, Marvis. Personal interview, January 31, 2019.

Gardener, Greg. "The Surfing Spine Surgeon." *Indian River Magazine*, Fall 2015. https://www.indianrivermag.com/articles/fall15/surfingsurgeon .html

Gilbert, Martin. *The Holocaust: The Jewish Tragedy*. New York: Harper Collins, 1986.

Gioia, Ted. *The History of Jazz*. New York: Oxford University Press, 2011.

Guimont-Guillaume, Laurie, Personal interview, February 23, 2019.

Hauser, Thomas, with cooperation of Muhammad Ali. *Muhammad Ali: His Life and Times*. New York: Simon & Schuster, 1991.

———. Personal interview, June 21, 2019.

Hess, Mickey. *Icons of Hip Hop: An Encyclopedia of the Movement, Music, and Culture*. Santa Barbara, CA: Greenwood Publishing Group, 2007.

Holmes, Larry. Personal interview, February 21, 2019.

Julian, Jeff. Personal interview, June 19, 2019.

Katz, Rick "Cubby." Personal interview, April 22, 2019.

Kilgannon, Corey. "Once the King of Harlem Hairdressers, Now Nearly Forgotten." *New York Times*, March 24, 2013. https://cityroom.blogs.nytimes.com/2013/03/24/sugar-rays-barber/?mtrref=www.google.com&gwh=73A54307CA25CD19517F26AB94805042&gwt=pay&assetType=REGIWALL

———. "Sugar Ray's Harlem, Back in the Day." *New York Times*, November 25, 2009. https://www.nytimes.com/2009/11/26/nyregion/26sugar.html

Kilroy, Gene. Personal interview, January 28, 2019.

Kindred, Dave. *Sound and Fury: Two Powerful Lives, One Fateful Friendship*. New York: Free Press, 2006.

Kram, Mark. *Ghosts of Manilla: The Fateful Blood Feud Between Ali and Frazier*. New York: HarperCollins, 2002.

———. "Smokin' Joe: The Life of Joe Frazier." New York: HarperCollins, 2019.

Levowitz, Irwin. Personal interview, June 18, 2019.

Light, Alan. *The Vibe History of Hip-Hop*. New York: Three Rivers Press, 1999.

Margolick, David. "Max Schmeling, Heavyweight Champion Caught in the Middle of Nazi Politics, Is Dead at 99." *New York Times*, February 5, 2005.

Muhammad and Larry. Dir. Bradley Kaplan and Albert Maysles. Perf. Muhammad Ali, Larry Holmes, Drew Bundini Brown. ESPN 30 for 30 Films, 2009.

Muhammad Ali: Float Like a Butterfly, Sting Like a Bee. YouTube, January 3, 2014. https://www.youtube.com/watch?v=bNpFiZDqcog

Muhammad Ali: The Greatest. Dir. Tom Gries and Monte Hellmen. Perf. Muhammad Ali, Drew Bundini Brown, and James Earl Jones. Columbia Pictures, 1977.

Muhammad Ali: The Whole Story. Dir. Joseph Consentino and Sandra Consentino. Perf. Muhammad Ali, Khalilah Ali, Rahman Ali. Turner Home Entertainment, 1996.

Myler, Patrick. *Ring of Hate: The Fight of the Century*. New York: Arcade Publishing, 2005.

"Navy 'A Family Affair' for Ali's Ex-Aid Bundini Brown and Jet Pilot Son," *Jet*, December 26, 1983.

"New York Beat," *Jet*, January 25, 1968.

Newfield, Jack. *The Life and Crimes of Don King: The Shame of Boxing in America*. New York: Harbor Publishing, 1995.

Ortegon, Randy. "Where Are They Now?: Taryn Brown." University of Texas website. https://texassports.com/news/2009/9/9/090909aaa_255.aspx

Owens, Darryl. "42 Reminds Us that Sanford, U.S., Haven't Crossed Home on Race." *Orlando Sentinel*. April 14, 2013. https://www .orlandosentinel.com/opinion/os-xpm-2013-04-14-os-darryl-owens -jackie-robinson-sanford-20130414-story.html

Pacheco, Ferdie. *Muhammad Ali: A View from the Corner*. New York: Birch Lane, 1992.

Penitentiary III. Dir. Jamaa Fanka. Perf. Leon Isaac Kennedy, Anthony Geary, Drew Bundini Brown. Cannon, 1987.

Plimpton, George. *Shadow Box: An Amateur in the Ring*. New York: Lyons Press, 1977.

Rafiq, Fiaz. *Muhammad Ali Conversations*. New York: HNL Publishing, 2010.

Remnick, David. *King of the World: Muhammad Ali and the Rise of an American Hero*. New York: Vintage, 1999.

Romero, Peter. "Muhammad Ali, Restaurateur." *Restaurant Business*. June 13, 2016. https://www.restaurantbusinessonline.com/muhammad-ali -restaurateur

Rougin, Gilbert. "A Battle of the Lionhearted." *Sports Illustrated*, April 11, 1966. https://www.si.com/vault/1966/04/11/608824/a-battle-of-the -lionhearted

Schmitz, Brian. "He Was the Spirit of a True Champion." *Orlando Sentinel*, October 4, 1987. https://www.orlandosentinel.com/news/os-xpm-1987 -10-04-0150170197-story.html

Shaft. Dir. Gordon Parks. Perf. Richard Roundtree, Moses Gunn, Drew Bundini Brown. Metro-Goldwyn-Mayer, 1971.

Shaft's Big Score! Dir. Gordon Parks. Perf. Richard Roundtree, Moses Gunn, Drew Bundini Brown. Metro-Goldwyn-Mayer, 1972.

Shavers, Ernie. Personal interview, January 30, 2019.

Shrake, Edwin. "Bundini: Svengali in Ali's Corner." *Sports Illustrated*, February 15, 1971. https://www.si.com/vault/1971/02/15/554295/bundini -svengali-in-alis-corner

Smith, James. Personal interview, January 24, 2019.

Solano, Victor. Personal interview, July 27, 2019.

Sugar Ray Robinson: Bright Lights and Dark Shadows of a Champion. Dir. Ross Greenburg. Perf. Sugar Ray Robinson, Dave Anderson, Evelyn Nelson. HBO Sports, 1998. https://www.usatoday.com/story/news/2018 /02/19/1968-project-muhammad-ali-vietnam-war/334759002/

Telegram, Drew Bundini Brown, Jr., to Drew Timothy Brown III, Ensign, U.S. Navy, August 21, 1981.

Tillis, James "Quick." Personal interview, January 25, 2019.

The Color Purple. Dir. Stephen Spielberg. Perf. Whoopi Goldberg, Oprah Winfrey, Danny Glover. Warner Brothers, 1985.

This is Your Life: Muhammad Ali. YouTube. Accessed June 28, 2011. https://www.youtube.com/watch?v=ZWZOBX1vE7A

Toner, Jim. "Sanford Kid's Charm, Vision Inspired Ali." *Orlando Sentinel*, January 10, 2002. https://www.orlandosentinel.com/news/os-xpm-2002 -01-10-0201100299-story.html

Torres, Jose, with Bert Randolph Sugar. *Sting Like a Bee: The Muhammad Ali Story*. Lincoln: University of Nebraska Press, 1971.

Wolfson, Andrew. "Muhammad Ali Lost Everything in Opposing the Vietnam War. But in 1968 He Triumphed." *USA Today*, February 19, 2018.

When We Were Kings. Dir. Leon Gast. Perf. Muhammad Ali, George Foreman, Drew Bundini Brown. Polygram Entertainment, 1996.

X, Malcom, with Alex Haley. *The Autobiography of Malcolm X*. New York: Random House, 1987.

NOTES

Introduction: Requiem for a Hype Man

[1] My student is referring to a direct quote from the introduction to our textbook: Light, Alan. *The Vibe History of Hip-Hop*. New York: Three Rivers Press, 1999.

[2] I am, of course, paraphrasing my conversation with Chuck D to the best of my ability.

[3] Hess, Mickey. *Icons of Hip-Hop: An Encyclopedia of the Movement, Music, and Culture*. Greenwood Publishing Group, 2007.

[4] Edwards, Paul. *How to Rap: The Art and Science of the Hip-Hop MC*. Chicago: Chicago Review Press, 2009.

[5] This story comes from my personal conversations with Chuck D. However, this story has been widely reported and is also featured in my course textbook: Light, Alan. *The Vibe History of Hip-Hop*. New York: Three Rivers Press, 1999.

[6] Hauser, Thomas, with the cooperation of Muhammad Ali. *Muhammad Ali: His Life and Times*. Simon and Schuster. New York: 1991.

Chapter 1: Do the Best You Can for Him

[1] In this book, every quote from Drew Timothy Brown III comes from our series of recorded interviews (spanning from January 12, 2019, to August 31, 2019). We recorded over fifty interviews during our time together. All dialogue, even when appearing in personal conversations, was read back to Drew and approved. I wanted to present the most authentic dialogue possible to my readers.

[2] Bryne, Jason. "Lynched in Longwood: The Brutal Killing of John West." *Medium*, June 6, 2017.

[3] "The Seminole Wars." Florida Department of State. https://dos.myflorida .com/florida-facts/florida-history/seminole-history/the-seminole-wars/

[4] Drew Brown Sr. married Ellen in 1930, after Elbert's birth.

[5] Elizabeth Brown's dialogue is taken from my interviews with Drew Timothy Brown III. This story was also relayed to me by other members of the Brown family.

[6] Bundini's quotes, in this portion of the chapter, come from Edwin Shrake's "Bundini: Svengali in Ali's Corner." *Sports Illustrated*, February 15, 1971.

[7] Myler, Patrick. *Ring of Hate: The Fight of the Century*. New York: Arcade Publishing, 2005.

[8] Margolick, David. "Max Schmeling, Heavyweight Champion Caught in the Middle of Nazi Politics, Is Dead at 99." *New York Times*. February 5, 2005.

[9] Myler, Patrick. *Ring of Hate: The Fight of the Century*. New York: Arcade Publishing, 2005.

[10] "NAS History." www.nassanfordmemorial.com

Chapter 2: A Rosebud in Harlem

[1] In the early 1990s, Drew Timothy Brown III attempted to write a screenplay about his father. He gave me a few pages of the screenplay to read. Drew opened the manuscript with a fictionalized account of a Jewish boy and a Black boy, in Russia and in Sanford, witnessing terrible crimes. I was moved by this account and, with Drew's permission, attempted to historicize this time period rather than fictionalize it. In this first paragraph, I am referencing actual historical events that took place in Russia. In gathering this data, I am relying on Martin Gilbert's *The Holocaust: The Jewish Tragedy*. New York: Harper Collins, 1986, pp. 30–33. In the second paragraph, I am referencing the lynching of John West, another true-life event that occurred during the same time period. Here, I am relying on Jason Byrne's "Lynched in Longwood: The Brutal Killing of John West." *Medium,* June 6, 2017.

[2] Fletcher, Tony. *All Hopped Up and Ready to Go: Music from the Streets of New York: 1927–77*. New York: W. W. Norton & Company, 2009.

[3] The direct quotes in this paragraph come from Ted Gioia's *The History of Jazz*. New York: Oxford University Press, 2011.

[4] During my first visit to Atlanta, Drew Timothy Brown III gave me a collection of his mother's high school essays. I wanted to share, at the

very least, one of these writings with the world. I wanted my readers to get a true sense of Rhoda Palestine's intellect.

[5] All dialogue attributed to Rhoda Palestine comes from Drew Timothy Brown III's interviews with his mother, in preparation for his own book: Brown, Drew T., III. *You Gotta Believe!: Education + Hard Work – Drugs = The American Dream*. New York: William & Morrow Company, 1991.

[6] In this chapter, Bundini's dialogue comes from Rhoda Palestine's comments to her son during their interview sessions, in preparation for Drew Timothy Brown III's own book: Brown, Drew T., III. *You Gotta Believe!: Education + Hard Work – Drugs = The American Dream*. New York: William & Morrow Company, 1991.

[7] Throughout this book, all boxing records and boxing-related dates come from the BoxRec official website. BoxRec, as fans well know, is the number-one record keeper of the sport. https://boxrec.com

Chapter 3: Honey and Sugar

[1] For the dialogue in this scene, I am relying heavily on my interviews with Drew Timothy Brown III. This encounter shows up in a number of my sources but I wanted to hear the story directly from Bundini's son. I allowed him to shape the dialogue to best fit the story, as it was told to him by his father and Norman Henry.

[2] For the dialogue in this scene, I am, once again, relying on my interviews with Drew Timothy Brown III.

[3] Kilgannon, Corey. "Once the King of Harlem Hairdressers, Now Nearly Forgotten." *New York Times*, March 24, 2013.

[4] Unless otherwise indicated, any dialogue between Bundini and his son comes from my recorded interviews with Drew Timothy Brown III.

[5] The dialogue found in this section is quoted directly from the following documentary film: *Muhammad Ali: The Whole Story*. Directed by Joseph Consentino and Sandra Consentino. Turner Home Entertainment, 1996.

[6] The dialogue found in the Bundini–Robinson meeting leans heavily on two key sources: (1) Edwin Shrake's previously mentioned *Sports Illustrated* article and Muhammad Ali's 1975 biography, written by Richard Durham. My goal was to shape the scene by using these sources. Next, I read the scene to Drew Timothy Brown III and asked him to draw on his memories of his father to make the dialogue more authentic. Drew said that his father told him this story many times and was very confident that our

end product represents the actual events as they unfolded in Shelton's Rib House.

Chapter 4: Metamorphosis
[1] The dialogue in this scene is directly quoted from *This Is Your Life*. The episode can be found on YouTube. https://www.youtube.com/watch?v=ZWZOBX1vE7A

[2] Ali, Rahaman with Fiaz Rafiq. *My Brother, Muhammad Ali: The Definitive Biography*. London: John Blake Publishing Ltd., 2019.

[3] This is quoted directly from *Muhammad Ali: Float Like a Butterfly, Sting Like a Bee*. YouTube. January 3, 2014. https://www.youtube.com/watch?v=bNpFiZDqcog

[4] All quotes from the Liston–Clay weigh-in scene come from the following source: Hauser, Thomas, with the cooperation of Muhammad Ali. *Muhammad Ali: His Life and Times*. New York: Simon & Schuster, 1991.

[5] I am quoting Muhammad Ali via the following source: Eig, Jonathan. *Ali: A Life*. New York: Houghton Mifflin, 2017.

Chapter 5: Blue Eyes and Brown Eyes, See Grass Green
[1] All dialogue in this section is directly quoted from Michael Mann's 2000 Muhammad Ali biopic, *Ali*.

[2] Pacheco's quotes, in this section, do not come from his book but rather from his interview in Thomas Hauser's Muhammad Ali biography.

[3] *Ali-Frazier 1: One Nation Divisible*. Directed by Dave Anderson. HBO Sports, 2000.

Chapter 6: Bundini's World
[1] While in Atlanta, researching for the book, Drew Timothy Brown III provided me with the actual copy of the speech that he read. I wanted to include the speech because it was written by Rhoda, providing readers with a window into her intellect.

Chapter 7: Make Sure You Be There, Waitin'
[1] This quote comes from the following source: Hauser, Thomas, with the cooperation of Muhammad Ali. *Muhammad Ali: His Life and Times*. New York: Simon & Schuster, 1991.

[2] I am referencing Don Quixote's famous sidekick in Miguel de Cervantes's literary classic *The Ingenious Gentleman Don Quixote of La Mancha* (1605, first edition).

Chapter 8: Road to Heaven

[1] All postfight interviews and quotes from color commentators are directly quoted from the actual fight broadcasts. I was able to access each of these fights via YouTube and my own DVD collection.

[2] I am indirectly quoting Drew Brown III's coach from a passage included in the following source: Brown, Drew T., III. *You Gotta Believe!: Education + Hard Work – Drugs = The American Dream.* New York: William & Morrow Company, 1991.

Chapter 10: Everyone Sees but Only a Few Know

[1] Here, I am referencing Sisyphus, the figure in Greek mythology who was punished by Hades, having to repeatedly roll a stone up a hill only to have it roll back down again as soon as it reached the summit.

[2] Here, I am referencing Beowulf, the warrior king from the epic poem. I compare Ali to Beowulf because they were both warrior-kings who were driven by both bravery and bravado (the myth of their own legends).

[3] At Drew Timothy Brown III's request, I have added this footnote. Drew felt that Wali might have misspoken by using the word "greed." Ali was, of course, having financial problems at the time this fight was made. For Drew, this was the incorrect word.

Chapter 12: From the Root to the Fruit

[1] Drew Brown Senior passed away on April 21, 1973. His services were held at Perry Funeral Chapel in Sanford, Florida.

Bundini is set in 10-point Sabon, which was designed by the German-born typographer and designer Jan Tschichold (1902–1974) in the period 1964–1967. It was released jointly by the Linotype, Monotype, and Stempel type foundries in 1967. Copyeditor for this project was Shannon LeMay-Finn. The book was designed by Brad Norr Design, Minneapolis, Minnesota, and typeset by New Best-set Typesetters Ltd. Printed and manufactured by Maple Press using acid-free paper.